A Change in the Weather

D1569947

A CHANGE
IN THE WEATHER

Modernist Imagination,
African American Imaginary

Geoffrey Jacques

University of Massachusetts Press

AMHERST

LC 2008035406
ISBN 978-1-55849-688-0 (paper); 687-3 (library cloth)

Designed by Dean Bornstein
Set in Adobe Garamond by House of Equations, Inc.
Printed and bound by The Maple-Vail Book Manufacturing Group

Library of Congress Cataloging-in-Publication Data

Jacques, Geoffrey.
    A change in the weather : modernist imagination, African American imaginary / Geoffrey
Jacques.
        p. cm.
    Includes bibliographical references (p.   ) and index.
    ISBN 978-1-55849-688-0 (pbk. : alk. paper) — ISBN 978-1-55849-687-3
(lib. bdg. : alk. paper)
    1. American poetry—20th century—History and criticism.   2. American poetry—
African American authors—History and Criticism.   3. Influence (Literary, artistic, etc.)
4. Modernism (Literature)—United States.   5. African American aesthetics.   I. Title.
    PS310.M57J33 2009
    811'.509896073—dc22   2008035406

British Library Cataloguing in Publication data are available.

CONTENTS

PREFACE

THE THOUGHT EXPERIMENT that animates the ideas and arguments explored in this book comes from a lifelong engagement with modernist literature and culture.

Modernism is conventionally identified as a movement in art and thought that started in a few countries of Europe and the Americas, in the late nineteenth and early twentieth centuries. The story goes that modernism in the arts meant, among other things, nonobjective painting; free verse and the rise of abstraction, the image, and the vernacular in poetry; the emergence of film, recorded sound, and commercial sound recordings; dissonant, syncopated, and atonal music; and the psychological novel and stream of consciousness narrative. The movement also has been portrayed, until quite recently, as a phenomenon to which African American contributions were primarily in the field of music, with ragtime, blues, and jazz.

These developments in the arts expressed the "nonlogical, nonobjective, and essentially causeless universe" that constitutes the society and culture "in which," writes William R. Everdell, "we all now live" (11). However, most examinations of this movement told a story where, in the field of literature at least, African Americans were for the most part invisible. This seemed at odds with what I had long known about what black writers were doing at the time of modernism's emergence.

The problem was not just about the exclusion of personalities, or of artistic works, from the historical record. The historical recovery of works and personalities is important, but it often leaves unanswered the question of the relationship between African American artists and culture and the larger one. Was literary culture in the United States racially divided and segregated in quite the same way that we've come to understand public life to be divided generally during the late nineteenth and early twentieth centuries? If so, how to account, then, for those situations where black voices seemed so familiar to the larger culture? This is a question that erupts, like a symptom, when black culture or African American artists are mentioned, often as an aside or an echo, in some historical and first-person accounts by white artists. These stories, like the childhood memory William Carlos Williams recalls of his father reading aloud the "Negro dialect" poems of Paul Laurence Dunbar— "simple poetry but it had swing and rhythm and quiet humor" (*I Wanted to*

Write a Poem 2)–stirred my curiosity. I wondered if we could rethink modernism in a way that would reveal a more complex picture than that already known to readers of aesthetic theory and literary history.

This exploration began with an in-depth study of the Harlem Renaissance, the literary and cultural movement that arose in the years right after World War I, as the massive migration of African Americans from the South to the northern cities was transforming the Harlem neighborhood in New York City into the capital of black America. Nearly a decade of reading, teaching, writing, and thinking about the "New Negro" movement, however, raised a number of questions about the relationship of that movement to modernism as such. For one thing, many of the writers (and others) in this movement understood themselves to be modernist artists, and the significance of this fact seemed to be, for the most part, lost in the conventional studies of modernism. For another, I was very fortunate to be thinking about these questions at the very moment when these problems were part of a growing conversation within the field of literary studies, and within that part of literary studies which is focused on African American literature. As I hope the following pages make clear, I have benefited greatly from this scholarship. The scholarly effort to reconcile the apparent disconnection between the self-regard of the "New Negro" artists and the histories of modernism has given rise to a variety of interpretations. When investigating these problems, I was struck by how much the literature regarded the legal environment and customs governing race relations and racism as the controlling authority when it came to understanding the culture of modernism. I wondered what would happen if we questioned the dominance of custom and the law by critically interrogating a discourse whose starting point took law and custom as determinative when it came to the operation of culture.

Looking into these issues forced me to reconsider some long-held assumptions about aesthetics, social and literary history, and cultural studies. How, after all, are we to understand the significance of the childhood exposure of Williams to the dialect poetry of Dunbar? When I have taught the poetry of Dunbar, students have often told me how the poet's poems lived in their families. I remember, especially, one young woman who talked about a pair of aunts who had contests with each other reciting Dunbar's poems. These poems–Williams mentions his father reading, specifically, "Accountability" ("Folks ain't got no right to censuah othah folks about dey habits" [*Collected Poetry* 5]; Williams quotes the poem's last lines)–were widely understood as vernacular verse. The point Williams makes, that this was among the earliest poetry he knew, made me wonder if there was not a sort of "secret history" of modernist literature, in which writing by African Americans played a far more important role than we have been led to believe. This book is the result of thinking about these questions.

Although a book is ultimately the product of the thinking and reflections of one individual, a study like this, which took several years to write, doesn't happen without its author being part of a community. I am very fortunate, first of all, to have had good counsel and support of Meena Alexander, John Brenkman, and James De Jongh of the English Program of the Graduate Center of the City University of New York (CUNY) as I worked on early versions of the project. They were astute and generous readers who provoked and prodded me, always asking the most challenging questions. Dan North, my editor and colleague for many years during my earlier career as a journalist, is also a great writing teacher. His queries always strike at the heart of the matter.

The libraries of the City University are wonderful institutions. I thank the staffs of the libraries of City College (CCNY), Hunter College, Brooklyn College, and the Mina Rees Library of the Graduate Center, CUNY, for making it possible to conduct rewarding research at those institutions.

Several friends also read various drafts of the manuscript, and I thank Melba Joyce Boyd, Eugene V. Cunningham, Ira Dworkin, W. Kim Heron, Aldon Lynn Nielsen, Amina S. Parker, and James Smethurst for their valuable observations and comments. The friends I made at the CUNY Graduate Center, including (but not limited to) Rhona Cohen, Chris Iannini, and Tisha Ulmer, were great companions and study partners. David Sassian read portions of the manuscript, offered insightful advice, and made invaluable suggestions, for which I am profoundly grateful.

Clarence Lusane showed me how going to graduate school after having had another career was not only possible but could actually be fun.

Cheryl Hanna has been a special friend throughout this project, and I want to say, here, how much I value her generosity, kindness, patience, humor, and attentiveness.

Sherri Barnes created the index. I thank her for that, but also for her optimism and enthusiasm during the latter stages of the project, and most of all for her love, which means more to me than words can say.

Colleagues at the institutions at which I held faculty appointments while revising this book were especially helpful conversation partners as I talked through the ideas that were on my mind. Faculty of the University of Massachusetts Boston American Studies Program were wonderful colleagues. Judith Smith expressed early enthusiasm and urged me to submit the manuscript for publication. Rachel Rubin and Jeffrey Melnick have been wonderful friends throughout the process. Others I wish to thank include University of Massachusetts Boston faculty members Phil Chassler, Linda Dittmar, Lois Rudnick, and Susan Tomlinson; and, at Lehman College, CUNY, James Anderson, Lise Esdaile, Jeannette Graulau, and Anne Humpherys.

Portions of this book served as conference presentations. Part of chapter 1 was delivered at an annual meeting of the American Studies Association, and part of chapter 2 was delivered at an annual Works in Progress conference sponsored by the Institute for Research in the African Diaspora and the Caribbean and the CUNY African American Network (IRADAC/CAAN). The facilitators and audiences at both of these conferences contributed significantly to helping me crystallize my ideas.

Finally, I want to thank three people who are no longer here: my late aunt and uncle, Lessie and Howard Douglas, and my friend and intellectual mentor, the late Edsel Reid. My aunt and uncle were always sources of great encouragement and were happy that I found joy in pursuing the life of the mind. This book is dedicated to Reid, who introduced me to the art of Bert Williams and other African American modernist masters, and pointed the way toward a comprehensive understanding of the power and scope of the African American Imaginary. I hope his spirit lives on in these pages.

A Change in the Weather

Introduction

IT MAY SEEM AN unlikely gesture to start a discussion about the relationship of modernist literature to African American culture by invoking the American barbershop. Nevertheless, I want to offer the barbershop as a point of departure from which we can renew our understanding of the origins of modernism, and especially modernist poetic language. This book is about poetic language, and about the impact both African American culture and black artists had on the emergence of a particularly modernist poetic language. In order to see that impact more clearly, I begin by taking a new look at the cultural and social conditions that prevailed, particularly in the United States, at the moment of modernism's emergence.

Modernism came about in a moment of social transition when, in the cities at least, a small minority of African Americans lived among whites within a shared public space. It was a moment—the half-century after emancipation—when the color line was being redrawn. It was the moment before the emergence of the racial ghettoes in the United States which came to be inhabited primarily by African American people, a moment when mass urban life was a relatively new phenomenon in the country. It is from this world that the jangled syntax of modernist poetry arose; it is from this environment that modernist literature takes its form as syncopated language.

Neither legal racial segregation and lynch terror nor the ideology that they engendered among individuals could stop the rise and impact of black culture on the culture as a whole. That is in part because the relationship between black culture and modern American culture generally is deeply rooted and interrelated with the social conditions in which the people who were involved in making such culture lived. The culture and the artists of modernism were born and grew up at the same time and, in ways that may seem surprising, in the same place as modern African American culture. Indeed, it is not a far-fetched suggestion to say that many American modernist artists, both black and white, would have had close and intimate exposure to black culture in the late nineteenth and early twentieth centuries by simply getting a haircut.

The barbershop is barely remembered now as a major point of interracial contact at the turn of the twentieth century, nor is it generally known that barbering was an occupation widely held by African Americans for many decades after the Civil War. In looking at service occupations held by men in cities outside the South in 1900, Stanley Lieberson found that blacks accounted for a quarter of all barbers and hairdressers in those cities where the workforce was at least 12 percent black; and in those southern cities where the population was at least one-third African American, some 60 percent of barbers and hairdressers were black (Lieberson 309, 324). As James Weldon Johnson reminds us, in his preface to *The Book of American Negro Spirituals*, these shops were also cultural centers. Here he is, remembering his Florida boyhood:

> In the days when such a thing as a white barber was unknown in the South, every barbershop had its quartet, and the men spent their leisure time playing on the guitar—not banjo, mind you—and "harmonizing." I have witnessed some of these explorations in the field of harmony and the scenes of hilarity and backslapping when a new and peculiarly rich chord was discovered. There would be demands for repetitions, and cries of "Hold it! Hold it" until it was firmly mastered. And well it was, for some of these chords were so new and strange for voices that, like Sullivan's *Lost Chord*, they would never have been found again except for the celerity with which they were recaptured. In this way was born the famous but much abused "barber-shop chord." (35–36)

In this remarkable passage, we see one more place of unexpected and productive interracial contact. It is a site where the cultural influence of African Americans can be seen in a number of ways, and it is here, using the barbershop as a point of departure, that I want to expand on the concept—which motivates much of the discussion in this book—of the African American Imaginary.

But before doing so, a few preliminary remarks concerning Johnson's comments are in order. The first thing to notice is the ubiquity of two elements: the African American barber, and the assertion that "every barber shop had its quartet." The second point is the emphasis on the chord, on the word, the lyric moment of the song, and its elision into, indeed its subordination to, pure sound. The reason this is an important point is that we are hearing, in Johnson's memoir, the birth of two aspects of modernist poetic language and of popular musicmaking at the same time. As far as poetic language is concerned, this subordination of the word to its sound occurs at the same time as the rise of the cliché as a foundational characteristic both of popular music and of modernist poetry. (Later, I elaborate on the impact of the cliché on the creation of modernist poetic language.) As far as music is concerned, this moment can be seen as one when the same process occurs, in which the sound is suspended ("Hold it! Hold it!") until it overwhelms any logic, sense, or narrative that the lyrics may have "meant." The all-male, mixed, or all-female vocal harmony group has been a prominent factor in U.S. popular music for more than a century. Practically every genre of the music has such groups at its core, usually quartets but often of varying numbers: the Rhythm Boys, Mills Brothers, Boswell Sisters, Pied Pipers, Andrews Sisters, Ink Spots, Platters, Clovers, Marvelettes, Four Freshmen, Shirelles, Temptations, Miracles, the Mamas and the Papas, Supremes, Fifth Dimension, Dramatics, and thousands of other groups of twentieth-century artists are all, to some measure, derived from these amateur quartets that performed in black-owned barbershops. These shops were also a place where the entire male population of the South, black and white (and a significant portion in the rest of the country, too, at least in the cities and towns) had firsthand experience with black culture. In addition, the fact that these were *vocal* quartets has significance for my study, since it is, above all, poetic language that is this book's central concern.[1]

{ 1 }

Literary criticism and theory has, over the last generation or so, charged itself with rethinking what we know about the genealogy of modernist literature and culture. Such rethinking is both necessary and possible, now that modernism is becoming the backstory of contemporary culture, but it is also necessary if we are truly to understand how modernism is the ancestor of the cultures of the twenty-first century and beyond. This necessity arises because of the different and unexpected ways that contemporary culture, with its polyvocality and its characteristic cultural difference, turns out to have developed from what has come to be known as "Anglo-American" modernism.

The rethinking about modernist literature proposed in this study is also necessary because the understanding of modernism bequeathed to us by modernist and, to some extent, even postmodernist criticism has been inadequate as an explanation of the literature and culture of the last century. The critical literature on late nineteenth- and early twentieth-century culture was embedded within a framework defined by the dominant cultural and social values of the day. Though modernism saw itself as a culturally renovative force, there are ways in which this self-conception was contested by some of its earliest critics. Because some of modernism's early champions were embedded in what can fairly be called a conservative value system, one can think of their criticism as a symptom of repression; it was a criticism that repressed some of the major constitutive elements of modernist culture. Among the major elements repressed in what we might call a kind of critical neurosis are those concerning racial and gender difference. When one looks carefully at the historical relationship between African American culture and the broader culture within which it resides, one can immediately see that something is amiss in critical evaluations of our culture. What is needed now is an extension of the critical thinking that has long been under way in the growing field of study that includes what have been called "ethnic" literatures. What we need now is to reorder the framework within which we study modernist culture. This book is an attempt at such a reordering.

The approach to modernism I propose privileges the interaction—as opposed to the dichotomy—between African American and "white" culture. It proposes that this relationship is a defining characteristic of modernism at the level of the identity of the modernist project itself. Its premise is based on a claim that may seem surprising, given the increasingly high profile of African American studies within the larger fields of literary and cultural study: that there has been an insufficient accounting of the relationship between black culture, on the one hand, and literary modernism, on the other, an insufficiency that reflects a critical misunderstanding of that relationship.

What might happen if we elaborate a genealogy of modernism in Anglo-American literature that puts African American culture, and African American artists, at its center?[2] What particular issues might be cast into relief? Where might such an investigation lead? What might prompt some of the underlying assumptions and hitherto unacknowledged conclusions behind such an inquiry? There are pitfalls involved in a study of this kind. Indeed, Michel Foucault advises the genealogist to use history to "dispel the chimeras of the origin" ("Nietzsche, Genealogy, History" 144). Yet, given the contested terrain, one sees a need for a study that raises these questions in an attempt to understand the relationship between African American culture, on the one hand, and modernist literature, on the other.

This book argues for an understanding of modernism that sees a singular project, cutting across cultural lines. It seeks to demonstrate how the question of difference might be approached in a way that leads away from the apparent dichotomies between African American culture, on the one hand, and modernism, on the other.

This genealogical recasting also leads to a reconsideration of questions of performativity and self-fashioning in modernism, and of the idea that modernism's identity is inextricably tied to an alienating estrangement from popular, or "mass" culture. Consider the way African American culture haunts some famous modernist texts by writers who are not African American. How are we to understand Ezra Pound's complaint, "The pianola 'replaces' / Sappho's barbitos" (189), in the context of the larger complaint in "Hugh Selwyn Mauberley"? Or the reflection of Eliot's speaker, in "Portrait of a Lady," a poem that could be read as a musical landscape of Western culture: "Inside my brain a dull tom-tom begins / Absurdly hammering a prelude of its own" (*Complete* 9)? Let me suggest that "haunt" may be a useful way to account for the appearance of the pianola and the tom-tom in these two poems. (I use the term "haunt" as an analytical tool when I explore this question more fully in the next chapter.) Each is an instrument identified with black culture, and in each poem these specific instruments seem to work as symbols of cultural anxiety. It seems, however, that the "haunting" I identify not only signifies the impact of black culture on modernist culture in a broad sense but also reflects the impact of black cultural artifacts (the ragtime-era player piano, the modern "drum kit"), and of black artists, on the work and consciousness of modernism generally. This study attempts to expand this idea by examining its function at the semantic and symbolic levels, invoking the term "African American Imaginary" as an analytic tool. Here, the term is used to identify an aspect of the historical and cultural milieu in which modernism developed.

This study distinguishes itself from the argument advanced by Houston A. Baker Jr., that African Americans "have little in common with Joycean or Eliotic projects" (xvi), by proceeding from a point of view that investigates the role of black culture and of African American artists as catalysts of, and not just influences upon, modernism.

The ideas of Sigmund Freud about "the Uncanny," and about the symbiotic relationship between the "primitive" and the "modern," are critical to this inquiry, as is the work of both Homi K. Bhabha—"the stereotype is at once a substitute and a shadow" (82)—and Toni Morrison, who suggests in *Playing in the Dark* that we should pay close attention to the "carefully observed, and carefully invented, Africanist presence" in American literature

(6). This latter idea can be considered a version of the phenomenon that I identify with the term "haunted."

A Change in the Weather also seeks to distinguish itself from works such as those of Michael H. Levenson, Frederick R. Karl, Michael North, Ann Douglas, and Mark A. Sanders. Both Levenson and Karl, in their useful studies, limit their discussion to the generally accepted modernist canon. North seeks to develop an understanding of modernism that does include an agentive role for African American culture; indeed, North's concept of "racial masquerade" has prompted my inquiry, as has his assertion that "the new voice that American culture acquired in the 1920s, the decade of jazz, stage musicals, talking pictures, and aesthetic modernism, was very largely a black one" (7). From this beginning, however, it seems that a fruitful examination must go beyond the notion that the relationship between black culture and modernism is one where African American creativity's role was limited to, as North writes, "raw material for white writers to use" (*Dialect of Modernism* 135). What happens if we think of African American culture not as "raw material" but as a codeterminate agent of the modernist project? When North writes about the relationships examined here, he seems to take for granted that the existence of legal segregation should define and limit how we understand cultural interaction within modernism: "Despite its enthusiasm for Africa and Meso-America, despite its promises of a transnational America and a multiethnic American modernism, the avantgarde proved ill prepared to include within its conception of the new American writing any examples that actually stretched the old categories of race and ethnicity" (150).

Reading the relationship between cultures and artists solely or primarily as a function of the negative legal environment that these cultural actors found themselves in can sometimes lead to a limited understanding of how cultural interaction works. This is especially true when such readings focus on the period of the birth of modernism. To take the fixed nature of this environment for granted would have the racialized hyper-segregation of peoples and cultures in the United States that was characteristic of most of the twentieth century look as if it had always existed in its familiar form. A reading of the demographic and social composition of the United States in the years between the end of the Civil War and the emergence, just before the First World War, of the earliest modernist works and culture suggests that a broader view is in order. In the early twentieth century the rise of African American culture had the effect of changing the very character of

American culture. How was this possible? These were the years that historians, following Rayford Logan, have by consensus designated the "nadir" of African American life. Their emphasis is, rightfully, on the rise of Jim Crow, on the increasing restriction and banishment of African Americans from the national public sphere, a banishment that occurred within a regime of terror that included lynchings, race riots north and south, systematic disenfranchisement in the southern states, the abandonment of civil rights by the federal government, the rise of white supremacy as official policy in the former slaveholding states and the spread of white supremacy throughout the country generally, and in a few cases the wholesale destruction of African American communities, such as the 1921 razing of the black community in Tulsa, Oklahoma. In historical, political, and sociological terms, the narrative of the nadir, which starts with the end of Reconstruction, tends to culminate in the appearance of ghettos, especially in the northern cities, inhabited by African Americans as a result of the first wave of the Great Migration north during and after the First World War. In cultural terms, this narrative tends to culminate in the appearance, within these communities, of the great flowering of African American culture during the 1920s—especially in New York, with the Harlem Renaissance, and in Chicago, where the first full-fledged northern jazz bands appeared in the early years of that decade. The unanswered question, however, concerns the background of the modernist culture of the 1910s and 1920s. It is as if the jazz age, free verse, the modern novel, and the "discovery" of the Negro happened all at once. Yet it did not happen all at once. If we look broadly at the emergence of modernism, and especially of modernist poetic language, as containing at the same time the emergence of modern African American culture, and if we consider this double emergence as part of the core of our understanding of modernism as such, we will then be able to refresh our understanding of the genealogy of modernist culture.

{ 2 }

One way to better understand my argument is to reconsider the status of black people—in particular, but not exclusively, the African American middle class—within the larger culture during the years between, roughly, 1875 and 1915. Most of the works examined in this book were published during those years, or they are works that portray a lifeworld or engage in linguistic conventions that emerged during those years. In addition, as I hope to make clear in my discussion of the art of Samuel Beckett, a writer who published later, the culture his work draws upon has its roots in the period of modernism's emergence.

Literary representations of this period, as well as the social science of the late twentieth century, seem to be in agreement on one central demographic point: in the years before World War I, African Americans who lived in cities did not live in ghettos but were, in fact, spread throughout the urban landscape. David M. Cutler and his colleagues, looking at the demographics of American cities, concluded that as of 1890 "the average urban black lived in a neighborhood that was 27 percent black." Only Norfolk, Virginia, had a black community that could, they claim, be considered a ghetto. "In 1890," they say, "American cities were segregated but not exceptionally segregated." Even though African American people were "disproportionately concentrated in particular parts of cities," such areas "were not entirely or even mainly black." It is, they emphasize, the "spatial proximity of the races that most distinguishes the city of 1890" from the city of the late twentieth and the early twenty-first century (456, 462).

Northern cities were more segregated than southern cities, but the black population of northern cities was small, averaging about 2.5 percent of the total. This remained more or less the case for decades. As late as 1940, according to Cutler and his colleagues, the average urban black person lived in a neighborhood that was 43 percent black. In some instances, especially around the turn of the nineteenth to the twentieth century, African Americans were less segregated, in terms of where they lived, than were some groups of whites: "Late in the nineteenth century and as recently as 1910, blacks were less segregated than were a number of the new European groups," writes Stanley Lieberson (290). Douglas S. Massey and Nancy A. Denton argue that urban black people's residential patterns in these cities were not segregated by color. "To be sure," they write, "certain neighborhoods could be identified as places where blacks lived; but before 1900 these areas were not predominantly black, and most blacks didn't live in them."

This was true of large cities as well as small ones. Gertrude Stein, writing about Baltimore, where she spent part of her youth, described it as a place "where no one is in a hurry and the voices of the negroes singing as their carts go lazily by, lull you into drowsy reveries. It is a strangely silent city, even its busiest thoroughfares seem still and the clanging car-bells only blend with the peaceful silence and do but increase it. To lie on the porch, to listen to the weird strains of Grieg's spring-song, to hear the negro voices in the

distance and to let your mind wander idly as it listeth, that is happiness"
(qtd. in Brinnin 35, spelling as in original). This somewhat romanticized, if
patronizing, account nonetheless suggests how the lives of black people and
the lives of whites were intertwined in these cities and towns. Stein was writing about Baltimore in the 1890s. In 1910, the city government, by law,
created separate African American and white neighborhoods (Massey and
Denton 41). In Hartford Connecticut, where Wallace Stevens lived during
the years he wrote most of the poems in *Harmonium*, his first book
(Richardson 487; Stevens, *Harmonium*; *Collected Poems* 3–113), African
Americans lived in every one of the city's ten wards, even though 86 percent
of the black population was concentrated in just three wards (Johnson,
Negro Population of Hartford, 8–9; Tuckel, Schlichting, and Maisel 724).
Sometimes these streets were slums, or parts of slums, what W. E. B. Du Bois
referred to as "the narrow and filthy alleys of the city" (*Philadelphia Negro*
51; see also Tolnay, Crowder, and Adelman 992). These areas were often designated "Darktown," "Negro Town," or "Black Bottom" or given even less
dignified names. There is even a popular song from the period, "Darktown
Strutters' Ball" (from 1917), written by the African American composer
Shelton Brooks, that alludes to these enclaves. Mary White Ovington describes the impoverished living conditions of most of the Manhattan blocks
where black people lived in the early twentieth century (31–51); but she
also describes another reality. "In Brooklyn, the Bronx, and in the Jersey
suburbs, Negroes buy and rent houses, sometimes with but a few of their
race in close proximity, sometimes with white neighbors only on the block"
(172–73).

This meant that African Americans living in cities were not, by and large,
a group set apart by residence, and this had an impact on the shape of late
nineteenth- and early twentieth-century culture. "No matter what other dis-
advantages urban blacks suffered in the aftermath of the Civil War," write
Massey and Denton, "they were not residentially segregated from whites.
The two racial groups moved in a common social world, spoke a common
language, shared a common culture, and interacted personally on a regular
basis. In the north, especially, leading African American citizens often en-
joyed relations of considerable trust, respect, and friendship with whites of
similar social standing" (17–18).

It is easy enough to overstate this case; after all, as Karl E. and Alma F.
Taeuber remind us in their study of urban racial segregation, nearly three-
quarters of African Americans lived in rural areas as late as the end of the first

decade of the twentieth century (1). The fact, however, that Massey and Denton, in support of their argument, cite the life of novelist Charles Chesnutt suggests that the demographics outlined here are an important, if insufficiently examined, set of facts with interesting implications for a reinvestigation of early modernist culture. Chesnutt, they point out, was a respected figure in his Cleveland community; he "pursued a highly visible career as a court stenographer, lawyer, and writer, sending his children to integrated schools, and maintaining a close circle of white associates" (23). These findings can be confirmed by a reading of the most significant late nineteenth century study of urban African Americans, *The Philadelphia Negro* (1899) by W. E. B. Du Bois. Early in this book, Du Bois writes that he is making an inquiry "into the condition of the forty thousand or more people of Negro blood now living in the city of Philadelphia." His focus was a house-by-house survey of the city's Seventh Ward, which was, in the last decade of the nineteenth century, "an historic centre of Negro population, and contains to-day a fifth of all the Negroes in this city" (1). Du Bois goes on to show that although the Seventh Ward, with nearly nine thousand black people, had the city's largest concentration of African Americans, black people lived in significant numbers in almost every one of the nearly three dozen (as of 1890) wards in the city (59).

The implications of these phenomena for a reading of the beginnings of modernist literature are plenitudinous. For example, what is remarkable is the mix of despair and anxiety that seems to coexist with a sometimes barely perceptible but widely expressed hopeful mode within African American culture. The oscillation between hope and despair is a commonplace in cultural products of this period. Du Bois, in a famous passage (in the *Souls of Black Folk* chapter interestingly titled "On the Training of Black Men"), speaks of himself as freely assimilating the world's culture: "Across the color line I move arm in arm with Balzac and Dumas, where smiling men and welcoming women glide in gilded halls" (74). And yet, in the same book, we can read about the tragedy of the Freeman's Bureau and the Freeman's Bank (17–33), or the bittersweet story of Rev. Alexander Crummell, "the tale of a black boy who many long years ago began to struggle with life that he might know the world and know himself." Du Bois writes of the "three temptations" Crummell "met on those dark dunes that lay gray and dismal before the wonder-eyes of the child: the temptation of Hate, that stood out against the red dawn; the temptation of Despair, that darkened noonday;

and the temptation of Doubt, that ever steals along with twilight" (134–35). The story Du Bois tells is one of Crummell's struggle to find a place in the church in the United States, his abandonment of that struggle "half in despair" (140), his voyage to England to complete his education, and his twenty-year sojourn in Liberia as a missionary. Near the story's conclusion, Du Bois writes of Crummell: "Out of the temptation of Hate, and burned by the fire of Despair, triumphant over Doubt, and steeled by Sacrifice against Humiliation, he turned at last home across the waters, humble and strong, gentle and determined" (141).

This oscillation appears at the same time that the society at large is engaged in a progressively expansive absorption of elements of African American culture. One can see, then, the importance of the demographic facts outlined here by the way they assert themselves in both textual and cultural contexts. On the textual level, one need look no further than the first chapter of *The Souls of Black Folk*, where Du Bois introduces his concepts of the veil and of "double consciousness" (10–11). What is often overlooked in readings of this famous passage is its setting, and the situation in which its address takes place.

Later, I comment on this paragraph of *The Souls of Black Folk* more extensively, but here I just want to make some preliminary remarks. Although readers are often focused on the repeated rhetorical question "How does it feel to be a problem?" rarely is attention paid to the social situation portrayed. That Du Bois's speaker is in a room of white men seems obvious, yet there are elements in this passage that remain vague. The others are described as "all," or "the other world." Both the speaker and his interlocutor are in a social setting, and there is a seeming intimacy to their talk that may have been difficult to replicate even a quarter of a century later. When the essay was first published, in 1897, the phrase "I know an excellent colored man in my town" could be seen and, indeed, is presented here as a commonplace. It is true that the majority of urban African Americans at this time worked as unskilled laborers; however, the "excellent colored man," could also have been a caterer (a declining but still important force in Du Bois's late nineteenth-century Philadelphia), or a barber, or a grocer, or someone who practiced any of a number of the professional and semiprofessional occupations still open to black people in the country's cities and towns in the late nineteenth century. Du Bois is here describing the "talented tenth," his term for the emergent African American middle class. It was a small group; nevertheless, it was the section of the black population whose interactions with whites were the most likely to be on terms approaching those of (public) social equals.[3] The quality that makes this passage somewhat provocative, then, is precisely its social setting. The essay originally appeared as "The Strivings of the Negro People" in the August 1897 issue of the *Atlantic Monthly*, not quite two years after the September 18, 1895, "Atlanta Compromise" address that Booker T. Washington delivered at the Cotton States Exposition. "In all things that are purely social we can be as separate as the fingers, yet one as the hand in all things essential to mutual progress," Washington had said (*Up From Slavery* 221–22). Yet here is Du Bois, in a purely "social" setting, suggesting that what Washington takes as an accomplished fact, the "purely social" separation of the races, has not yet fully occurred.

Scenes of interracial social intimacy, mainly in public space but sometimes even in private space, such as the home, are not unknown to American literature of this period. These are often rendered as scenes of transition, of the color line being redrawn. One thinks, for instance, of the scene in *Iola Leroy*, the novel by Frances E. W. Harper, in which Iola's suitor, Dr. Gresham, visits the protagonist in her urban home. Leroy's rejection of his marriage proposal revolves around differing perceptions of the social reality surrounding them. For Leroy, the visibly white but legally "colored" heroine, the fact of the descending color line is clear. "The prejudice against the colored race environs our lives and mocks our aspirations," she says. But for the legally white Gresham, the opposite appears to be the case: "The color line is slowly fading out in our public institutions," he claims (232–33).

Another such scene of transition occurs in Chesnutt's novel *The Marrow of Tradition*. Dr. William Miller is stopped and roughly interrogated by his once friendly white neighbors as he passes through riot-torn Wellington:

> Miller stepped down from his buggy. His interlocutor, who made no effort at disguise, was a clerk in a dry-goods store where Miller bought most of his family and hospital supplies. He made no sign of recognition, however, and Miller claimed no acquaintance. This man, who had for several years emptied Miller's pockets in the course of more or less legitimate trade, now went through them, aided by another man, more rapidly than ever before, the searchers convincing themselves that Miller carried no deadly weapon upon his person. Meanwhile, a third ransacked the buggy with like result. Miller recognized several others of the party, who made not the slightest attempt at disguise, though no names were called by any one. (288)

Here we see the moment of fissure, with social interracialism in the process of breaking down. The narrator's memory is focused on the recent past, when public social interracial relations were still a fact of everyday life.

It is worth noting here that the action in this novel takes place in a southern city, whereas, although Du Bois is not specific about where the action in his anecdote occurs, it is true that when "Strivings of the Negro People" was first published, he was living in Philadelphia. Both texts exhibit an anxiety on the narrator's part about such situations. Where Du Bois's narrator reduces his boiling blood "to a simmer," Chesnutt's narrator is forced into a stance of nonrecognition vis-à-vis his interlocutors. It is, however, the play between the acts of nonrecognition, on the one hand, and lack of disguise, on the other, that is most intriguing about the Chesnutt passage. Here again we witness a moment of transition, a moment when one culture (that never truly finished being born) was being supplanted by another. If, for Du Bois, the opening moment of interracial sociability is not repeated in *Souls*, in *The Marrow of Tradition* the moment of interracial bonding that concludes the novel is tentative and takes place amid the ruins of tragedy.

{ 3 }

In order to understand more fully how the change in poetic language that happened with modernism is tied to the popular culture of the twentieth century, it is also necessary to understand the way that African American music influenced popular music, and how that influence was able to spread so easily in the days before commercially recorded music was widely available. One of the reasons I point to the rise of African American–style barbershop music is to suggest just how widespread such popular music was in the days of modernism's emergence, an indication that, at least at the level of everyday life lived in public, black America and white America were more racially integrated in the late nineteenth and early twentieth centuries than much scholarship tends to assume.

The title of this book means to evoke three of the ideas under examination here. "A Change in the Weather" comes from the lyric to one of the earliest hits of the jazz age, "There'll Be Some Changes Made." The song, with music composed by W. Benton Overstreet and lyrics by Billy Higgins, was a hit for Ethel Waters. Here is one of the song's two choruses, transcribed from Waters's August 1921 recording for the Black Swan label.

Why, there's a change in the weather, there's a change in the sea,
So from now on there'll be a change in me,
Why, my walk will be different, and my talk, and my name,
Nothing about me gonna be the same;
I'm gonna change my way of living, and that ain't no shock,
Why, I'm thinking about changin' the way I gonna set my clock,
Because nobody wants you when you're old and gray.
There's gonna be some changes made today,
There'll be some changes made.

The lyric is emblematic of some of the concerns explored in this book. It is a famous lyric, so much so that it was still occasionally used in the late twentieth century as a theme song for television commercials.[4] I am attempting to place the popular song, and popular song lyrics, at the center of the discussion about modernist poetic language. This is a largely neglected subject but one that needs to be explored in order to account more fully for the "revolution of the word" which was a hallmark of modernist poetics. I explore the importance of the "coon song" and the blues for understanding the emergence of the new poetic language of modernism in an attempt to demonstrate how the chorus of the popular song developed into its dominant feature and how this feature relied primarily on the mobilization of clichés for its power. The song lyric quoted above, for example, relies on such clichés as "a change in the weather" and "from now on there'll be a change in me" just two examples of the sort of oft-repeated, commonplace phrases that we have come to view as clichés. The development of a lyric art based on clichés has important implications for the concurrent development of modernist poetics (see chapter 2). The popular song was a transmitter of vernacular language, and with the development of recorded sound and the commercial recording industry, this means of transmission became universal.

As significant as the popular song and the sound recording were for the spread of vernacular language, another feature of Waters's performance deserves attention as well: the fact that the female singing subject is asserting herself as an autonomous individual intent on shaping her own reality. The song is, in a word, about self-fashioning. This is true in another sense as well, in that the song was recorded for the Black Swan label, the first African American–owned record company. Harry Pace, who had been a business partner of W. C. Handy, founded Black Swan, and the company had many prominent African Americans on its executive board, including W. E. B.

Du Bois. Besides Waters, the company recorded early works by Fletcher Henderson and classical music by African American singers. It was one of the earliest of the "New Negro" institutions, and its history is an example of the idea of self-fashioning as it came to characterize black America from the end of the First World War onward.[5] The idea, most famously articulated by Stephen Greenblatt, that self-fashioning is a hallmark of the individual in modernity is well known. In the context of modernist culture, and also of African American culture, this idea is central and is a distinguishing characteristic of the blues and other African American song forms. It is invoked here as an emblem of the modernist imagination.

One significant achievement of modernism was its ability to "decreate" meaning in ordinary language, to use the word in the sense that Frederick R. Karl suggests. "Language is no longer the primary agent in its old form of communication or as creating subject-object relationships," Karl writes. "The page or territory is primary, on which language wanders like a lonely adventurer hoping to survive emptiness and whiteness." Language, Karl adds, "turns into a form of music, becoming not only a visual image but an aural one as well" (16). The tactility of language suggested here came about in many ways and from many sources, and continued to be hallmark of experimental poetics throughout the twentieth century. One source of such "decreation," considered in its relationship with modernism, was African American vernacular speech. Others have explored this matter, their discussion usually centering on the 1920s, but the process of decreation had been underway for decades by the time the first blues and jazz recordings became available. African American vernacular speech had been part of the larger culture for a very long time, but when Paul Laurence Dunbar began to publish in the 1890s, he brought to the form a sensibility that was distinctive, and, as I argue, one that had many affinities with the earliest modern poets. The poems Dunbar wrote in "Negro dialect" were considered the best of their kind in his own day. These poems have suffered a decline in esteem from some critics, who, following the criticisms of J. Saunders Redding (*To Make a Poet Black* 36–67), seem to be influenced by the assessment of dialect works made by James Weldon Johnson in his preface to *The Book of American Negro Poetry* (xxxiii–xxxv; xxxix–xiii). The art of Dunbar, however, deserves reconsideration. His poetry—the works written in standard English as well as his dialect poems—has, because of its significant affinities with Symbolism, qualities that have hitherto been overlooked in the study of the development of modern poetry.

Among the central ideas of this book is the claim that in the years before the first wave of the Great Migration of African American people north and into the cities, there emerged in the United States—and to some extent in Western culture generally—a cultural formation I have chosen to call the "African American Imaginary," and that this "Imaginary" had already made its indelible mark on society, and especially on the culture and on modernist poetic language, before the first works of the "New Negro" 1920s were even published. This idea draws on two interrelated but distinct concepts. The first relies on a rethinking of the status and role of black culture within American culture generally, at the level of literary discourse and poetic language. The second is an elaboration of the concept of the "imaginary" as it has been developed by a select group of thinkers. This latter concept I have adopted as an analytical tool in order to understand and rethink the impact of black culture on the larger culture during the years of the "nadir."

In his examination of the discursive relationship between Africans, African Americans, and the dominant discourse of the West in the eighteenth and nineteenth centuries, Henry Louis Gates Jr. employs the idea of the "Discourse of the Black Other" (*Figures in Black* 49). He is referring to "the literature that persons of African descent created as well as the non-black literature that depicts black characters." Gates traces this idea from such "Noble Negro" narratives as *Oroonoko*, by Aphra Behn, through the slave narratives. He also uses this figure when he draws a parallel history, tracing the line from the emergence of the harlequin to the "American Minstrel Man" (51). He is interested in the signifying relations between these figures and those of the dominant culture. It is worth drawing attention to the fact that the relationship Gates describes is one whose main content is domination. The figure of the black other exists in a subordinate position to the (white) figures to which it has what Gates calls a "signifyin(g)" relationship. This relationship reflected the position of Africans in the Americas during the period Gates examines.

Similarly, Eric Lott, in studying the emergence of minstrelsy in the early nineteenth century, has many useful things to say about the ways in which introjection and substitution were important to the development of the minstrel show. These served, among other things, to help Jacksonian-era minstrelsy play a role in consolidating the country. One function of minstrelsy, Lott argues, "was precisely to bring various class fractions into contact with one another, to mediate their relations, and finally to aid in the construction of class identities over the bodies of black people." Blackface performance by whites, he adds, "provided a convenient mask through which to voice class resentments of all kinds—resentments directed as readily toward black people as toward upper-class enemies" (67–68). He also convincingly argues that there was, among the antebellum minstrel show's audience, "the public perception of the minstrel show as black" (97). He hastens to add that the minstrel show was not black culture but "a structured set of white responses to it which had grown out of northern and frontier social rituals and were passed through an invisible filter of racist presupposition." This "iconography of racial difference" had many uses for both performers and audiences (101). But these did not include an effort to gain knowledge of the real African American community or its culture.

All that began to change after the Civil War and accelerated, ironically, just as legal segregation came to dominate the South and just as the urban ghettos populated by African Americans arose in the early decades of the twentieth century. A post-Emancipation surge in the significance and influence of African American culture on the culture as a whole began in the late nineteenth century, demonstrated most obviously by the rise of new musical forms: the spirituals, the barbershop quartets, and, especially, ragtime. Scholars of ragtime, ranging from Rudi Blesh and Harriet Janis to Edward A. Berlin, have outlined this influence. Alec Wilder has written about the relationship between ragtime song and American popular song generally. I undertake to build on those findings, and investigate how ragtime-era songs helped "decreate" English by introducing African American vernacular speech forms that were subsequently used by modernist poets ranging from Gertrude Stein to T. S. Eliot and that formed a basic element of modern poetry and poetics. In addition, I identify a whole range of cultural products, from songs to the modern minstrel character, as elements of the "African American Imaginary," a collective cultural milieu characterized not by relations of domination but by relations that can best be identified as involving (to borrow a term from Jacques Lacan), "imaginary interplay." For Lacan, this interplay takes the form of two pairs of actions: "expulsion and introjection" and "projection and absorption" (82).

These ideas are important for understanding what is meant here. The imaginary can be seen in a number of ways: as a faculty of mind, as the source of creativity, or as a kind of public space in which notions of difference are allowed to, as it were, speak and picture and know themselves and the other.

Drucilla Cornell offers the concept of "the imaginary domain" as a way of conceptualizing women's equality; this domain is "the moral space necessary for equivalent evaluation of our sexual difference as free and equal persons." The idea of the imaginary domain, she adds, "can help us see that questions of what it means for sexed beings to be included in the moral community of persons as an initial matter must be explicitly addressed before principles of distributive justice can be defended by the moral procedure" (14–15). The key ideas I take from this are the "equivalent evaluation" of difference and that the imaginary domain helps address "what it means for sexed beings to be included in the moral community of persons."

If we apply these concepts to the ideas of "race" and the emergence of modernism, they can help us see more clearly what was at stake when the public idea of black culture was not the minstrel masquerade alone but the emergence of the "raced" being who was, simply by taking part in the public sphere, demanding an "equivalent evaluation" of his or her personhood. But how could this take place in an environment where such a demand was met, as often as not, with ostracism, civil discrimination, denial of rights, and violent civil repression? One answer involves the African American Imaginary that emerged as a new cultural formation in the late nineteenth and early twentieth centuries. This was a space where questions of how racialized, or "raced," beings could be included in the moral community of persons could be threshed out at the level of cultural production itself. "What we know as perception and idea, dream and daydream, phantasm and hallucination bear witness to a multifarious manifestation of the imaginary" Wolfgang Iser notes (182). "If the imaginary," he adds, "conjures up a range of nonactual perceptions, it simultaneously moves as a differential between that range and the actual perception, and, being indeterminate, allows for the determinacy of the actual perception that acquires its individual stability against the backdrop of the nonactual ones" (183). African American culture emerged as a new part of the national culture after the Civil War not only against the masquerade of minstrelsy but also against the idea of black culture created by that masquerade. At the same time, black culture carried with it, into this new cultural formation, the ideas imposed on it by the old culture. It was the agentive role of black artists that was now new, however, and that role made claims for itself, and for the society as such, in the name of black people. Those claims were not simply regional; they were national or social as well. From them emerged the idea that black culture, in some sense, belonged to all; it is this last idea that is at the heart of the concept of the African American Imaginary, and it is this idea that is among the driving concepts this book seeks to examine.

{4}

Thinking through the African American Imaginary helps us see how Louis Armstrong became the most significant United States–born artist of the twentieth century, or how ragtime became a national music almost before anyone truly knew it to be of African American origin; or how a figure like Bert Williams could be so important to the emergence of modernism. In his performances, Williams played, simultaneously, both the despised Negro and the "universal man;" he played the "darky" stereotype while being, at the same time, in the words of W. C. Fields, "the funniest man I ever saw and the saddest man I ever knew" (qtd. in Rowland 128). Each of these categories is suggestive of a relationship between the African American artist and the surrounding culture more complicated than one that can be defined, in Henry Louis Gates's term, as the "Discourse of the Black Other" (*Figures in Black* 49). In such a discourse, the possibility of "knowing," the "Other" (in the intimate sense suggested by Fields) is limited.

One can also see that black culture was a constitutive element in the construction of modern culture as it was articulated by white people, and nowhere is this fact clearer than in the creation of literary modernism itself—one of the major themes of this study. And there is probably no better illustration of the early appearance of the African American Imaginary in literary modernism than in the poems of Marianne Moore. These may seem a surprising place to begin, but Cristanne Miller, among others, has already commented significantly on "race" in Moore's poetry, and the remarks I offer are aimed at building on that commentary.

The poet symbolizes black people as, among other things, carriers of a kind of romanticized, idealized myth that allows the poetry to articulate an implied, discreet critique of a contemporary society whose values are undermined by its own formal rituals and material abundance. Consider "The Hero" (Moore, *Complete Poems* 8–9). The setting of the poem is George Washington's Mount Vernon, Virginia, estate. Its centerpiece is an anecdote concerning an exchange between an African American man, presumably a tour guide, and a woman tourist whose race is not mentioned but who is presumably white.[6] This anecdote follows a long meditation on the qualities of heroism, beginning with those qualities that the hero does not like. These include "suffering and not / saying so; standing and listening where something / is hiding." Next come a few words about a group of "vexing" figures—Joseph, Cincinnatus, Regulus—and, significantly, these words about hope: "hope not being hope / until all ground for hope / has vanished."

Then there follows the anecdote about the uniformed black guide, "a decorous, frock-coated Negro" who informs the "fearless sightseeing hobo" of the location of George and Martha Washington's graves.

This exchange is of interest for two reasons: the poem's descriptions of the characters in the "play,"[7] and the language of each of the three speakers— the anecdote's narrator, the Negro, and the sightseer. The narrator describes the Negro as "decorous"; the sightseer is both "fearless" and a "hobo." For the poem's contemporary readers, the irony of this passage would have been apparent: it is elevating the guide and mocking the sightseer, and even in the Great Depression the figure of the hobo would have lost little of its earlier connotation of decadent vagabondage. The black tour guide, when he addresses the woman, is described as:

> speaking
> as if in a play—not seeing her; with a
> sense of human dignity
> and reverence for mystery, standing like the shadow
> of the willow.
>
> (9)

"As if in a play." This key phrase helps us read back into the entire poem what part of "a play" we are witnessing; for the poem is both a depiction of and a meditation on what Bertram Wilber Doyle calls "the etiquette of race relations in the South." Doyle's interesting and obscure study oscillates between an apparent defense of the racial status quo, on the one hand, and on the other an exposé, in some detail, of the humiliating social environment endured by African Americans in everyday life in the South after white supremacy and public racial segregation were firmly reestablished. These social rituals were at all times aimed at reminding black people that their status in the South was "generally as a menial and that [they] must look and act the part" (154). These rituals covered all manner of social interactions in public. African Americans "normally greet white men with the title 'Mister'"; "well known" white people were to be addressed "by the intimate 'Mr. John' or 'Miss Mary,' as the case may be." On the other hand, white persons are not expected to address Negroes as 'mister'; but 'boy' is still good usage as a term to address Negro males of all ages," Doyle writes. And further: "The rule is that shaking hands, walking together, and otherwise associating in public, except on terms of superior and inferior, are not done" (142–43). Doyle, especially in his chapter on the then contemporary scene of the 1930s (135–59), addresses all aspects of public social relations in the South during that period in which Moore's poem was first published, and his study can give us some insight into the portrayal in "The Hero" of social interactions during one day in Mount Vernon.

Seen in this light, the tour guide, the sightseer, the poem's narration of the anecdote and reaction to it, all assume a definite character. There is, for one thing, the "decorous" tour guide and the sightseeing "hobo." This reversal of status ascribed to each character, then, appears to be a deliberate subversion of social norms. The tour guide's nonrecognition of the sightseer is described in the poem as a dignified, heroic, reverent, and mysterious stance. This all takes place after Moore's poem has told us what heroes do and do not like, from having to put up with unjust social mores ("suffering and not / saying so") to having to endure "vexing" characters like Joseph, who "made himself strange" to his brothers (Gen. 42.7, King James version), and through all this the poem's hero is "lenient, looking / upon a fellow creature's error with the feelings of a mother—a / woman or a cat" (9). The poem's speaker, finally, just before unveiling the central hero of the poem, identifies with that figure and ascribes "female" characteristics to him. "The Hero," then, can be read as a commentary on and a critique of the racialized social mores of the early twentieth-century South and, to some extent, of the state of public interracialism generally.

"The Hero" can also be seen as an exemplar of the African American Imaginary at work. The African American tour guide is both emblem and agent. He embodies noble characteristics and is in no way to be pitied. In fact, the poem seems to call on the reader to feel a little diminished for, in a sense, consenting to and tolerating the social relations it reveals. It is by catalyzing the African American through a process of projection and absorption that the sort of interplay characteristic of the African American Imaginary takes place in this poem. It is this sort of interplay, I argue, that is a characteristic of modernist poetics and poetic language, and of modernism generally. It is worth noting here that in a later poem, Moore describes several African American figures, including ragtime pianist Eubie Blake and jazz composer Thomas "Fats" Waller, as "champions" (163) and that still

later, in a short poem with a dedicatory title to African American dancer
Arthur Mitchell, she writes:

> Your jewels of mobility
>
> reveal
> and veil
> a peacock-tail.
>
> (220)

This poem is most interesting for the way it both approaches and steps away
from stereotypes. Its metaphor, in the opening lines, of the dragonfly for the
dancer ("Slim dragonfly / too rapid for the eye / to cage") approaches old
ideas about the relationship between black people and nature, then swiftly
moves off in another direction; thus the poem's reference to the veil in this
context is all the more intriguing, suggesting that more investigation is war-
ranted before ruling out a Du Boisian allusion here.

{ 5 }

At each juncture of the African American Imaginary, then, the stereotypes
and figures associated with the "Discourse of the Black Other" are invoked,
only to be undermined in the very process of invocation. The "comedian" in
Wallace Stevens's poem "The Comedian as the Letter C" (*Collected Poems*
27–46) is both New World explorer and a man whose own identity develops in an anxious relationship with the "Maya Sonneteers" who precede
him; the best explanation for the linguistic innovations of modernist poets
is to liken them to the syncopated rhythms of jazz; and a typical, if not key,
text of literary modernism (Jean Toomer's *Cane*) becomes, in the eyes of its
publishers, a "vaudeville."

In sum, this book is an exploration of the impact of African American
culture on modernist poetic language. It explores the work of Jean Toomer
(1894–1967), Wallace Stevens (1875–1955), Gertrude Stein (1874–1946),
James Bland (1854–1911), Paul Laurence Dunbar (1872–1906), Bert
Williams (1874–1922), and Samuel Beckett (1906–1989), plus the genesis
of ragtime and Tin Pan Alley–style song and of modernist criticism.

The idea that black culture haunts modernism was brought into contemporary literary studies by Toni Morrison. Whereas Morrison is primarily concerned with the means by which this haunting takes place as a function of

fictional rhetoric and character development, chapter 1 here, "Haunted," is concerned with this trope as a function of language. Through an examination of "The Comedian as the Letter C" (1923) the chapter shows how Freud's idea of the uncanny can be used to read Wallace Stevens's poem as an enactment of a specific type of anxiety that catalyzes the construction of modernist self-consciousness, which is a racialized self-consciousness.

Continuing in this vein, chapter 1 uses *Tender Buttons* (1914) by Gertrude Stein to demonstrate how even the most apparently opaque modernist texts are implicated in this dynamic of the racialized uncanny, and, using "Characteristics of Negro Expression" by Zora Neale Hurston (1934) as a primary guide, attempts to uncover the "black" voice of *Tender Buttons*. Finally, an examination of "The St. Louis Blues" by W. C. Handy (1914) provides an opportunity to explore further some roots of the linguistic decreation that became identified with modernist poetics.

Chapter 2, "Lyric," begins by arguing that the emergence of modernist lyric poetry in English was in part influenced by the changes in the character of popular song lyrics in the United States in the late nineteenth and early twentieth centuries. In examining the genealogy of American song through late minstrelsy, ragtime, and early Tin Pan Alley, the discussion singles out two characteristics of American songs: the development of the chorus as a self-contained utterance, independent of dramatic or narrative context; and the emergence of the cliché as a primary carrier of poetic heft within that utterance. One focus of the chapter is on the little-studied nineteenth-century African American songwriter James A. Bland, who introduced these characteristics into his songs in the 1870s. Bland's "Oh! Dem Golden Slippers" (1879), one of the first modern American songs, is examined here as an exemplar of the changes in poetic language that would later bloom more fully both in popular songs such as "Some of These Days" (1910), by Shelton Brooks, and in the canonical poems of literary modernism.

Although Paul Laurence Dunbar is not a modernist poet, I go on to argue that he is a little-examined but important precursor to modernism. Placing an exploration of the development of modernist poetic language within a context that privileges the innovations in lyric brought about by the emergence of American popular song shows that Dunbar was an important modernizer of American lyric language. The poems that chapter 2 studies include his "We Wear the Mask," "The Deserted Plantation" (both published in 1896), "The Poet" (1903), and song lyrics such as "Down de Lover's Lane" (1900) from *The Casino Girl*, the Broadway show on which Dunbar collaborated with composer Will Marion Cook. Dunbar is especially important for this study because he was among the earliest major U.S. poets to become popular both as a literary figure and as a writer of songs for the modern musical theater. Both Dunbar's "pure" English poems and his poems in "Negro dialect" can be seen to share certain affinities with that style of poetry that is associated with the term "Symbolist."

Chapter 3, "Minstrel," begins with a study of the relationship between performativity and lyric language in the art of Bert Williams, the early twentieth-century vaudeville comedian. This chapter argues for a view of Williams's performance personality as an archetypal modernist figure. His incarnation of the tramp manipulates racial stereotypes in such a way that it transcends the very stereotype it performs. The lyrics of his songs, especially his most famous song, "Nobody," written with lyricist Alex Rogers (1905), give voice to this modern urban tramp figure.

The influence of minstrelsy on the work of Samuel Beckett is the subject of the concluding section of this chapter. In each of two of Beckett's plays, *Waiting for Godot* (1953) and *Not I* (1972), the various elements derived from minstrelsy are reconfigured into his theatrical style. In the latter, these elements are joined by features of poetic language (fragmentation, the autonomous utterance, the cliché) that are objects of inquiry throughout this book.

Finally, chapter 4, "Vaudeville," explores the relationship, often described as contentious, between modernism and popular culture, with special reference to Toomer's *Cane*. The discussion begins with a consideration of the use of the words "vaudeville" and "jazz" as metaphors for modernism. Although the fact has received insufficient attention, it is important to understand that these metaphors were constituent elements of the language employed to describe and understand modernism. The chapter also attempts to come to terms with a larger question about the relationship between African American culture, as such, and modernism. If, as I claim, this relationship may be described as interdependent and, to some extent, filial, then why is this idea not a commonplace of our understanding of modernism? One answer might be found in the way modernist criticism, as exemplified by the writings of Clement Greenberg, has polarized "high" and "popular" cultures, setting these terms against each other as if the polarization were itself a commonplace understanding about modern art and literature. I question this view. The polarization is, I suggest, historically bound, and this chapter explores how it came to be socially constructed.

A discussion of the genealogy of modernist criticism by that focuses on Greenberg's 1939 essay "Avant-Garde and Kitsch," considers the fissure within that criticism which allows a prevailing consensus to relegate texts by African Americans and women to a "marginal" status. As in much modernist criticism, the essay renders this fissure through the polarities signified by such terms as "kitsch" and "popular culture."

The book's major themes are then explored through an examination of the modernism of *Cane* (1922). What qualities in Cane are "modernist"? Which are "African American"? These questions are posed in order to uncover the relationship of *Cane* to the blues, the idea of the aesthete, the uses of the pastoral, and the attendant interplay of the symbols of modernity in the text. The purpose of all this is to argue for a reconsideration of the place of *Cane* in the literary canon. The fact that the work has been kept alive primarily by African American literary criticism has in some ways obscured its relationship to literary modernism as a whole, yet a discussion of that relationship provides a means of coming to terms with the larger question of how to redefine the relationship between modernism and the art of African Americans in the modernist era. This study concludes with the position not only that African American culture is a constituent part of modernism but that modernism cannot be fully understood unless its African American element is fully explored. It is in this sense, as well, that the culture created by African Americans in the twentieth century can be seen as essentially modernist.

Thinking in this way calls for a new understanding of modernism. It means that those definitions and explanations that seek to place black literature and culture at the margins of our understanding of modernism end up misunderstanding modernism itself. Such definitions cannot fully account for modernist literature, its linguistic innovations, or its strategies of self-articulation and self-fashioning. Their result is often an array of explanations that seem emptied of heft. Many newer studies attempt to integrate the ways in which (white) modernist artists used African American culture in their work. But whether it is the enthusiasm of T. S. Eliot for (white) blackface comedians or the adoption by William Carlos Williams of jazz age black vernacular, most of these studies do not see African Americans as actors on the modernist stage in a relationship, if not of equality, at least of interaction. This study is distinctive in that it sees modernism as a scene of "play," not only in the sense outlined above but also in the sense used by jazz musicians. It is a scene in which the various actors "played together" to make modernism.

CHAPTER ONE

Haunted

{ 1 }

THE IDEA THAT black culture haunts American literature was suggested by Toni Morrison, who identified what she calls an "Africanist presence" (6) in American literature. Whereas Morrison is primarily concerned with the means by which this haunting takes place as a function of fictional rhetoric and character development, I am concerned with this trope as a function of poetic language and style. In an attempt to expand the idea of this "presence" by examining its function at the semantic and symbolic levels, this chapter explores how such language acts as a function of what I am calling the "African American Imaginary," the term I use to identify an aspect of the cultural milieu in which modernism developed.

This milieu is also a historical one, in which late nineteenth- and early twentieth-century culture in the United States was being reshaped by, in part, the migration of African Americans from the rural areas to the cities. Much of the influence on the larger culture that this migration produced can be seen in its reflection in popular culture, and part of the urbanizing African American culture's influence showed up both in the way popular culture "imagined" black people and in the way African American artists' artistic imagination impacted the larger culture. It was, as I try to show, a process marked by, to use Jacques Lacan's words, "an alternating mechanism of expulsion and introjection, of projection and absorption, that is to say from an imaginary interplay" (82).

The process works, I suggest, in two ways. At the symbolic level, it provides a means by which modernism defines the self in terms of its opposition to this Africanist presence, by proposing that this presence be understood as a kind of binary opposite to itself, a binary in which each side is, in effect, haunted by the other. At the rhetorical level, the process uses the forms of linguistic expression that African American people brought into the culture as a means of creating its own, "new" or "modernist" expression. Put another way, there is a relationship between the concept of the "colonial uncanny" and that of the "African American Imaginary." Modernism is, in part, constituted by an engagement between the racial self-consciousness of whiteness and the figure of the racialized other. This racialized other is not, as is often thought, a mute and unnameable presence but one whose works in the world are as present as those of the speaker, the "modernist."

The ways in which these relationships develop, either in culture in general or in the realm of artistic expression, are not straightforward. As I attempt to demonstrate, the mechanisms described by Lacan (and used, as I suggest below, by Homi K. Bhabha in his discussion of the stereotype) call for understanding this process as one characterized by an interplay of both mimetic and synthetic elements; that is, the song lyrics, dialect phrases, cultural artifacts, and iconography that make up the substance of these elements may or may not belong to the actual African American culture. Whether they are "real" or "copies," however, makes little difference to the substance of this inquiry, because the two forms together make up the "African American Imaginary" that I wish to explore.

Through an examination of "The Comedian as the Letter C" by Wallace Stevens (*Collected Poems* 27–46; hereafter "The Comedian"), one can see how Freud's idea of "the uncanny" can be used to read Stevens's poem as an enactment of a specific type of anxiety which catalyzes the construction of modernist self-consciousness, which is at the same time a racialized self-consciousness. And a discussion of *Tender Buttons* (1914) by Gertrude Stein demonstrates how even the most apparently opaque modernist texts are implicated in this dynamic of the racialized uncanny. Using "Characteristics of Negro Expression" (1934) by Zora Neale Hurston as our primary guide helps to uncover the "black" voice of *Tender Buttons*.

I begin with a consideration of what I call the "language of the colonial uncanny" as it is expressed in the voyage of Crispin in "The Comedian." This idea of the "colonial uncanny" is a way of thinking about how modernism can partially be conceptualized in terms of a performative relationship between the racial self-consciousness of whiteness and the figure of the racialized other. It is a relationship in which the connection can be said to involve an act of haunting. Following this discussion, I turn to another means of using language, that engaged in by Stein in *Tender Buttons*. That use, I argue, is rooted in what I have termed the African American Imaginary. This term is meant to identify that mixture of cultural influences derived from both real and imagined representations of black culture as they existed in the culture at large in the early part of the twentieth century, during the years Stein was composing her first experimental works. Finally, in an examination of the lyrics to the seminal blues song "The St. Louis Blues," I hope to demonstrate how the linguistic operations common to modernist verse are also shared by blues composers.

Those three texts are chosen not only because I am arguing that each one is implicated in the African American Imaginary but also because these works are exemplars of the modernist sensibility. The choice to insert the lyrics to a song based on the blues as a "poetic" text alongside two canonical and more conventionally "literary" ones may seem provocative, but this particular song first entered the culture as a text written on paper and was a major conduit (both as a text and as a representation of an aesthetic practice) for the interaction of African American expressive and creative culture with the majority culture.

{ 2 }

It has been a long time since the days when literary critics could ignore the racist epithet in the title of one of most famous and accomplished poems of Wallace Stevens, explicating that title with only a gloss calling it an "ellipsis" (Vendler, "Like Decorations" 136) or referring to its meaning in a footnote (Vendler, *On Extended Wings* 65–78, 321). This state of affairs dominated Stevens criticism historically, however, and the silence about his racialized language often shocks new readers of the poet's work (DuRose 6–8). At the same time, the attention paid to the way race and racialization figure in Stevens's work has its own peculiar features which tend to focus on thematics, treating the rhetorical strategies he employs as a secondary feature in enhancing our understanding of the poet's relationship to race and racism. To cite one example, Aldon Lynn Nielsen is concerned with Stevens's subjective attitude toward black people: "The black in America is Stevens' homeless cosmopolitan," Nielsen writes. Stevens's work is an example, he adds, of a poetry "in which black people simply carry things about while white writers experience them" (*Reading Race* 65, 76–77).

Lisa DuRose points out that critics have cited numerous incidents from Stevens's life which reveal a presumed "alignment with and sympathy for the African Other"; however, she adds: "No critic asks what Stevens gains, artistically, by embracing 'the primitive strength' of his African American characters or by experimenting in his poetry with the rhythm of ragtime music. Their tone suggests an admiration for the poet, for what he gives African Americans, namely a sense of legitimacy and a call for recognition of their gifts (all stereotypically framed, of course)" (7).

In examining this question, critics write about a handful of poems, including "Like Decorations in a Nigger Cemetery," "Exposition of the Contents of a Cab," "Nudity in the Colonies," "Nudity at the Capitol," "Prelude to Objects," "The News and the Weather" (DuRose 6–8), and, sometimes, "The Silver Plough Boy." When he talks about the poet's racializing tropology, Eric Keenaghan is interested in how Stevens's language allows "his narrators' perspectives to become *overdetermined* by what his contemporaries would interpret as perverse forms of sexual desire, ranging from miscegenation to voyeurism to homosexuality" (441; original emphasis). In all these interpretations, the focus is on Stevens (and Stevens's speaker) as poetic subject. Yet there remains the rhetoric of the poems themselves, which seem to call for explanations placing us outside a paradigm that focuses on the moral subjectivity of the poet. There is a sense in which both those critics who ignore Stevens's racial language and those who criticize the poet's racial stereotyping are united in privileging the poet, rather than the poems, as the center of critical attention. This privileging is not always presented as unmotivated—indeed, the idea that Stevens is at least somewhat motivated in presenting his racialized characters and tropes is a common thread in the criticism that addresses race—but critics often present this motivation as a means by which the poet achieves aesthetic goals. To ask what Stevens gains, artistically, through this racial tropology is the overriding mode of such inquiry.

The problem with this mode of inquiry is that it doesn't sufficiently examine what is at stake in the poet's deployment of a language that signifies racialized distancing. In ignoring or playing down this aspect of the poetry's language, much of the criticism that concerns Stevens has the effect of erasing the agency of the racialized figures the poet creates, which in turn poses problems for our own reading of the poems and especially for our reading of the ways in which the stereotypes and other racialized figures are being deployed. I seek to reverse this normative strategy of reading and to discover whether we can find some new way of explaining the role these figures have in the poetry. More generally, it is my aim to find whether we can more adequately explain how race and racializing language can be said to be a constituent element in the construction of the modernist literary artwork.

"The Comedian" is a poem that deploys language signifying the racialized other, but it is one in which that deployment is not necessarily obvious or normally a subject of inquiry. It has long been accepted that "The Comedian" is a quest poem, and its genealogy in this regard (its relationship to Shelley's "Alastor," and to Whitman's "The Sleepers," "Out of the

Cradle Endlessly Rocking," and "As I Ebb'd with the Ocean of Life") has been established by both Vendler and Harold Bloom. Bloom, not surprisingly, sees the poem as being primarily about the anxiety of influence. "It is a poem about those writers who induced such anxiety, however repressed, in Stevens," he writes (72). Rather than seeing the poem as primarily a literary argument, however, we might take its mythical burdens seriously and consider with which myths both the poem's speaker and the poem's character, Crispin, are contending.

We are confronted with this problem from the first stanza. The opening lines appear to be an assertion of the generic "man" and his domination over nature:

> Nota: Man is the intelligence of his soil,
> The sovereign ghost. As such, the Socrates
> Of snails, musician of pears, principium
> And lex.
>
> (Stevens 27)

This is a common enough theme in Stevens's poetry; but then the poem asks rhetorically whether man is "the preceptor to the sea"—whether, in other words, man is the instructor of nature. It is here that "man" becomes a specific man: Stevens's hero, Crispin. He is named and introduced as the eye whose gaze encompasses and, presumably, defines nature.

> the eye of Crispin, hung
> On porpoises, instead of apricots,
> And on silentious porpoises, whose snouts
> Dibbled in waves that were mustachios,
> Inscrutable hair in an inscrutable world.
>
> (27)

Though his gaze may be powerful, two adversaries confront Crispin at the beginning of the poem: his own limitations, and Triton; and though Crispin may be the "musician of pears," it must be remembered that Triton is a trumpeter of the seas. This conflict animates the first part of the poem, that part titled, "The World without Imagination":

> Against his pipping sounds a trumpet cried
> Celestial sneering boisterously. Crispin
> Became an introspective voyager.
>
> (29)

Triton is followed by even more significant adversaries, whose strength both frightens and challenges Crispin. They include the Maya Sonneteers, the storm that comes from "west of Mexico," and the visions of Crispin's sleep

> In which the sulky strophes willingly
> Bore up, in time, the somnolent, deep songs.
>
> (33)

Throughout the poem there stands, behind the conflicted but still-powerful voyager, a latent power that always threatens and sometimes challenges Crispin. There is an undercurrent of anxiety, signified, in one instance, by the Maya Sonneteers, the "green barbarism turning paradigm," who, despite the anxiety they produce for Crispin and his project,

> Came like two spirits parleying, adorned
> In radiance from the Atlantic coign
> For Crispin and his quill to catechize.
>
> (31)

In what is perhaps the most direct allusion to the nature of this anxiety, the voyager, in the poem's "Approaching Carolina" section, has left the parts where his gaze and his writing have conquered and has entered, as it were, a land where human labor power and its products predominate. The warehouse and railroad with their smells provide, for Crispin, the balance that "helped him round his rude aesthetic out" (36), but this Whitmanesque allusion immediately succumbs to one that would again signify a central set of anxieties animating this poem. Warehouse, railroad spur, "rotten fence" would have, so the speaker claims, a salutary effect on Crispin:

> It purified. It made him see how much
> Of what he saw he never saw at all.
>
> (36)

The allusion appears to be to a line from *Huckleberry Finn*: "It shows how a body can see and don't see, at the same time" (Twain 291), and it is this double nature of Crispin's vision that gives the poem, for all its fantastic language and its mapping of a linguistic terrain of self-discovery, an anxiety founded upon a rhetoric that I choose to call the language of the colonial uncanny.

For Freud, "the uncanny" refers to an emotional effect that is transformed, by repression, into a morbid anxiety which becomes uncanny by virtue of repetition. The repeated occurrence of this morbid emotional effect causes the sensation of being haunted. This idea animates much of the modernist project, and in "The Comedian," Stevens's first major long poem, as in many other such works, the idea of the racialized other is often an active agent, pushing forward the anxiety of the presumed modernist subject. The important thing to remember, however, is exactly the point that this just-below-the-surface agent is an active, constitutive part of the construction of the identity of the modernist work of art. The "other" is only an other if we don't pay attention to what the figure is saying. In Stevens's "The Comedian," this "other" figure appears as the Maya Sonneteers, who challenge the primacy of the poem's voyager with a presence of their own, one that commands the forces of wind and storm which the "introspective voyager" with his catechizing quill can barely tame. Yet we must observe not simply the conflict enacted between the various and repeated manifestations of the obstacles erected against the voyager but the way the language projects these obstacles as elements of the fantastic—of, perhaps, even fantasy.

Homi K. Bhabha writes about the essential role of fantasy in the construction of colonial discourse: "Not itself the object of desire but its setting, not an ascription of prior identities but their production in the syntax of the scenario of racist discourse, colonial fantasy plays a crucial part in those everyday scenes of subjectification in a colonial society which Fanon refers to repeatedly." Such fantasy is the substance of the racialized stereotype, which Bhabha, drawing his language from Jacques Lacan, describes in the following way: "Stereotyping is not the setting up of a false image which becomes the scapegoat of discriminatory practices. It is a much more ambivalent text of projection and introjection, metaphoric and metonymic strategies, displacement, overdetermination, guilt, aggressivity; the masking and splitting of "official" and phantasmatic knowledges to construct the positionalities and oppositionalities of racist discourse" (81–82). "The Comedian" deploys a whole array of fantastically described insects, flora, and fauna to depict the terrain through which Crispin travels, and it is within this terrain that the eruptions of storms, mysterious counterpoetics, and the "somnolent, deep songs"—perhaps an allusion to black music that's as stereotypical as it is complex—occurs. The term suggests the African American ("Negro") spiritual, those songs that W. E. B. Du Bois called the "sorrow songs," and in the phrase itself is the suggestion of one such song, "Deep River," which was beginning to achieve popularity in the 1920s through performances and recordings.[1]

Freud talks about a second part of the uncanny, in addition to the recurrence of the repressed emotional effect: the uncanny, he says, is "nothing new or foreign, but something familiar or old–fashioned in the mind that has been estranged only by the process of repression." He adds, "An uncanny experience occurs either when repressed infantile complexes have been revived by some impression, or when the primitive beliefs we have surmounted seem once more to be confirmed" (148, 157). The stereotype, and the figure that haunts, must be, above all, something familiar, and it is this familiarity that gives the figure its characteristic as a fetishized thing. Avery F. Gordon cites three characteristics of haunting:

> The ghost imports a charged strangeness into the place or sphere it is haunting, thus unsettling the propriety and property lines that delimit a zone of activity or knowledge. I have also emphasized that the ghost is primarily a symptom of what is missing. It gives notice not only to itself but also to what it represents. What it represents is usually a loss, sometimes of life, sometimes of a path not taken. From a certain vantage point the ghost also simultaneously represents a future possibility, a hope. Finally, I have suggested that the ghost is alive, so to speak. (63–64)

The problem with reading "The Comedian" as an autobiographical poem of discovery, or as simply an argument over literary influence, is that such readings repeat and reinforce the repression that the poem itself enacts only with great tension and anxiety. The price of Crispin's anxiety is his own uncertainty, his own ambivalence in a world in which he is the discoverer, the voyager, but a world the ownership of which, for all his exertion of power over it, ultimately eludes him.

The section titled "The Idea of a Colony" is the turning point of the poem, as the voyager now has to devise the parameters of his domination. As Edward Marx observes, "Crispin's half-serious poetic ideology concocted in 'The Idea of a Colony' is beset by conflict and irresolution as he grapples with the question of imposing some kind of order on the cultural producers of his colony" (272). Here is where the language of the uncanny becomes plenitudinous. Throughout the poem, the reader has been treated to the eruptions of anxiety visited both on the speaker and on Crispin, as he navigates his way through this territory in which he is both discoverer and the figure that's being "discovered." Now, however, we come up directly against the anxiety that has been with us all along:

The natives of the rain are rainy men.
Although they paint effulgent, azure lakes,
And April hillsides wooded white and pink,
Their azure has a cloudy edge, their white
And pink, the water bright that dogwood bears.
And in their music showering sounds intone.

(37)

These "rainy men" with their "showering sounds" threaten to engulf Crispin, even as he establishes himself in this colony, whose "idea" is to replace the "natives of the rain" with other colonizers: "The man in Georgia walking among pines / Should be the pine-spokesman." The poem then continues with a striking verse that signals the link I am attempting to demonstrate between the concept of the "colonial uncanny" and that of the "African American Imaginary." My use of both terms is an attempt to show the ways in which modernism is, in part, constituted by an engagement between the racial self-consciousness of whiteness and the figure of the racialized other, which is not, as is often thought, a mute and unnameable presence but one whose works in the world are as present as those of the speaker, the "modernist." It is important to consider that when Stevens's speaker identifies the "man in Georgia," this "man" lives in a world with other men, such as the Maya Sonneteers, or with the artists whose presence is hinted at in the following:

The responsive man,
Planting his pristine cores in Florida,
Should prick thereof, not on the psaltery,
But on the banjo's categorical gut,
Tuck, tuck, while the flamingoes flapped his bays.

(38)

To be "responsive," then, is to be responsive—in particular, by means of imitation—to the African.

A key to this passage, I would argue, is the appearance of the banjo as a symbol. It is not uncommon for the mechanism of this uncanny that I have been discussing to appear in the form of a musical instrument, or as a specific musical genre that is identified with African Americans. The banjo, in this instance, like Crispin, signifies travel and exploration. The instrument has a long history in the Americas. Though its exact provenance is a source of dispute, its appearance among slaves brought from Africa to the Americas has been noted as far back as the seventeenth century. In an often cited footnote, Thomas Jefferson, in the midst of the diatribe against black people that he published in *Notes on the State of Virginia*, wrote: "The instrument proper to them [black people] is the Banjar, which they brought hither from Africa, and which is the original of the guitar, its chords being precisely the four lower chords of the guitar" (135; cf. Courlander 212; Epstein 354). The footnote and the book of which it is a part are also intriguing for another reason. Like "The Comedian," Jefferson's *Notes*, as Floyd Ogburn Jr. points out, is a text in which the quest metaphor plays a significant role (142–43). Others have pointed to Jefferson's racist rationalizations in the section of *Notes* that the "banjar" footnote annotates (Magnis).

That scholars seem to have paid scant attention to the way black Americans haunt Jefferson's text is perhaps due to the effect this text is presumed to have had on African American culture, an effect described this way by Henry Louis Gates Jr.: "Asserted primarily to debunk the exaggerated claims of the abolitionists, Thomas Jefferson's remarks on Phillis Wheatley's poetry, as well as on Ignatius Sancho's posthumously published *Letters* (1782), exerted a prescriptive influence over the criticism of the writing of blacks for the next 150 years" (*Figures in Black* 5). Whatever the truth of Gates's assertion, it is also true that Jefferson's *Notes* is an exemplar of the ambivalence that Bhabha assigns to the trope of the stereotype. Jefferson's mixture of supposition and superstition in attributing inferior status to Africans in the Americas is fraught with the necessity of naming figures whose very existence poses a threat to the scaffold of ideas he is trying to construct. "Religion, indeed, has produced a Phillis Whatley [*sic*]; but it could not produce a poet," Jefferson writes (135). Why, however, must he be engaged enough to name her if, as he continues by saying, that her poems are "below the dignity of criticism?" This mention of Wheatley occurs during one of two discussions of poetry in *Notes*, and Wheatley is the only American poet Jefferson mentions by name in the entire text. Through this very acknowledgment, then, Jefferson betrays an anxiety which is at the heart of my concerns here: the way in which a relationship of "charged strangeness," to use Avery Gordon's words, exists between African American culture and modernism (and, in the case of Jefferson, the culture of modernity), and how this strangeness is not founded on an acknowledgment of this relationship

but is based on what might be called an "anthropological" model of the discovery of artifacts. It is a relationship that acknowledges itself in the form of
direct address, by the naming of artists and the instruments of art and by its
incorporation of forms of language used by African Americans. This is what
is meant here by the term African American Imaginary. By naming Wheatley and the banjo, Jefferson engages this imaginary even while rejecting it at
the level of the text's foregrounded exposition.

The same is true for the speaker of "The Comedian," whose own evocation of the banjo is made in the context of the tasks that the poem's explorer
must undertake to become the man who is "responsive" to his environment.
The very evocation of the banjo here, however, reveals the anxiety at the
heart of the poem's language. It is not only the natural environment and the
people within it which the poem's explorer must conquer; to be truly responsive, the explorer must conquer as well the art forms and the instruments of art making that he finds within that environment. He must learn
to play the banjo. Despite such mastery, however, the anxiety never goes
away for Crispin, because he knows that the colony is, after all, only an idea:

> He could not be content with counterfeit,
> With masquerade of thought, with hapless words
> That must belie the racking masquerade . . .
>
> (39)

Understanding the dilemma that haunts Crispin, and the poem's speaker,
cannot be, as Eric Keenaghan rightly observes, limited to identifying a "sim-
plistic return of the racialized repressed" (441), if for no other reason than
that the return is itself not so simple. Implicated within the lyric exposition
of this voyage is the question of what to do with the fact that the figures and
voices which Crispin (and the poem's speaker) seek to repress are not, in
fact, repressed at all but are themselves constituent (if unconscious) parts
and voices of the poem. It is a question that the poem itself repeatedly asks
and one that modernist poems find themselves asking quite a bit. Repeating
an image we find also in T. S. Eliot's "Portrait of a Lady," the poem's speaker
uses an object which itself signifies the very anxiety I've been attempting to
identify:

> Was he to company vastest things defunct
> With a blubber of tom-toms harrowing the sky?
>
> (41)

In Eliot's poem, the speaker is plagued with the sounds of competing strands of music, each representing, presumably, the differing directions in which modern society is being pulled:

> Among the windings of the violins
> And the ariettes
> Of cracked cornets
> Inside my brain a dull tom-tom begins
> Absurdly hammering a prelude of its own,
> Capricious monotone
> That is at least one definite "false note."
> (Eliot, *Complete Poems* 9)

In each poem, what is at stake is the speaker's attempt to resolve the conflict between the values of his present life and the voice of the racialized other, which threatens the stability of that presence. This anxiety, this conflict, is at the very core of modernism. It is, in a sense, a constituent part of the modernist identity itself, an identity that we can only understand as one that's split into a racialized "subject" and "other" (as opposed to one whose racialized tropology is an object of fantasy) if we refuse to listen.

{ 3 }

If Wallace Stevens's Crispin can be said to enact his voyage in a language of the colonial uncanny, in Gertrude Stein's earliest experiments with poetic language a fissure seems to open between the language on the page and its linguistic antecedents. Although I have argued so far that within Stevens's language we can find an echo of an anxiety in the wake of the emergence of the racialized "other," an anxiety that then produces that fissure, my argument now attempts to uncover the contents of the fissure by exploring whether we can find an unconscious African American language within the apparent opacity of Stein's *Tender Buttons* (1914). It is a work particularly useful for this investigation because of its increasingly acknowledged place in the canon of American modernist poetry.

The work's appearance came at a moment that was significant for modern culture for another reason: the year 1914 was also the year in which "The St. Louis Blues," W. C. Handy's seminal blues song, was published. Although I do not seek to claim a linkage between the two, the coincident temporal appearance of these two works of modern culture seems to suggest lines of investigation into the making of modernist culture that would demand attention to what Adele Heller and Lois Rudnick call "the cultural moment."

For Heller and Rudnick, that moment is the year 1915, when the Provincetown Players were born. We need not argue for prioritizing one year over the other, however, when we point to *Tender Buttons* and "The St. Louis Blues" as objects of our investigation. My point, in focusing on what I am calling the "African American linguistic unconscious" in *Tender Buttons*, is to deepen the discussion of the "language of the colonial uncanny" that I deployed earlier. The aim, here, is to deepen our understanding of how Stein's linguistic experimentalism can be said to be a product, in part, of an interaction with black American culture, an interaction which, however much it has been acknowledged at the thematic level, is rarely investigated by looking at the style in which *Tender Buttons* is written.

To aid in this investigation, I pay some attention also to a work that appeared twenty years after Stein's but stands as one of the earliest popular and literary investigations into African American vernacular language: "Characteristics of Negro Expression" (1934) by Zora Neale Hurston, which originally appeared in *Negro*, an anthology published by Nancy Cunard.

Commentators have often acknowledged the influence of African American culture on Stein's work. "While Stein is arguably one of the most radical innovators in early twentieth century literature, her work at the same time contains some of the most openly racist descriptions of characters," writes Laura Doyle (256). Aldon Lynn Nielsen's comment that "Stein's own attitudes toward the nonwhite are everywhere problematic" (22) seems to be confirmed by numerous biographical and exegetical examinations of her life and work, including his own summary account. Most discussions of Stein's racism begin, as does Doyle's, with an examination of her story "Melanctha" from *Three Lives*. Jamie Hovey, for instance, examines the ways in which "Melanctha" deploys primitivist tropes as a means of rewriting (and at least partially obscuring) the lesbian sexuality that is present in the story's source: Stein's early, autobiographical novel, *Q.E.D.* (1903), which was never published during her lifetime.

A few critics, such as Nielsen and Lorna J. Smedman, point to the presence of racist epithets in *Tender Buttons*, drawing particular attention to the phrase "needless are niggers" (494) from the poem "Dinner" in the "Food" section of the work. Rarely do these discussions also point to the one-line poem "White Hunter" in "Objects": "A white hunter is nearly crazy" (475).

Nevertheless, this search for the racist epithet in Stein's work has its own problematic dimension. Doyle suggests that the poet's racist remarks were an intentional provocation: "These lines are calculated to offend. They are indistinguishable from contemporary racist assumptions among many educated, established whites about blacks and new immigrants but are pushed a step further than 'polite' white society (which Stein knew well enough) would like to read in print or hear out loud" (263).

Given that Stein began her writing career during the heart of the years Rayford Logan calls the "nadir" of African American life, it is difficult to agree with Doyle about what could be said aloud in "polite" society. Nevertheless, in the context of "Melanctha"—whose main character is a young African American woman whom Stein portrays more sympathetically and in a less stereotypical and derogatory manner than was typical for white writers at the time—one could understand how Doyle could come to such a conclusion. Such a claim would be more difficult to support in the context of *Tender Buttons*, a text whose reputation as one of the most linguistically obscure of all modernist works would seem to make any talk of intentionality on the writer's part speculative at best. At the same time, the phrases quoted above would seem to call upon readers to inquire whether in *Tender Buttons* there is more to Stein's engagement with African American culture than a few epithets. What if there is, within this apparently opaque language, a reflection, and perhaps a continuation, of Stein's engagement with a perceived African American linguistic universe that began with "Melanctha"? The question of Stein's style in *Buttons* has long puzzled readers. Yet there seems to have been no inquiry into whether there is some relationship between that style and the African American speech—either real speech or cultural artifact—which would have been part of Stein's everyday milieu.

That everyday milieu included Baltimore, where Stein attended the Johns Hopkins medical school. Carla L. Peterson has written in detail about the African American culture of Baltimore in the last decade of the nineteenth century and its influence on *Q.E.D.* and *Three Lives*. Indeed, Peterson claims that to write "Melanctha," "Stein turned to black cultural forms with which she had come into contact during her Baltimore years" (145). The city was a major site of modern African American music and particularly well known as a center of ragtime music. The title of one of the best-known ragtime songs, "Baltimore Buzz" (recorded as a piano solo by Eubie Blake in 1921), gives a fair indication of the importance of the city to the development of African American musical culture.

The suggestion made by Peterson that the black music of the time had some influence on Stein's early work is an intriguing one. In particular, Peterson argues that readers should pay close attention to the phenomenon known as the "coon song" in order to uncover some of the sources of Stein's experimental literary language: "Perhaps the earliest Negro sound that Stein would have heard in Baltimore in the 1890s was the coon song, sung by whites and blacks alike, that had developed out of earlier minstrel and road show traditions. Its lyrics relied on caricature and racist stereotyping in order to ridicule and lampoon blacks as uncivilized and primitive people" (146). This song form constituted a major style of popular music in the last two decades of the nineteenth century, prefiguring the rise of ragtime at the end of the century. Many of the important popular singers of the era were coon singers (or "coon shouters," as they were often called). Among the major singers associated with the form were African American singers such as Ernest Hogan and Bert Williams, and white singers such as Arthur Collins (the so-called "King of the Coon Shouters"), Dolly Connolly, Billy Murray, May Irwin, Al Jolson, and Sophie Tucker (Clarke 62; Wondrich 81–111). All these performers, both black and white, performed in blackface makeup.

This could have been one of the genres of popular music that Stein and her contemporaries listened to and played at home on the piano during her youth and young adulthood. As Peterson writes, the coon song deployed many of the most outlandish racial stereotypes in its lyrics. Peterson suggests that many of Stein's characters in "Melanctha" are based on stereotypes made popular by the coon songs: "It is to this tradition, I suggest, that Stein turned in order to portray Melanctha's father, James Herbert, her last lover, Jem Richards, and her friend, Rose Johnson," Peterson writes (146). The sheet music of these enormously popular songs sold well throughout the United States and abroad. Their popularity was in large part based on the simultaneous rise, in all media, of anti-black racist stereotypes as a major social discourse. As James H. Dormon points out: "The coon song craze in its full frenzy was a manifestation of a peculiar form of the will to believe — to believe in the signified 'coon' as represented in the songs — as a necessary sociopsychological mechanism for justifying segregation and subordination" (466).

Dormon begins his examination of this phenomenon by calling our attention to the rise of what he calls "an essentially new etymological departure: the pervasive use of the word 'coon' as a designation for 'Afro-American'" (452–53). He calls the emergence of this term a "linguistic coup"

(453), and, indeed, many of these songs seemed to rest on this word as their main identifying feature. It was a conduit for the pervasive use of insulting and degrading language and scenes in the song, at the same time serving to identify the songs as, in some sense, belonging to African America. This genre comprised songs written by both blacks and whites (a point I return to later).

It is sufficient for my present purpose to take note of just a few basic characteristics of this genre. First, these were humorous songs set to syncopated melodies. The humor, however, was often deployed in the interest of portraying the most intensely derogatory racial stereotypes. As Dormon writes, in the coon songs, "blacks began to appear as not only ignorant and indolent, but also devoid of honesty or personal honor, given to drunkenness and gambling, utterly without ambition, sensuous, libidinous, even lascivious. 'Coons' were, in addition to all these things, razor-wielding savages, routinely attacking one another at the slightest provocation as a normal function of their uninhibited social lives" (455). But perhaps the "single most threatening [aspect] of the new ascriptive 'coon' stereotypes," continues Dormon, "was the implied threat to the hallowed racial caste system protected in the past by slavery, and now, in the early 1890s, devoid of clear sanction in law. This most threatening of all themes—threatening at least in its encoded subliminal message—was the theme of the black who wants to become white" (461). This theme was related to the possibility of racial "passing" and its collateral assault on the ideas of white racial purity that animated so much white supremacist discourse.

Here we begin to see, in the development of the song styles emerging at this time, themes that hint at the idea of African Americans as familiar, yet also strange and threatening. It seems, then, that one element giving the coon song its power was its capacity to play on the very anxieties that constituted so much of white supremacist discourse. Dormon gives numerous examples from songs of the 1890s, but it is useful to recall that variations on this theme remained in African American popular music for a long time afterward. One derivation appeared, perhaps most famously, in a song of the jazz age, a song written in 1929 by Andy Razaf, which Louis Armstrong later used as a theme song in performances during the civil rights era:

> I'm white, inside, but that don't help my case,
> Cause I can't hide what is in my face.
> (Armstrong, "Black and Blue")

This is perhaps a far cry from the way the sentiment had been expressed some thirty years before Razaf wrote "Black and Blue" by the chorus of one of the most famous of the coon songs:

> Coon! Coon! Coon!
> I wish my color would fade:
> Coon! Coon! Coon!
> I'd like a different shade.
> Coon! Coon! Coon! Morning, night, and noon.
> I wish I was a white man!
> 'Stead of a Coon! Coon! Coon!
> (Qtd. in Dormon 463)

The combination of racist stereotypes with an obsessiveness with whiteness and the possibilities of racial passing was pervasive in the language of the coon songs, which were expressive of these anxieties among white people just as often as they portrayed a set of supposed analogous anxieties among black people. This kind of doubling masquerade that was embodied in the coon song was characteristic of minstrelsy, which initially based itself on the idea of whites masquerading as blacks. The coon song was a product of late minstrelsy, as it was beginning to give way to vaudeville, an era in which black performers such as Ernest Hogan, George Walker, and Bert Williams began to gain national attention through variations on this masquerade.

Black minstrels had long used blackface makeup, imitating white minstrels who imitated black people; but in the coon song, black and white songwriters and singers were imitating, on the national stage, the psychological anxieties attendant on the rising racism of the time. It was a case of the emergent African American Imaginary using humor and parody both to give voice to and to signify upon the paranoia that lies at the heart of racist discourse.[2]

One way of thinking about this doubling masquerade is in terms of Judith Butler's idea of the performative, which has to do with the way gender is not an ontological category but a socially constructed one. Its use here must carry with it an appropriate set of qualifications.[3] Nevertheless, her idea that in the construction of gender, "acts, gesture and desire" produce the appearance of gender identity "on the surface of the body" is quite useful in understanding the cultural discourse catalyzed by the emergence of the "coon" song. Butler adds: "Such acts, gestures, enactments, generally construed, are *performative* in the sense that the essence or identity that they otherwise purport to express are *fabrications* manufactured and sustained through corporeal signs and other discursive means" (173; original emphasis).

Minstrelsy and the coon song created an *idea* of racialized expression and of the racialized body that reflected primarily the set of social restrictions and customs characterizing the legal regime of racist segregation that was then emerging in the United States. At the same time, the idea, as expressed in the song quoted above, of the black singer's desire to be white was itself expressed in terms of an African American culture whose primary existence was as a *staged* event. What relationship did this staged event have to social reality as it was lived by black people? To what extent did it reflect a social reality or a social paranoia? It is easy to say that minstrelsy and the coon song were fabrications, and leave it at that; but the fact is that these "fabrications" were also part of an expressive, artistic culture then emerging from the black community. It is from within the nexus of this contradiction that the African American Imaginary (which can be said to be a site where "black culture" is "performed" by the culture at large) emerges. These issues surrounding the performance of blackness in the United States in the late nineteenth and early twentieth centuries, the period that Rayford Logan calls "the nadir of the Negro's status in American society" (52), seem also to be ones that were crucial in the formation of the culture we call "modernist." It is here, then, that we can productively read the interplay of the African American Imaginary with Gertrude Stein's early experimental texts such as *Tender Buttons*, since these issues and the linguistic representation of them appear to have been central concerns for Stein as well. For Lorna Smedman, who has written about the use of the word "coon" in Stein's work, the importance of Stein's use of such words is illustrative of a contradiction embedded in her experimental language project:

> Stein's use of racialized language is best understood in the context of her focus on difference and relation in the arenas of semantics and syntax. Racialized signifiers, which foregrounded the issue of difference by embodying America's brutal racist history, posed the greatest challenge to Stein's project: to unlink the signifier from the signified, to foster a plurality of meaning, to reformulate relations between words outside the laws of grammar. If she was drawn to racialized terms and references again and again, it was because, unlike many others, these signifiers could not be separated from what they signified. (570)

If Stein's use of these terms was prompted primarily by their challenge to her artistic project, then one can be justified in reading them within a historically and sociologically bound narrative which helps explain Stein's personal tastes and prejudices. Smedman's account of the meaning for Stein of this racialized language, however, suggests also another interpretive possibility. One could argue that in Smedman's description, Stein's project has certain similarities to the way African American culture (and the imitators of African American culture) used language both in everyday speech and in such venues as the coon song. Indeed, it is possible that Stein's very attempt to use this racialized language to accomplish her aesthetic ends had the effect of (at least partially) wrenching these terms from their moorings. This effect can perhaps be more clearly demonstrated by looking not at how she uses the language that racializes African Americans but at how her language discourses on "whiteness."

In some of the earliest pieces in *Tender Buttons*, "A Substance in a Cushion," "A Box," and "A Piece of Coffee," Stein uses the word "white" in alluding to both color and stereotype. White is deployed in a meditation on the idea of cleanliness, which arrays the color against counter-concepts of colors associated with dirt:

> A closet, a closet does not connect under the bed. The band of it is white and black, the band has a green string. A sight a whole sight and a little groan grinding makes a trimming such sweet singing trimming and a red thing not a round thing but a white thing, a red thing and a white thing. (462)

> So then the order is that the white way of being round is something suggesting a pin and is it disappointing, it is not, it is so rudimentary to be analyzed and see a fine substance strangely, it is so earnest to have a green point not to red but to point again. (463)

> Dirty is yellow. A sign of more in not mentioned. A piece of coffee is not a detainer. The resemblance to yellow is dirtier and distincter. The clean mixture is whiter and not coal color, never more coal color than altogether. (463)

> All the seats are needing blackening. A white dress is in sign. A soldier a real soldier has a worn lace a worn lace of different sizes that is to say if he can read, if he can read he is a size to show shutting up twenty-four.

> Go red go red, laugh white. (475)

The association of yellow with dirt, the idea that the band of white and black "does not connect under the bed," and the idea that coffee's "resemblance to yellow" is "dirtier," and that "the clean mixture is whiter and not coal color" can all be read as racialized signifiers, used here for the purpose of scrambling the normative relations of syntax. And yet their use is also consistent with the way these terms appeared in such popular language arenas as advertising and the coon songs of the day. Shades of skin color were among the subjects of several coon songs, and the association between black skin and dirt was widely used by advertisers of soap and detergent products.

The language of advertising is of interest for another set of reasons. Richard Ohmann has traced changes in the discourse of print advertising during the late nineteenth and early twentieth centuries and finds that the language of advertising became, over this period, less text-heavy, and more reliant on images to carry the burden of persuasion (175–85, 218). As the amount of text in advertisements diminished, the burden of persuasion came to rest more on slogans, on clichés. It is useful to keep in mind that the emergence of the slogan as the carrier of the main burden of persuasion in advertising took place right at the moment that Stein was composing *Tender Buttons*.

The advertising slogan tended to raise the poeticity of advertisements. Samuel Jay Keyser has looked at how modern advertisements use poetic devices as means of persuasion; he cites such devices as syllable repetition, poetic format, and rhyme, chiasmus, exemplification, and compression, among others, as common features of magazine advertisements. At the beginning of the twentieth century, when the modern phase of advertising was developing, these features were just coming into wide use. Modern advertising was aimed primarily at female consumers, and its language and imagery were focused on selling domestic products: soap, foodstuffs, household goods, and new technology such as washing machines and modern stoves. Moreover, as Marilyn Mannes Mehaffy has demonstrated, advertising trade cards of the late nineteenth and early twentieth centuries were part of a racialized discourse, much like the coon songs. In trade-card advertisements this discourse was realized by the pairing of "black domestic labor and white (consuming) domesticity," which, Mehaffy, says, constitute the "primary iconography" of such cards: "This prevalent pairing can be attributed, in part, to the trade card's representational participation in a larger national discourse—of plantation literature, the visual arts, and politics—mythologizing antebellum slavery as a more coherent, tranquil era 'lost' to the uncertainties and upheavals of postwar urbanism, industrialism, and commercialization" (142).

These ads, like the songs, were a fundamental part of the popular culture of the day. It was not only their iconography that took part in this racialized discourse but the text of the ads as well. In many, the texts were written in a style that approximated the African American theatrical and literary dialect of the day. This ersatz African American speech, in both advertisements and songs, was part of the environment of the African American Imaginary which constituted part of Stein's environment—the environment that she drew from in her experimental texts, where she used these racialized words and associations to create her poetic language of dissociation. One of the ways she uses such language is not far removed from its use in the African American community as a means of fostering (in Smedman's words) "plurality of meaning."

For a further understanding of this linguistic strategy, another text can help us see more clearly some aspects of Stein's experimental texts. Though it was published some twenty years after *Tender Buttons*, "Characteristics of Negro Expression" (1934) by Zora Neale Hurston is an important interpretive tool for the present discussion because that essay is a literary (as opposed to strictly linguistic) analysis of the sort of African American speech with which Stein would have been familiar. It is an attempt to codify and characterize some elements of African American speech. Indeed, it is one of the earliest texts of any sort to attempt a serious examination of that speech, since "significant research on Black English in the United States is almost entirely a product of the 1960s," claims J. L. Dillard (*Black English* 6).[4] One aspect of Hurston's essay is the way it seems to complement some of the concerns that occupied Stein during the time she was writing *Tender Buttons*.

In what might be seen as a somewhat ornate analysis, given the way it employs terms that were commonly accepted by anthropologists of the time (such as "primitive"), Hurston's claims for the distinction of African American vernacular language revolve around a number of characteristics. The first is the use, in African American language, of "picture words" (she gives examples such as "sitting chair" and "cook pot"), in which "the speaker has in his mind the picture of the object in use" (50).[5] Second is the "will to adorn" (50), the use of ornamental expressions and words. She cites several, at least one of which remains a part of the language: "bodaciously."[6] Hurston goes on to write about what she calls "the Negro's greatest contribution to the language," including "(1) the use of metaphor and simile; (2) the use of the double descriptive; (3) the use of verbal nouns" (51). She lists numerous examples of each category, and this is where her text begins to enter the realm of modernist poetic language. Here is a sample from the "metaphor and simile" section:

> One at a time, like lawyers going
> to heaven.
> You sho is propaganda.
> Sobbing hearted.
> I'll beat you till: (a) rope like okra,
> (b) slack like lime, (c) smell like onions.
> Fatal for naked.
> Kyting along.
> That's a rope.
>
> (51)

Such syntax, in which the adjectives appear to substitute for nouns and verbs, seems not so very different from the sort of linguistic operations Stein employs in such lines as "A white dress is in sign," or "Go red go red, laugh white." Hurston's list of "nouns from verbs" shows a remarkable affinity with Stein's language:

> Won't stand a broke.
> She won't take a listen.
> He won't stand straightening.
> There is such a compliment.
> That's a lynch.
>
> (53)

Here we see a distinctive mixing of word functions. Lisa Green has shown how some verbs in African American vernacular English can also function as adjectives (50–53). Some of Stein's sentences can be read in this way as well, especially those that come closest to the sort of syntax we've come to hear from speakers of African American vernacular English. Her sentence "All the seats are needing blackening," for instance, can be read as a variant of "all the seats be needing blackening."

This African American characteristic of allowing words to perform multiple functions may not be unique *in* the English language but might be unique *to* English: "This faculty of using one and the same form with different values, while the context shows in most cases what part of speech is meant, is one of the most characteristic traits of English, and is found to a similar extent in no other European language" (Jespersen 73).

Otto Jespersen calls such expressions "grammatical homophomes" (73). Although such forms may not be unique to African American speech, it is nevertheless true that black speakers used them in radical ways. In "Characteristics of Negro Expression," Hurston also helps us consider how nouns are used in African American English. One of her categories is the "verbal noun" ("Taint everybody you can confidence" is one of her examples (52). Her discussion, here, recalls the discussion by Salikoko S. Mufwene about how nouns are used by speakers of African American vernacular English. Mufwene shows how black English speakers use nouns in a variety of ways: as "mass" nouns ("that's a food he don like") and "countable" nouns ("A Cadillac's too much car for me"); and he shows how proper nouns can be used as common nouns ("Billy wearing Calvin Klein") (72–73). Hurston also calls attention to two other aspects of African American expression: "angularity" and "asymmetry" (54). She uses the term "angularity" to describe African American dancing ("Every posture is another angle") and visual sensibility ("The pictures on the walls are hung at deep angles. Furniture is always set at an angle"); for the term "asymmetry" she quotes a verse from the poem "Evil Woman" by Langston Hughes:

> I ain't gonna mistreat ma
> Good gal any more.
> I'm just gonna kill her
> Next time she makes me sore.
> (*Collected Poems* 120)[7]

"It is the lack of symmetry," Hurston asserts, "which makes Negro dancing so difficult for white dancers to learn. The abrupt and unexpected changes. The frequent change of key and time are evidences of this quality in music," she concludes (55). She gives "The St. Louis Blues" as an example of this point.

All these linguistic operations were a part of African American popular culture and its artistic expressions, as well as of everyday speech, and although some of them were certainly present in the coon songs, they came more clearly to cultural prominence with the blues. Perhaps the most famous blues song ever written was published the same year as *Tender Buttons*. "The St. Louis Blues" by William Christopher Handy shares with Stein's text some of the same linguistic operations that Hurston summarizes in her essay.

That at least some of these operations were known and identified with black culture during the time Stein was composing *Tender Buttons* can be demonstrated by the popularity of Handy's song and by the scholarship existing at the time on African American music. In 1911, Howard W. Odum published "Folk-Song and Folk Poetry as Found in the Secular Songs of the Southern Negroes" in the *Journal of American Folklore*. There, he characterized the style of the African American work songs and blues that were the subjects of his study: "The language is neither that of the whites nor that of the blacks, but a freely mingled and varied usage of dialect and common speech. Colloquialisms are frequent. The omission of pronouns and connectives, asyndeton in its freest usage, mark many negro verses, while the insertion of interjections and senseless phrases go to the other extreme" (Odum, qtd. in Tracy, 145).

These operations have striking affinities with those used by Stein. The sentences of her prose poems seem to defy sense precisely to the degree that they use colloquialisms, that they omit pronouns and connectives, and that syntactical units or phrases seem not to make sense because of missing conjunctions. What is most significant for my purposes is that the particular ways that African American speakers made multivalent use of the parts of speech, and, perhaps just as important, the means by which those methods were put to use by writers and performers of song lyrics, became widely known in the United States at about the same time as Stein was composing *Tender Buttons*. Here is an example from Stein's book:

> It was a way a day, this made some sum. Suppose a cod liver a cod liver is an oil, suppose a cod liver oil is tunny, suppose a cod liver oil tunny is pressed suppose a cod liver oil tunny pressed is china and secret with a bestow a bestow reed, a reed and a reed to be, in a reed to be.
>
> Next to me next to a folder, next to a folder some waiter, next to a folder some waiter and re letter and read her. Read her with her for less. (496–97)

At the very beginning of the poem, the pronoun seems to be placed in the subject position in the sentence. The second pronoun, "this," refers to "it," whose referent is absent from the utterance. Neither part of the sentence seems to refer directly to the other, giving the sentence the sense of a list of disconnected phrases, a case of asyndeton "in its freest usage." (An asyndeton is, according to the Oxford English Dictionary, "a rhetorical figure which omits the conjunction.") The second sentence seems governed by wordplay between the set of nouns "cod liver," "oil," "tunny," "china," "secret," and "reed." Here, nouns become verbs by virtue of punning ("cod liver"), but the verbs then revert back to nouns. The poem is a model of the asymmetry and angularity that characterizes this book as a whole. Only in the second paragraph are we given a hint of a setting, and that hint is quickly undermined by the poem's incessant wordplay, as the second paragraph refers, again by pronoun, to a "her" that may have as its referent "waiter" (wait her). The use of internal rhyme and of phrases that rely on common constructions ("suppose A is B"), may be reminiscent of advertising copy. In any case, the "meaning" of the poem is secondary to the sound of the words playing against each other, in a manner that is reminiscent of some of the better-known African American songs of the day.

{ 4 }

I have been arguing that to read Stein's experimental texts from within the context of the African American Imaginary is to read for those affinities these works have with the emergent urban African American culture of the early twentieth century.

To demonstrate this point more clearly, I turn now to that other canonical text I have already referred to, "The St. Louis Blues," for several reasons. For one thing, it marks the best-known example of an African American popular song lyric of its time. For another, its very canonicity allows us to see it alongside Stein's texts and to demonstrate how African American culture forms a crucial part of the context of modernism, and of the context within which modernist texts were created. More to the point, this song demonstrates the very qualities I have been pointing to in Stein's verse. Here are the first four stanzas of Handy's song.

> I hate to see de ev'nin sun go down,
> Hate to see de ev'nin sun go down,
> 'Cause my baby, he done lef dis town.

> Feelin' tomorrow lak ah feel today,
> Feel tomorrow lak ah feel today,
> I'll pack my trunk, make ma gitaway.

> St. Louis woman, wid her diamon' rings,
> Pulls dat man roun' by her apron strings.
> 'Twant for powder an' for store-bought hair,
> De man ah love would not gone nowhere, nowhere.

Got de St. Louis Blues jes as blue as ah can be,
Dat man got a heart lak a rock cast in the sea,
Or else he wouldn't have gone so far from me.
(Handy, "The St. Louis Blues" 89)

Although it is not the most radical set of blues lyrics, "The St. Louis Blues" demonstrates some of the disjunctive qualities that characterize modernist texts. The verses constitute a set of laments that hardly add up to a coherent narrative. An especially disjunctive feature of the lyric is the use of the word "feelin'" (feeling). Standard American English would have the sentence read: "If I feel tomorrow as I'm feeling today"; however, the conjunction and the pronoun are absent, and the tenses of the word "feel" are reversed. The melody of the song is just about all that keeps the verse from sounding like nonsense. As the song progresses through another fourteen stanzas, the lack of narrative connection appears even more dramatic. In recorded renditions, singers have chosen almost randomly from among the verses to make up their versions of the song. In the classic version, recorded by Bessie Smith and Louis Armstrong on January 14, 1925, Smith sings the first four verses printed above, with two word substitutions—"grip" for "trunk" in line six, and "wouldn't go" for "would not gone" in line ten—and a different line three: "It makes me think I'm on my last go-round" (Smith).

"The St. Louis Blues" is "by far the most performed and recorded individual blues of all time" (Friedwald 42). In the years between the two world wars it was one of the most recorded and performed American compositions. Among its most distinctive features is the degree to which its origins and organization reflect a modernist aesthetic sensibility. The song is essentially a pastiche. Musically, it is a traditional blues combined with a tango, which enlivens the chorus.[8] It is the song's manifestation as a linguistic product, however, that most concerns us here. What is remarkable about "The St. Louis Blues" from this point of view is the means by which the composer sought to create his song.

It is important, for my analysis, to remember that "The St. Louis Blues" is, in part, a commodity and a literary product. Its primary manifestation was as a musical composition written and sold as sheet music. This is significant because most writing about the blues, since the days of Howard W. Odum, treats it as primarily a product of an oral culture. Though this is true of the music generally, it is important to remember that the form entered the consciousness of modern society as the product of literacy. This is one reason why, in attempting to understand "The St. Louis Blues" as a product of a modernist sensibility, I turn to the circumstances of its composition to help sort out how it came into existence as a product of language. An especially rich source for this investigation, is W. C. Handy's own memoir.

"The St. Louis Blues," it seems, came about not only as the composer's response to the vagaries of the capitalist marketplace; its writing was also preceded by an engagement with a form of literary "nonsense." Handy's "Memphis Blues" of 1912 was a big hit, one of the first blues songs to be a commercial success. Soon after writing the song, Handy lost the rights to it, and he was determined to write another hit with which to make back some of the money he lost as a result. His first attempt was with a song called "Jogo Blues." Handy tells the story of that song's origins:

> The inspiration for the new composition was a curious Negro custom that could be traced to the Gullahs[9] and from them all the way back to Africa. I had first noticed it among the troupers of the minstrel company. Whenever these fellows wanted to say something to one another—something not intended for outside ears—they used words invented by themselves for this purpose. Sometimes they simply attached new means to familiar words. For example, a white person was always "ofay," a Negro "jigwawk." The terms, as pliable as silk, were also extended to cover fine distinctions. Thus if the girl you were sparking at the moment was light colored, you might describe her as ofay jigwawk. If she was the stove-pipe variety, you might have to hear her called a jig-wawk-jigwawk. I recalled that back in the nineties Ben Harney wrote a ragtime song entitled *The Cake Walk in the Sky*. But when the jigs sang it, the audience heard something like this: *The Kigingy Kikake Wyging-wawk Higin The Skigy*.
>   Of course, in the theatrical profession one meets alert ears and sharp wits, and the public early became familiar with words like "ousylay" and "umbay." To meet this cleverness, we used throw-offs to confuse them. "Siging Sigwatney" was one such a throw-off—it meant nothing whatever. "Jogo" did have meaning, however. It meant colored and was a synonym for jigwawk. I decided to call my new composition the *Jogo Blues*. (116–17)

Handy is careful to authenticate the provenance of his composition by placing the origins of its structural concerns in Africa. In this context, it is necessary to remember how much African American popular culture from these years harked back to Africa for just such authentication—even among coon song writers, despite the fact that many of their compositions were racially insulting. Some of the most famous songs and theatrical productions of the era, such as Bert Williams and George Walker's Broadway musical *In Dahomey* (1905), evoked just such a context.

Next, Handy couches his composition within the context of a language maneuver, one that is similar to the practice that came to be known as "signifying" (Gates, *Signifying Monkey* 54). The maneuver as described by Handy relies on nonsense for its effect: "It meant nothing whatever." What seems distinctive, however, about these word games is that they base themselves on the *effects* of "meaningless" sounds. This use of nonsense was to become a major trope in African American artistic practice, especially among musicians, during the twentieth century, resurfacing most notably with Louis Armstrong's 1926 recording of "Heebie Jeebies" and again, two years later, with his introduction in "West End Blues" of what came to be called "scat singing." After World War II, African American musicians would spark a whole musical style whose name, bebop was a nonsense word. As important as this genealogy is, it is just as important to see Handy's evocation of "jigwawk" as an experiment that stands in the same arena of artistic production as Hugo Ball's sound poems at the Café Voltaire in Zurich, and the Zang Tumb Tuuum of F. T. Marinetti (which he premiered in St. Petersburg in 1914), as well as of Stein's experimental texts (both cited in Perloff 45–79).

"Jogo Blues" was not the hit Handy wanted. For one thing, it was an instrumental composition, too obscure and too difficult: "Only Negro musicians understood the title and the music," he writes (119). He wanted something with the complexity of "Jogo Blues" but written so that sheet-music-buying amateurs as well as professionals could play it. He also needed a song with words, and his story of how he went about writing it is striking, in light of how I have been trying to convey the sense of the "African American Imaginary": "This number would go beyond its predecessor and break new ground. I would begin with a down-home ditty fit to go with twanging banjos and yellow shoes" (118). We are brought once again into the center of this Imaginary through the use of one of its important symbols. Handy's story of origins is filled with tropes attesting to the authenticity of the work. For one thing, he suggests that "The St. Louis Blues" is, like its predecessor, rooted in Africa: among its more unusual features is the tango rhythm in the introduction and the middle strains, of which Handy says, "Indeed, the very word 'tango,' as I now know, was derived from the African 'tangana,' and signified this same tom-tom beat" (120).

In the first of two allusions to coon songs, the "down-home ditty" he was looking for is identified with a song made popular by May Irwin, a white singer of coon songs. He then tells the story of one of the song's key verses. As he sat in a rented room in Memphis, he was remembering a long-ago visit to St. Louis: "There was the picture I had of myself, broke, unshaven, wanting even a decent meal, standing before the lighted saloon in St. Louis without even a shirt under my frayed coat," when he saw a woman "whose pain seemed even greater." She was drunk and disheveled: "Stumbling along the poorly lighted street, she muttered as she walked, 'Ma man's got a heart like a rock cast in de sea'" (119). Handy didn't know what she meant, and stopped another woman to ask for a translation. "She replied, 'Lawd, man, it's hard and gone so far she can't reach it.'" It's not clear whether this "translation" enlightened Handy, but the song's lyric remains as mysterious as ever. "Thus," writes Friedwald, this section of the song "opens with a curious 'Mona Lisa' kind of a line that few people who hear it, or even sing it, quite understand, yet it certainly makes the song more interesting than your average drawing-room drama of 1914" (49). This is where Handy shows what was really revolutionary about his new composition: "Her language was the same down-home medium that conveyed the laughable woe of lamp-blacked lovers in hundreds of frothy songs, but her plight was much too real to provoke much laughter" (119). "The St. Louis Blues," in other words, had taken the medium of the coon song, and made it a modern means of expression. "I resorted to the humorous spirit of the bygone coon songs," Handy writes (120), and thereby he recreated the African American vernacular as a medium for high art.

It's hard to overestimate the impact of "The St. Louis Blues" on twentieth-century culture. The song came to be identified with both African American and American culture generally in the years between the world wars, as a veritable sign of the modern. It became, in a sense, the visible sign of the African American Imaginary and its relationship to modernism. It became part of the standard repertoire in orchestras throughout the world during these years, whether jazz bands or simply dance bands. That this was true was shown by Langston Hughes, who wrote about the song in connection with his 1933 visit to Japan: "Blues were not unknown in Japan. 'The St. Louis Blues,' W. C. Handy's classic, was very popular. The words had been translated into Japanese—'I hate to see de evenin' sun go down"—and records of it were whirling on Tokyo jukeboxes. The Tokyo jazz bands, with a number of Filipino musicians in them, played good jazz (*I Wonder as I Wander* 242).

This examination of Handy's song has focused on the language of the lyric in an attempt to demonstrate that the rhetorical operations commonly identified with the modernist lyric were also being developed by writers of modern African American song lyrics. The next chapter examines another aspect of this problem, as it relates to the use of the cliché and to some aspects of symbolism in black American poetry. Here, however, my purpose has been to demonstrate how the blues and their coon song antecedents can be said to stand in an uneasy, uncanny relationship to the texts of canonical modernism. "The St. Louis Blues," published the same year as *Tender Buttons*, can be seen, then, as using language in a way that foreshadowed the coming out of this vernacular from behind the minstrel mask of the coon shouters and into the mainstream of modern culture—helping, along the way, to create modernism.

{ 5 }

I have used the terms "uncanny" and "haunted" to characterize the relationship I've been trying to describe, but I want to clarify one important fact. The relationship between canonical modernism and African American culture should by no means be construed as one in which black culture stands as docile, or inert. In the sense used here, African American expressive, creative culture must be seen as itself modernist and a full-fledged agent of the modernist project. The use of the terms "haunting," "uncanny," "African American Imaginary" attempts to describe the multiple means by which the same phenomenon occurred. With Stevens and Stein, their work of making a modernist artwork took place within a context that required them to engage African American culture and its products, even if they did not name the real-life artists behind those artifacts. It was enough to name articles (musical instruments) or to invoke racial myths and white America's obsession with whiteness for this engagement to create productive elements in their art. This engagement without naming is the mechanism that I have referred to with the term "haunted."

Yet all this does not, by any means, indicate that the "unnamed" agent of the uncanny did not exist in real life, within the very culture that Stevens and Stein lived in. One could fairly say that by the early twentieth century, in the United States at least, the presence of African American people and their culture had ceased to be, as they had been since the early days of minstrelsy, mainly mediated to the white majority through imitation and ascription. As the culture became more urbanized, and as black people became an increasing proportion of that urbanizing majority, so their culture became, in a real sense, a part of that majority culture. That is at least one meaning of the emergence of ragtime as a national art form, and it certainly accounts for the increasing use of a (presumed) African American dialect both in the mainstream theaters and in the emergent national advertisements of the late nineteenth and early twentieth centuries.

As I have argued, one reason why the relationship between the "minority" and "majority" cultures has been obscured by many commentators is an apparent confusion between the legal-historical framework in which artists worked, on the one hand, and the mechanisms of cultural transition and translation, on the other. These latter often worked around and between the legalistic barriers erected against them. After all, it was at the height of racial segregation that an African American musical form, jazz, became the country's first truly national music, and it was at exactly this moment when it became clear that an American way of speaking English would be at least partially based on a real or imagined African American dialect: the dialect of the coon songs, one of the early manifestations of the African American Imaginary that I have been discussing. It was an Imaginary that came to have an anxious, uncanny relationship with the "majority" culture throughout the twentieth century.

This anxiety can be said to be characteristic of the century. Michael Rogin and Jeffrey Melnick have each written about the way black culture was used by some immigrant cultures during this era as a tool of "Americanization." The distinction I am attempting to show here, however, is that these phenomena not only were social and historical (in any case, the changes that many scholars identify with the 1920s were already in place nearly a generation earlier) but also took place at the level of poetic language and rhetoric. The importance of the distinction can be clarified by looking into the poetics of what is commonly understood to be the "lost" years of American poetry.

CHAPTER TWO

Lyric

{ 1 }

At least one overlooked point of departure for modernist poetry in English can be found in an old saloon in Sedalia, Missouri. It was at the Maple Leaf Club, on Main Street in that city, at the end of the nineteenth century, that one of the major revolutions in the English-language lyric began to stir. It was a revolution that would soon find its way into the body of twentieth-century poetry. It is not quite a story of modernism popping, like a genie, out of a bottle of rye; rather, it is an attempt to unpack the assertion made by Michael North that the voice of modernism "was very largely a black one" (*Dialect of Modernism* 7). North examines the collaboration between Pablo Picasso and Gertrude Stein, which resulted in the construction of what he calls "Modernism's African Mask" (59–78). He also looks at the "racial masquerade" practiced by T. S. Eliot and Ezra Pound (79–99) in an exploration of how these artists used African and African American culture.

I have argued that modernist literature is "haunted," both thematically and structurally, by the African American Imaginary. Here, I want to call attention to the nature of the lyric, of poetic language, as it emerged both from within the arena of the literary and from "outside," as it were: that is, from the realm of popular music. That is why I am starting with a meditation on the Maple Leaf saloon, proposing that we imagine the site of the Maple Leaf Club as a kind of metaphor, the examination of which can help us understand what happened to the English-language lyric in the early part of the twentieth century. I want to extend North's assertions somewhat by looking outside the strictly literary domain to help explain the demotic turn this poetry made as it became what we now call modernist.

Before doing so, however, I want to call attention to what Denis Donoghue identifies as one of the unique qualities of the poetic language of American twentieth-century poetry: "The modern revolution in such American poems as 'The Waste Land,' 'Hugh Selwyn Mauberly,' 'Paterson,' 'The Maximus Poems,' and 'The Changing Light at Sandover,'" he writes, "depends on a different sense of life and a different syntax." He adds:

> One's first reading of these poems leaves an impression of their poetic quality as residing in their diction: the animation of the verse arises from the in-

calculable force of certain individual words or phrases that stay in the mind without necessarily attracting to their orbit the words before or after. The memorable quality of those phrases seems to require a clear space on all sides. The relations that the words of an American poem enact are not prescribed or predictive but experimental. Around each word is a space or a void in which nothing is anticipated, nothing enforced. Every relation must be invented, as if the world had just begun (114).

By suggesting that the diction of these poems is particularly American (as opposed to British), Donoghue is observing a quality that is at the heart of my concerns here. In addition, his pointing to the phrase as a constitutive element of the poetry is of interest, because it is important to remember that modern American poets very often use the phrase as a unit of measure in the poetic line. A focus on the phrase can also lead us to consider how important speech rhythms are to American poetry. Phrases, modern speech rhythms, and the "black" voice are widely understood to be distinctive qualities of twentieth-century verse in English as practiced in the United States (Olson; Damon; Nielsen, *Black Chant*). What is less understood is how all this came to be. This chapter explores some implications of North's claims about the "black" voice of modernism.

The Maple Leaf Club serves as a metaphor for an inquiry into lyric poetry and modernism because it is here that some historians locate one of the beginnings of ragtime (Blesh and Janis 14–19). Ragtime is the entry point for this inquiry because it focuses my argument that too little attention has been paid to the ways in which the lyrics of ragtime-era songs have influenced modernist poetry. Sedelia, Missouri, serves as a fitting location for reexamining of the rhetoric of early modernist poetry: its geographic proximity to where several modernist poets spent their childhood (especially T. S. Eliot in St. Louis), and its site as a crossroads between Ezra Pound's Hadley, Idaho, birthplace and his childhood in Philadelphia provide ground for investigating a question which has rarely been posed in literary studies. What connection can one draw between the emergence of ragtime music, especially ragtime song, and the modernist lyric as developed by American poets in the early twentieth century? The question is posed as a kind of thought experiment, the aim of which is to help us understand more fully the idea, as put forward by Donoghue, of the importance and distinction of diction in American poetry.

The character of ragtime-era songs is what strikes us, first of all. Edward A. Berlin points out that ragtime music during the early twentieth century was mainly perceived by its contemporary public as vocal music, a music of songs (5–17). The public perception that ragtime was mainly piano music is a product of the rise of jazz, and especially of the twentieth-century rediscovery of the music of pianist-composer Scott Joplin. It is with ragtime-era song and its precursors, however, that I am most concerned.

Ragtime song emerged at about the same time as that genre of American song associated with Tin Pan Alley (Hamm 284–325; Wilder 3–28). Indeed, in their earliest days the two forms were often indistinguishable. What made them differ from earlier forms of the popular song—and made them distinctly American—were two things: their adherence to spoken diction, and the emergence of the chorus as a self-contained element.[1] These developments have a long history, which has only partly been uncovered by music historians. One of the most prominent of these historians, Charles Hamm, locates the beginning of the verse-chorus form in American popular music in the 1840s. It came to dominate American song some fifty years later. But though the verse-chorus form had become standard by the late nineteenth century, Hamm points out that during the turn to the twentieth century an important difference arose:

> The "chorus" is given to the solo voice, rather than to a quartet of mixed voices. And the relationship between verse and chorus, in length and importance, has changed: in the majority of these songs, verse and chorus are of equal length, and in some the chorus is longer than the verse. More importantly, the chief melodic material is now in the chorus, not the verse. A person knowing any of these songs from memory, upon being asked to play or sing it, will invariably respond with the music of the chorus, not the verse—and may not even be familiar with the latter. (292)

One of the earliest manifestations of this form in American popular music was in the work of African American songwriter James A. Bland (1854–1911). Bland, whose major work dates from the late 1870s and early 1880s, was an important precursor to the ragtime era and an important, if now largely overlooked, transitional figure. Bland was born a free person. His father, Allen, was "one of the first college-educated blacks in the United States" with a degree from Wilberforce (Jasen and Jones 8); he became a Howard University law graduate and a Reconstruction-era federal appointee, as an examiner at the U.S. Patent Office. James A. Bland dropped out of Howard to pursue a career on the minstrel stage. He was a major influence in popular music for over two decades and on two continents. While living in England in the 1880s, he was known as "the Idol of the Music Halls"

(Southern 234). He gave command performances before Queen Victoria, and one of his songs was for many years the official song of the state of Virginia, the only such official song written by an African American.[2]

Bland traveled to Europe in 1881 with a minstrel troupe and remained there, living mainly in England, for over a decade, dispensing with the black-face makeup of the minstrel shows and "performing as an elegantly dressed singer-banjoist" (Southern 236). He has often been described as trading in racialized and degrading minstrel stereotypes, a charge that has been effectively refuted by William R. Hullfish. The song that won him fame in Europe was "Oh, Dem Golden Slippers" (1879):

> Oh, my golden slippers am laid away,
> Kase I don't 'spect to wear 'em till my weddin' day,
> An' my long-tail'd coat, dat I love so well,
>   I will wear up in de chariot in de morn.
> And my long white robe dat I bought last June,
> I'm gwine to git changed Kase it fits too soon,
> And de old gray hoss dat I used to drive,
>   I will hitch him to de chariot in de morn.
>
> (Chorus)
> Oh, dem golden slippers!
> Oh, dem golden slippers!
> Golden slippers I'm gwine to wear,
> Because dey look so neat;
> Oh, dem golden slippers!
> Oh, dem golden slippers!
> Golden slippers I'm gwine to wear,
> To walk de golden streets.
>
> Oh, my old banjo hangs on de wall
> Kase it ain't been tuned since way last fall
> But de darks all say we will hab a good time
>   When we ride up in de chariot in de morn.
> Lats ole Brudder Ben and Sister Luce
> Dey will telegraph de news to Uncle Bacco Juice
> What a great camp-meetin' dere will be dat day.
>   When we ride up in de chariot in de morn.
>
> (Chorus)

Oh, it's good-bye, children, I will have to go,
Whar de rain don't fall or de wind don't blow,
And yer ulster coats, why, yer will not need,
  When yer ride up in de chariot in de morn.
But yer golden slippers must be nice and clean,
And yer age mus' be Just sweet sixteen,
And yer white kid gloves yer will have to wear,
  When you ride up in de chariot in de morn.

(Chorus)[3]

This is a key point in the transition of the American song lyric from its dependence on its British, Scottish, and Irish origins to something more particularly based in U.S. culture. "Oh, Dem Golden Slippers" doesn't quite fit, historically speaking, within the period of ragtime (roughly 1895–1917) but comes from an earlier era just after the Civil War, when black performers were first appearing in the minstrel shows. Yet formally and aesthetically, some of the features of "Golden Slippers" are of interest to the study of the diction of the American lyric because, structurally, its lyrics prefigure the major innovation, the most important difference that would characterize, first, the ragtime song at the turn of the twentieth century and, later, the Tin Pan Alley song. Both forms would have decisive impact on the emergence of American modernist poetry.

Perhaps the most important sign of this difference is in the nature of the chorus of "Golden Slippers." Though written for multiple voices, as was common for pre–Tin Pan Alley American songs, the chorus of this song shares a distinguishing feature of the later genre: people familiar with it often demonstrate their knowledge of the song by beginning to sing the first phrase of the chorus.[4] The chorus and the verses are both dependent on and independent of each other; the chorus can, and often does, stand alone as the part most often remembered. The chorus stands apart as an independent utterance. It is not necessary to know the rest of the song in order for the chorus to cohere; even though the verses add to a dramatic, or narrative, understanding of the piece as a whole, the chorus conveys enough of a sensation on its own to make it a pleasing verbal object. Among the ways it does so is its concentration on the utterance as a means of communication.

In "Golden Slippers," the first utterance, the title phrase, is a repeated exclamation that claims our attention both for its simplicity of phrasing and for its evocation of an image. The term "golden slippers" contains no dramatic content of its own, and the sentence that follows ("Golden slippers Ise gwine to wear, Because dey look so neat") adds little to any consideration of the chorus as an example of dramatic or narrative content. The thematic content of the chorus, at this stage, is simply that the speaker admires the slippers for the sensation provided by their appearance alone. We are reminded, here, of Immanuel Kant's idea of the importance of form in generating an understanding of what is beautiful. For Kant, it is the play of figures in space, or the play of sensations, that claims our appreciation, our sense of beauty. This claim, which appears to have "merely formal purposiveness, i.e., a purposiveness without purpose, is quite independent of the concept of the good," writes Kant (61–62). This idea is useful for my inquiry in that it allows one to better appreciate the autonomy given the chorus of "Golden Slippers" by its assumed context. For many of those familiar with the song, the theme of the text is less about getting dressed up for a party than it is about the aesthetic appreciation, *for its own sake*, of a pair of slippers.

With these qualities of familiarity, autonomy, individual expression, and joyful intonation, the chorus assumes the characteristics of an independent utterance, one that is not contingent on a narrative frame to produce the sense of a meaning.[5] And yet the utterance itself only suggests a meaning. The evocation of pleasure does not derive from the subject of the chorus. The chorus is itself the evocation of pleasure.

Another way of looking at this chorus is to divide it into a pair of utterances that have, as it were, a formulaic quality that encourages memorization. Walter J. Ong, drawing on the work of Milman Parry, has pointed out the important role played by such formulaic utterances in the transition from oral to written culture. Ong discusses Parry's discovery that the Homeric poems are structured in a way that suggests their origin in oral culture. This structure provides a clue as to how to think about the relationship between the utterance in American popular song of the late nineteenth and early twentieth centuries and the modernist innovations in literary verse during that same period. "Parry's discovery might be put this way," writes Ong. "Virtually every distinctive feature of Homeric poetry is due to the economy forced on it by oral methods of composition" (21). It appeared that Homer, writes Ong, "had some kind of phrase book in his head. Careful study of the sort Milman Parry was doing showed that he repeated formula after formula." Homer "stitched together fabricated parts" that consisted of phrases garnered from the oral tradition (22). Ong then adds a striking comment: "This idea was particularly threatening to far-gone literates. For literates are educated never to use clichés, in principle. How live with the fact that the Homeric poems, more and more, appeared to be made up of clichés, or elements very like clichés? By and large, as Parry's work had proceeded and was carried forward by later scholars, it became evident that only a tiny fraction of the words in the *Iliad* and the *Odyssey* were not parts of formulas, and to a degree devastatingly predictable formulas" (22–23).

Writing in the 1920s, Parry was concerned with the transmigration of the oral epithet into the written verse of Homer. Nearly sixty years later, Ong uses the term "cliché" to characterize these formulaic phrases. That term has come into use in English only in the last century or so. H. W. Fowler identifies it with the term "hackneyed phrases" (602), and the Oxford English Dictionary's earliest citation of the word is from the last decade of the nineteenth century.[6] Cliché is, then, a very modern concept and, writes Anton C. Zijderveld, a term intricately bound up with late industrial and post-industrial modernity itself. According to Zijderveld, the distinction between the use of the cliché in traditional literature and speech and its modern use has to do with how the utterance carried meaning. The cliché-like epithet once had a distinct meaning; it had "symbolic vigour and semantic power." The modern cliché, on the other hand, is distinguished by the absence of such vigor and power: it is "a traditional form of human expression (in words, thoughts, emotions, gestures, acts) which—due to repetitive use in social life—has lost its original, often ingenious heuristic power. Although thus it fails positively to contribute meaning to social interactions and communication, it does function socially, since it manages to stimulate behavior (cognition, emotion, volition, action), while it avoids reflection on meanings" (12, 10).

This definition, with its emphasis on repetition, avoidance of reflection, and what Zijderveld calls the "supersedure of original meanings by social functions" (10), coincides with my argument about the relationship between the emergence of twentieth-century popular song in the United States and the syntactic change identified with modernist poetry—especially if one adds to the definition cited above two more of Zijderveld's points. The first concerns the autonomy of the cliché. Because they "can be set apart as distinct entities," that is, because of their "reified nature, and because of their repetitiveness, clichés have a tendency to acquire a momentum of their own, i.e., to become relatively autonomous vis-à-vis the individual in society" (15–16). This autonomy stimulates memory and is one reason why the most memorable element of modern American songs, the chorus, gradually assumed the character of an autonomous expression, abstracted from its original dramatic or narrative context and meaning.

The second point concerns the idea that the rise of the cliché in modern social life coincides with the decline of the "aura" in art, a decline identified by Walter Benjamin as one of the hallmarks of modernism. For Benjamin, the "aura" is identified with the historical authority and authenticity of the work of art. It is the aura that "withers" in the age of mechanical reproduction (221). This loss of aura is characterized by the loss of distance, uniqueness, and the authority and authenticity of the traditional work of art, a loss occasioned by the subjection of the work of art to mechanical reproducibility. For Benjamin, the prime example of this process is film. The decline of the aura can be likened to the decline of meaning in that form of poetic utterance I am identifying with the word cliché. In "Golden Slippers," for instance, this decline is reflected in the ambivalence that is attendant on the identification of the genre of the song. When it was first published, it was marketed as a minstrel song. In the twentieth century, however, it has been performed both as a spiritual (Waller) and as a country and western song. In this hybridity of genre the song's original status as a historically situated work of art has been lost.

By pointing to the aesthetic autonomy of the chorus in "Golden Slippers" and the relationship of the song's lyrics to the concept of the cliché, I am attempting to locate the "incalculable force of certain individual words or phrases that stay in the mind" which Donoghue says is so characteristic of American poetry. This force was very much a characteristic of the way American song developed as it moved away from its original United Kingdom models, adopting and transforming the traditions inherited from the minstrel stage and from African American spirituals that had their first national (and international) hearing in the decades after the Civil War. The American song would continue to develop in this direction, to the point where the autonomy of the chorus, its existence as an aesthetic "object of sense" in its own right, to use Kant's phrase, would become a dominant characteristic of the genre.

By the turn of the twentieth century the form of the American song had long settled into its introduction–two verse–chorus form; but most significantly, with the rise of ragtime and Tin Pan Alley in the 1890s the chorus had matured into the most important element of the song. The revolution in song form that Alec Wilder wrote about as having emerged around 1910 may also be seen as the victory of the chorus. Wilder identifies "Some of

These Days," a 1910 song by Shelton Brooks, as "the landmark song" of the transition era in popular music between turn-of-the-century sentimentalism and that form generally associated with the heyday of Tin Pan Alley (14). Brooks, an African American, introduced the song to Sophie Tucker, who sang it throughout her career. Here is the chorus:

> Some of these days, you'll miss me honey.
> Some of these days, you'll feel so lonely;
> You'll miss my hugging,
> You'll miss my kissing,
> You'll miss me honey,
> When you go away.
>
> I feel so lonely,
> Just for you only,
> For you know honey,
> You've always had your way;
> And when you leave me,
> I know it will grieve me;
> You'll miss your little baby;
> Yes some of these days.

The lyric is composed almost entirely of clichés. It appears to be a set of commonplace utterances strung together, and even though its meaning is apparent, there is no narrative or dramatic context that the lyric fits within. (That some people see "narrative" in these lyrics might well reflect the fact that, after nearly a century, we are accustomed to these songs and their idiom and read "stories" in them. Their original audiences, however, often heard them as having little or no narrative content. This is at least one source of the sense of wonder with which these songs were greeted.) Indeed, its function is not to provide any such context, but simply to be a set of phrases that carry the musical melody. This is the function of the chorus of the early twentieth-century American-style popular song—a function that would soon come to dominate much modernist poetry in English as well.

In noting the use of "Negro dialect"[7] in Bland's song, is not necessary to rehearse here the debates around the origins of African American dialect speech, which have been exhaustively covered elsewhere (Dillard, *Black English* 73–138). What is important is the understanding that Negro dialect (as distinct from the actual speech of African American people) had, by the mid-nineteenth century, become a literary and theatrical language whose relationship to actual speaking was somewhat arbitrary. The entry of African Americans onto the minstrel stage in midcentury did not radically alter this situation; in fact, black performers often created exaggerated versions of the racist stereotypes initiated by white minstrels. Nathan Huggins, speculating on the reasons, suggests that such versions were efforts to empty the stereotypes of their racist content: "Some black performers attempted to achieve the distance between the stage character and themselves by the very extremities of the exaggeration. Grotesques, themselves, could allow black men, as they did white men, the assurance that the foolishness on stage was not them" (258).

This "grotesque" took place at the level of language, as well, with the appropriation by black minstrels of the white minstrel's Negro dialect. The relationship between the stage dialect and the actual speech it was supposed to represent is a matter of debate (Huggins 197, 255; Redding, *To Make a Poet Black* 62–64), but as William J. Mahar argues, there is some basis for supposing that the stage dialect reflected an attempt to imitate real speech. It is in any case true, as Gavin Jones shows, that Negro dialect was among the most popular of the many ethnic dialects used on the minstrel and vaudeville stage. Whatever the relationship between black speech and minstrel speech, the rise of the black minstrel troupes in the latter decades of the nineteenth century added something to the linguistic veracity of minstrelsy.

In addition, use of Negro dialect by performing artists became something more than reflection, something in addition to mimesis. In their representation, dialect performers often saw themselves as paying tribute to a despised caste, or they saw themselves (especially after the Civil War) as reflecting a past that was rapidly slipping from memory. At the same time, however, the use of dialect reflected an additional impulse: an attempt to create verbal art out of a language that more closely resembled contemporary spoken dialect and at the same time sought to fragmentize and—to borrow a term that Frederick Karl uses in relationship to Stéphane Mallarmé—to "decreate" ordinary language. This impulse to recreate an authentic speech through the use of what was, after all, primarily a theatrical convention was a major feature of literary discourse as well. It became a major characteristic not only of American fiction writers—in particular with its use by Mark Twain and Joel Chandler Harris, among others—but of poets as well. Although African American poets do not seem to have used dialect in their verse until the 1870s (that is, after the emergence of black minstrel performers on the American stage), their application of it did not seem to be very different in character from that of white writers (Sherman xxviii–xxix). Although Paul Laurence Dunbar, the most famous African American poet of the period to write in dialect, was not, strictly speaking, a modernist poet, an examination of his work can reveal several points of transition toward modernism, points which, I argue, have been virtually ignored in the critical literature on this poet.

{ 2 }

Few readers seem to evaluate the poetry of Paul Laurence Dunbar in terms that privilege its aesthetic content. Critics have often followed Sterling Brown in classing Dunbar as an imitative poet, indebted to Thomas Nelson Page, Irwin Russell, or James Whitcomb Riley (Brown 32). Even as sympathetic a reader as J. Saunders Redding follows the general line of opinion that divides Dunbar's work along lines of qualitative evaluation, judging his dialect poems to be better than those written in "standard" English: "Though certain of his pure English lines are frequently quoted," writes Redding, "in general they are overlooked; not because they are poor, but because they do not distinguish him from dozens of other poets" (*To Make a Poet Black* 67). The fact that Redding excludes nearly a dozen of Dunbar's "pure English" poems from this criticism doesn't lessen that criticism's impact. Each of these critics judges Dunbar's work by the standards of a succeeding generation. By lumping the poet with the sentimental popularizers of his day, they also seem to be enacting, from within the precincts of black literature, the general modernist rejection of the verse of the late nineteenth century.

Later critics are no less involved in evaluating Dunbar's poetry primarily in terms of its presumed limitations. Henry Louis Gates Jr. invokes not only the standards of the New Negro rejection of the Negro dialect convention (*Figures in Black* 167–87) but also those of African American authenticity derived from the aesthetics of the Black Arts Movement of the last quarter of the twentieth century. Gates suggests that what is ultimately at stake in Dunbar's poetry is the debate over "the absence and presence of the black voice in the text" (*Signifying Monkey* 174). At the same time, Houston A. Baker Jr. finds that "Dunbar offered the example par excellence of a tragic hemming in of Afro American *artistic* aspiration" (39; original emphasis). The "example" offered by the poet, Baker suggests, derives from Dunbar's facility in using standard, inherited forms to enact a strategy of concealment and subversion of stereotypes. But in the end, Baker judges Dunbar—as a poet, at least—as "naïve, politically innocent, or simply 'spoiled'" (40).

One major source for these opinions can be found in the writings of the poet himself, plus reminiscences of friends, acquaintances, and even from those who were connected, if only distantly, with Dunbar's circle. Dunbar is said, by James Weldon Johnson, to have disliked being pigeonholed into writing dialect verse. "I didn't start as a dialect poet," he told Johnson. "I simply came to the conclusion that I could write it as well, if not better, than anybody else I knew of, and that by doing so I could gain a hearing. I gained the hearing, and now they don't want me to write anything but dialect" (qtd. in *Along This Way* 160). This sentiment is reinforced, in many commentators' minds, by the following lines of Dunbar:

> He sang of love, when earth was young,
> And Love, itself, was in his lays.
> But ah, the world, it turned to praise
> A jingle in a broken tongue.
> (*Life and Works* 275)

Before beginning any aesthetic consideration of Dunbar's poetry, then, one must acknowledge the absolutely terrifying circumstances under which the poet lived and worked, the toll they took on him, and the profound existential dilemma they produced, which is reflected in the work itself. The period during which Dunbar worked and published his major works (1895–1906) was coincident with Logan's "nadir" of African American life. Over 1,200 black people were lynched in the United States during the decade 1890–1900. In 1896, the year the poet's first major publication, *Lyrics of Lowly Life*, appeared, the United States Supreme Court decided *Plessy v. Ferguson*, the case that codified legal racial segregation (Aptheker 792; *Statistical History* 218; Sundquist, 225–70).[8] This period of extreme racism and terrorism against the African American population placed an artist like Dunbar under extraordinary pressures. Though he was a popular artist who read his poems in "literary concerts" before both black and white (though rarely before mixed) audiences, the consequences of that popularity took an emotional toll. In a speech given at a literary conference organized to celebrate Dunbar's centenary, J. Saunders Redding repeated an anecdote he heard from the poet's widow, Alice Dunbar-Nelson, who was a family friend and one of Redding's childhood schoolteachers. The story tells of a public reading the poet gave before an audience of wealthy white people:

After one such literary concert in Newport, Rhode Island, a staid and imperiously aristocratic white lady rose while the all white audience was still applauding, waited for silence and said, "Paul"—she had never seen him before much less met him—"Paul," she said, in a most complimentary and gratified tone, "I shall never again wax impatient and cross at the childish antics of my servants, members of your race. Tonight, you have made me understand and love them." Following this remark, the applause was resumed more enthusiastically than before, and Paul Dunbar fled through a side door to an anteroom where his wife waited. There he dropped to his knees before her, buried his head in her lap, and wept convulsively. (Redding, "Portrait Against Background" 42)

This episode, in many ways, exemplifies the transitional nature of the emergence of modern American culture. In this nexus of praise and humiliation, of adulation and pathos, we see both the power of the African American Imaginary and the moment when it was, at the same time, beginning to give way to the more restricted and racially segregated social reality that was coming into being. Here is Dunbar, appearing as star at a literary salon (such as few other black writers would do over the next several decades), and yet the humiliation he faces is but a foreshadowing of the hypersegregated society that was being implanted. Dunbar's appearance at the Newport salon attests to his status as a poet with a national reputation, not only as a "representative" of black people. Yet the reaction of the "aristocratic white lady"—calling him by his first name, and praising not his poetry as such but only his status as a "representative" poet—shows just how fraught with anxiety, and just how intertwined was the reality that made it possible for him to be, as it were, a star in "white" society, while facing the increasingly harsh social conditions that awaited African Americans as the period of nadir (which can also be seen as a period of transition) began to give way to the "separate but equal" society of the first half of the twentieth century.

It is no wonder, then, that readers of Dunbar's poetry have such difficulties reading his work in a way that privileges its aesthetic value. Karl Marx's comment that the "tradition of all the dead generations weighs like a nightmare on the brain of the living" (*Eighteenth Brumaire* 15) can serve as an allegorical signifier of the wall that seems to stand between the poet and his readers. From another point of view, it is also, in a sense, the wall that stands between Dunbar's own remark, about the audience which praises only a "jingle in a broken tongue," and the manifestation of such praise in the

Newport literary concert that Redding wrote about in "Portrait Against Background."

This problem plagues approaches to Dunbar and his poetry because readers are often driven, given the historical circumstances in which the artist worked, toward making the poems into what Theodor Adorno calls "objects with which to demonstrate sociological theses" ("On Lyric Poetry and Society" 37–38). Adorno's attempt to lead readers out of such a circumstance may be helpful in reading the poems of Dunbar.

For Adorno, the significance of lyric poetry lies with the supposition that the lyric poem "hopes to attain universality through unrestrained individuation" (38). The lyric poem's universality is social in nature, however. Speaking with an individualized voice is itself an act that posits the poem against society but in a way that reveals its own contradictory nature: "Even the solitariness of lyrical language itself," Adorno writes, "is prescribed by an individualistic and ultimately atomistic society, just as conversely its general cogency depends on the intensity of its individuation." The discovery of this intensity, Adorno suggests, must lie outside a consideration that limits itself to "the so-called social perspective or the social interests of the works or their authors. Instead, it must discover how the entirety of a society, conceived as an internally contradictory unity, is manifested in the work of art, in what way the work of art remains subject to society and in what way it transcends it. In philosophical terms, the approach must be an immanent one. Social concepts should not be applied to the work of art from without but rather drawn from an exacting examination of the works themselves" (38–39).

If Adorno seems to be advocating a kind of New Critical approach, it should be noted that what is at stake here is the discovery of how the work of art not only functions as an "internally contradictory unity" but also functions aesthetically. Adorno is, perhaps, less explicit about this than he might be; his concern, however, is with developing a means of social interpretation that bases itself on keen attention to the lyric poem's aesthetic qualities: "[N]othing that is not in the works, not part of their own form, can legitimate a determination of what their substance, that which has entered into their poetry, represents in social terms" (39).

To extend Adorno's point somewhat, we can say that it is within the poem itself that we can find the source of its transcendence. The poem is not simply a reflection of protest against a society that would stamp out its presumably utopian aspirations; it is a work that enacts the act of protest itself by the operation of its very structure as a lyric work. It accomplishes this by the way it operates upon and, in a sense, challenges our normative view of how language produces meaning, as well as the very meanings produced by poetic language: "The lyric reveals itself to be most deeply grounded in society when it does not chime in with society, when it communicates nothing, when, instead, the subject whose expression is successful reaches an accord with language itself" (43).

There are objections to Adorno's sweeping generalizations. We could say, along with John Brenkman, that discovering the veracity of these claims does not depend on general assertions but must rest on the individual examination of individual poems (108–11). This is a welcome and necessary caution, apparently aimed at guiding readers toward a more exacting and fruitful reading of the poems at hand. I would question whether the "accord" Adorno writes about is even possible, whether one of the tensions that give the lyric poem—and especially the Romantic and post-Romantic lyric poem—its power is precisely the *inability* of the lyric subject to reach a successful "accord with language itself." These reservations do not, however, detract from our ability to use Adorno's insights to in approaching Dunbar's poetry. Even Adorno's provocative idea that lyric poetry is most deeply grounded in society "when it communicates nothing" can be extremely helpful in showing what is at stake in a body of poetry such as that of Dunbar, which, presumably, draws its power from what readers have come to believe it communicates.

No one seems to have paid more attention to the pessimism in the work of Dunbar than Dickson D. Bruce Jr. Dunbar's best poems, writes Bruce, "were distinguished by their pessimism and by a sense of ambiguity that was equally uncommon in black writing." In his thoroughgoing and penetrating reading of the poetry, Bruce portrays Dunbar as a poet whose skepticism and pessimism provide major themes for his work. He points out that this is particularly true of Dunbar's poems on religious themes. "In many of his poems," writes Bruce "skepticism is stronger than piety," and, he adds, "Although Dunbar was, in many ways, a sentimental poet in standard English, his writings often showed a studied rejection of the bases for sentiment found in earlier black writing" (*Black American Writing from the Nadir* 79–81).

Bruce is right to point out that the skepticism in Dunbar's work distinguishes it from earlier African American poetry and, it should be noted, also distinguishes him from his generally accepted influences, Riley and Russell.

At the same time, it should be noted that both Edgar Allen Poe and, possibly, William Blake were important to Dunbar, according to at least one of his biographers (Cunningham 66).[9] When Bruce searches for the sources of this pessimism, however, he goes outside the poems themselves and cites the poet's marital problems and the historical situation of his times. These circumstances were no doubt influential, yet depending on them for an explanation of the poetry's power is ultimately unsatisfying, not necessarily because they are the wrong explanations but because, I would argue, they are incomplete.

An examination of Dunbar's poetry will reveal a rich element that has heretofore been missing from the thinking about the premodernist history of American poetry. Not only can Dunbar best be seen as the most important black American poet of the turn of the twentieth century, but also, it appears, his poetics contained elements of a style that bore some similarities to the poetics associated, in other contexts, with the term Decadence, and with the Symbolist aesthetic. I argue, further, that what Bruce calls Dunbar's pessimism reflects a kind of emptying-out of language which can be found in the poet's work, that what gives his work at least some of its power is, to use Adorno's words, that it "communicates nothing." Put another way, his poetry, especially to the degree that his diction argues with itself, tends toward a kind of fetishization of language, toward a dependence on clichés. This is true in both his standard English and his dialect poems, though it may be more apparent in the latter. In considering these aspects of Dunbar's poetry, it must be kept in mind that he was not only a man of letters but also a writer of librettos for the Broadway stage. His collaborations with Will Marion Cook on such Broadway productions as *The Casino Girl* (1900) and *In Dahomey* (1902) place Dunbar at the center of the transformations taking place in American lyric song as well as in poetry.

Controversy over Dunbar's dialect verse has dogged his reputation from the beginning. Dickson D. Bruce has amply demonstrated that it was popular with African American readers during the poet's lifetime ("On Dunbar's 'Jingles'"), yet modern readers are mostly familiar with James Weldon Johnson's criticism as it appears in *The Book of American Negro Poetry*, which takes to task the (by then) older generation's tradition of dialect verse.

An examination that looks beyond humor and pathos, the "two stops" of Johnson's complaint, can see, however, why the dialect poems resonated so well with Dunbar's African American as well as white audiences. Despite his misgivings about the form, Dunbar himself knew that he wrote dialect

poems better than any of his contemporaries; and though they constitute
only about a third of his published poetry, they contain some of his most intriguing work. In addition, Dunbar seems to have been aware, as Marcellus
Blount suggests, of how his use of vernacular dialect "could serve to subvert
the constraints of literary convention." He remarks that, "in writing in the
vernacular, black poets like Dunbar donned their stereotypical guises as a
way of deceiving white audiences." He adds that Dunbar "challenged his
audience's assumptions by revealing that the use of such language, depending on the rhetorical and ideological contexts, could be liberating" (586).
Blount demonstrates this liberating effect with a subtle reading of one of
Dunbar's most famous vernacular poems, "An Ante-bellum Sermon" (Dunbar, *Collected Poetry* 13–15), in which he shows how the poem "is self-
consciously angled and refracted as Dunbar risks rhetorical instability." The
poem *"performs* the devious agenda of African American cultural practices"
(590; original emphasis), while it "invites us to theorize" about the practices of African American poetry. Blount roots his reading of "An Ante-
bellum Sermon" in a historical interpretation of the sermons of slave
preachers and is able to provide some rich insight into the poet's use of
African American vernacular dialect.

There is, however, an additional means we can use to see how Dunbar, in
his vernacular dialect verse, performs this agenda, and that is by reminding
ourselves of what I have been suggesting are rhetorical affinities in Dunbar's
verse with the language we've come to associate with the Symbolist aesthetic. In two of his best-known dialect poems, "The Deserted Plantation"
and "When Malindy Sings" (*Lyrics of Lowly Life* 158–60, 195–99), he
employs some of these subversive strategies to great effect, through a use of
language which, while coming from within the nostalgic-plantation tradition, transcends that tradition with an almost modern poetics. In "The
Deserted Plantation" the speaker introduces a barren, empty place whose
former natural and human abundance is signified by the marshaling of a
rhetoric of absence:

> In de furrers whah de co'n was allus wavin',
> Now de weeds is growin' green an' rank an'
> tall;
> An de swallers roun' de whole place is a-bravin'
> Lak dey thought deir folks had allus owned it
> all.
>
> (159)

This absence is contrasted only by nature, including birds (swallows and whippoorwills), and the voice of the speaker who is describing the scene. The poem opens as a catalogue of absence: an empty house, a barn without a carriage or driver, a (musicianless) banjo and the lack of a singer to accompany it. All that's left is the natural world, which the speaker describes wearily:

> But de murmur of a branch's passin' waters
> Is de only soun' dat breaks de stillness dere.
>
> (159)

At this point it may be tempting to read the catalogue as one of nostalgia, but the speaker offers us little ground for that assumption. The voice's description is without affect, even when describing the banjo and the hymns that no longer inhabit the scene. The speaker describes a "rustin'" hoe, a plow that's "a-tumblin down" in the field, a house without "a blessed soul." And despite the prominent place of the banjo in the scene, "D' ain't a hymn ner co'n-song ringin' in de / air" (158–59). All that's left is the sound of the waters. Even the change of mood announced by the next stanza fails to fully counteract the world-weariness of the speaker's voice. At this point it becomes clear that the poem has been deploying clichés all along to create its mood. Through a series of interjections posed as rhetorical questions, the speaker leads the reader through a second catalogue, this time through a group of racially stereotypical tropes: "Whah's de da'kies, dem dat used to be a-dancin' / Evry night befo' de ole cabin do'?" (159). These lines, with their alternating syllabic stresses, seem to dance, performing the function of enacting the very racially charged stereotypes they signify; but in the hands of Dunbar, they also reveal the emptiness of the gesture, as the series of questions resolves itself into an exclamation that brings the reader back to the significance of the poem's title: "Gone! not one o' dem is lef to tell de story" (160).

The speaker reports that all the inhabitants of the plantation—ex-slaves as well as ex-slavemasters—have abandoned the place "to de swallers." All that's left is the speaker, "a lover till de las'," who will tend to and live on the land. But the emphasis is on the evacuation of all other human inhabitants from the premises, its subsequent deterioration, and the fact that this evacuation is being told by a speaker who is left with a language devoid of any productive meaning other than to perform its own absence. It is, in a word, the language of clichés.

Dunbar also deployed the language of clichés in lyric art in his work in the Broadway theater. The lyrics he wrote in collaboration with composer Will Marion Cook were full of clichés, and the strategies he used there were similar to those he had been using in his poetry. Lyrics such as those from "Down de Lover's Lane," a song he wrote with Cook for the Broadway show *The Casino Girl,* show just how familiar Dunbar became with the use of the cliché. The song was labeled a "Plantation Croon":

> Summer night an' sighin' breeze,
> Long de Lover's Lane—
>
> Friendly, shadder-makin' trees,
> Long de Lover's Lane—
>
> White fo'ks wu'k all done up gran',
> Me an' Mandy han' in han',
> Struttin' lak we owned de lan',
> Long de Lover's Lane.

Here the cliché is deployed liberally, and to great effect. Narrative is virtually suppressed, leaving little more than a series of images. The song is, in sense, a satire on the coon song. This evacuation of meaning in lyric language in favor of impressions, symbols, and images would, as the twentieth century progressed, become a commonplace in poetry. Here we see a prescient presentation of these concerns in a vaudeville song (though, significantly, in the verse, not the chorus) written by a literary poet.

In "When Malindy Sings," Dunbar poses a set of questions about the relationship of the emergent free African American culture to the larger one. In that poem, the poet asserts the contents of the challenge made to the "majority" culture by the "minority" one:

> G'way an' quit dat noise, Miss
> Lucy—
> Put dat music book away;
> What's de use to keep on tryin'?
> Ef you practise twell you're
> gray,
> You cain't sta't no notes a-flyin
> Lak de ones dat rants and rings
> F'om de kitchen to de big woods
> When Malindy sings.
> (*Collected Poetry* 82)

Throughout the poem, music as written text is contrasted to music as human expression, with the songs of Malindy clearly having the upper hand. Indeed, to push the point, the poem's speaker extols Malindy's supremacy over the musicmaking capacities both of other humans and of nature:

> Fiddlin' man jes' stop his fiddlin,
>   Lay his fiddle on de she'f;
> Mockin'-bird quit tryin' to whistle,
>   'Cause he jes' so shamed hisse'f.
> Folks a-playin' on de banjo
>   Draps dey fingas on de
>   strings—
> Bless yo' soul—fu'gits to move
>   em,
> When Malindy sings.
>   (*Collected Poetry* 82)

Though both the fiddle and the banjo would remain staples in African American music for another two generations, they were already being identified with the ideologically contested ground of the minstrel stage and its purported antecedent, the plantation entertainers.

If, in the nineteenth century, African American music would be most closely identified with minstrelsy and with instruments such as the fiddle and the banjo, in the twentieth century American culture would be dominated by African American vocal music. The song Malindy is identified as singing at the end of the poem, "Swing Low, Sweet Chariot," would first come to international prominence in the 1870s and 1880s with the Fisk Jubilee Singers. It is also a song that could be said to presage the dominance of the music of Malindy's heirs in American, and world, musical culture over the next century.

Moreover, the poem thematizes the birth of the ragtime–Tin Pan Alley era in American music history. It is a history that I have been exploring through its relationship to the emergence, among American poets in the first years of the twentieth century, of that new type of poetic lyric identified with the term "modernist." Dunbar was, I have attempted to demonstrate, a significant forerunner of modernism, in part because of the self-reflexivity and symbolic heft of his language, particularly in its deployment of the cliché. He was the only major American poet to have participated as a full-fledged professional artist both in the emergent American musical theater and in the international world of letters. That he was a figure of international renown can be demonstrated by his 1897 trip to London, where he read

"When Malindy Sings" and other poems at the Southplace Institute (Wiggins 67–68), lived with Alexander Crummell, and met Henry Morton Stanley and Samuel Coleridge-Taylor, the latter of whom set some of Dunbar's poems to music (Cunningham 159–71). This trip of Dunbar's has received far too little attention in the available scholarship on the poet and deserves much more detailed study, especially in light of the aesthetic concerns I have been attempting to trace here.

To continue our inquiry into Dunbar's poetry, here is "The Poet," the non-dialect poem quoted from earlier, in full:

> He sang of life, serenely sweet,
> With, now and then, a deeper note.
> From some high peak, nigh yet remote,
> He voiced the world's absorbing beat.
>
> He sang of love, when earth was young,
> And Love, itself, was in his lays.
> But ah, the world, it turned to praise
> A jingle in a broken tongue.
> (Dunbar, *Life and Works* 275)[10]

In this poem, in diction and meters reminiscent of A. E. Housman, Dunbar deploys clichés throughout. The language appears almost opaque until the wholly original last line, which compels us to read back into the poem to unravel its meaning and significance.

The opening phrases present the speaker's alienation, as he refers to himself in the third person, and the phrases themselves seem hackneyed, but with a hint of obscurity, and of despair. The speaker is aloof from the world. The language is itself remote, the nouns lacking in specificity, the tone in the past tense. The poet seems alienated from his own poem. The second quatrain mirrors the first, with the same qualities of distance, alienation, weariness, discontent, and even boredom. The projection into the eternal past of the speaker ("He sang of love, when earth was young") has the effect of sharpening the distance of the speaker from his own voice, from his own presence. The vagueness communicated in the first quatrain is due to the dominance there of adjectives, adverbs, prepositions, and the three-word interjection ("now and then"), which together make up half the stanza. This burden of vagueness is only slightly relieved in the second stanza, which, in almost mirrorlike fashion to the first, is dominated by nouns, verbs, and pronouns. The formulaic phrases ("He sang of life"; "He sang of love, when earth was young") only add to the weariness evoked by the poem. While he speaks of his attempts to win the world's favor through the time-honored themes of poetry, he is also a speaker whose poem is about the exhaustion of poetry itself, even as it contains a complaint about the world's refusal of the poet's work.

What makes the poem's last line so remarkable is the way it seems to refer to both a song outside the poem itself—which the world "turned to praise"— and to the present poem. The key to this understanding is a consideration of the word "jingle." Among the definitions given by the Oxford English Dictionary are "any arrangement of words intended to have a pleasing or striking sound without regard to sense," and "a short verse or song in a radio or television commercial or in general advertising." The poem appears to use the word in both senses.[11] The word, here, signifies nonsense, empty expression, just as the poem enacts a series of empty expressions, a series of aporia, to signify upon itself. The poem doubles back on itself, as it were, in a rhetoric not inconsistent with the Symbolist aesthetic. "The symbolist imagination consistently employs the mirror as an icon for the ambivalence of existence, because of its mysterious betrayal of uncertainty in what is perceived and the strangeness of its shadowed world," writes Margaret Stoljar (364). Although "The Poet" does not explicitly use mirror imagery, the poem's rhetoric is in a self-reflective mode, with such self-reflexivity being named as the subject of poetry as such: "And Love, itself." The self-reflexivity and ambivalence of "The Poet" can serve, then, as a useful beginning from which to explore the affinities between Dunbar's poetry and poetic avant-garde of the late nineteenth century.

At this point I need to clarify some terms. Having introduced the term "Symbolism," and having attempted to read Dunbar as a poet who worked with a poetics that had at least some affinities with the work of those poets associated with the term, I would like to consider some further characteristics of the style I am attempting to identify. This is not as simple as it may at first appear. The terms "Decadence" and "Symbolism" have come to be identified, in literary studies, with certain sets of historical coteries of artists, each identified with a set of (mainly European) nations or nationalities, with a poetics tied to a certain set of historical figures, and, perhaps only secondarily, with a means of making poetry. Once one begins to examine the poetics of this late nineteenth-century avant-garde, however, the possibilities of reading a poet like Dunbar in new ways open up tremendously. A detailed exegesis of symbolism would be out of place here, but a brief statement of the style's central aesthetic problem, as given by Paul de Man, is useful:

The symbolist poet starts from the acute awareness of an essential separation between his own being and the being of whatever is not himself: the world of natural objects, of other human beings, society, or God. He lives in a world that has been split and in which his consciousness is pitted, as it were, against its object in an attempt to seize something that it is unable to reach. In terms of poetic language—which as an agent of consciousness is on the side of the subject (or poet)—this means that he is no longer close enough to things to name them as they are, that the light and the grass and the skies that appear in his poems remain essentially other than actual light or grass or sky. The word, the logos, no longer coincides with the universe but merely reaches out for it in a language that is unable to *be* what it *names*—a language that, in other words, is *merely* a symbol. (150, original emphasis)

It is from this standpoint that we get the vagueness, aporia, and ritualization of language whose most telling residue is the cliché, the split between the subject and the objects in the real world that appear in the poet's verse, and the poetry's weary acceptance of a state of affairs that cannot be changed, a weariness that often appears as a nostalgia for an imagined past and perfect world. The exemplary poet in English in this regard is William Butler Yeats. The language and the style, however, have become so normalized as features of modern poetry that their distinctiveness is often overlooked, in particular in poets whose value is assumed to reside not so much in their style as in their presumed "message." The split in consciousness described by de Man, which manifests itself in the way objects are treated in Symbolist poetry, is a central feature of some of Dunbar's best poems. It is not only the existence of this split that figures in the poetry; the set of choices the poet makes with regard to the split is an important feature of this style as well. In de Man's view, the Symbolist poet chooses either to maintain the split through the use of metaphor or to make the language itself an objective, malleable thing. In the latter alternative, one pursued by Mallarmé, language reflects the "ambiguity" of being. It is "handled very much as if it were an object, with considerable attention given to its objective qualities of sound, visual appearance, and form" (159). Elsewhere, de Man writes that Symbolism "transfers attributes of consciousness onto the natural object" (*Rhetoric of Romanticism* 154) as a means of attempting to achieve the unity of subject and object.

These problems become apparent in some of Dunbar's best-known poetry. "We Wear the Mask" is a poem familiar to all his readers:

We wear the mask that grins and lies,
It hides our cheeks and shades our eyes,—
This debt we pay to human guile;
With torn and bleeding hearts we smile,
And mouth with myriad subtleties.

Why should the world be over-wise,
In counting all our tears and sighs?
Nay, let them only see us, while
    We wear the mask.

We smile, but, O great Christ, our cries
To thee from tortured souls arise.
We sing, but oh the clay is vile
Beneath our feet, and long the mile;
But let the world dream otherwise,
    We wear the mask!
                  (*Collected Poetry* 71)

In comments already alluded to, Houston A. Baker Jr. considers that this poem reveals Dunbar's naiveté:

> Rather than recognize that the black soul's eternal indebtedness is a result of *white* guile, the speaker *accepts* an indebtedness to "guile" as a force—not un-like a cosmic spirit making life bearable—that enables stoicism. In other words, it is as though Dunbar's speaker plays the masking game without an awareness of its status as a game. It seems that he does not adopt masking as self-conscious gamesmanship in opposition to the game white America has run on him. And he surely does not have as one of his goals the general progress of the Afro-American populace. (39)

Baker is here concerned with Dunbar as a historic figure and with his poem as an expression of a historical condition. This is fair enough, if one decides, as Baker has done, to place the poem within a racialized discursive frame that can be supported only by referring to historical and biographical circumstances that exist outside the poem but are not referred to directly by the poem at all.

The poem is a rondeau, a verse form that comes from medieval French prosody (Turco 239–40). It was first brought to English prosody by Sir Thomas Wyatt, and, far from echoing William Ernest Henley, as Baker suggests, "We Wear the Mask" seems to be a rewriting and recasting of one of Wyatt's Egerton manuscript poems ("What vaileth trouth? or, by it, to take payn?") (Wyatt, *Collected Poems* 3).[12] That Dunbar chose to take this form, and perhaps that poem, for his model can be seen as a deliberate rhetorical strategy, aimed at placing himself face to face with his nemesis, human guile, as an equal and at confronting his opponent from the standpoint of one who, like that nemesis, is rooted in the very culture whose language they share. The mention of guile, here, is a direct echo of Wyatt. Here is the last stanza of Wyatt's poem, from the edition edited by Kenneth Muir:

> Deceved is he by crafty trayn
> That meaneth no gile: and doeth remayn
>   Within the trappe, withoute redresse
>   But for to love, lo, suche a maistres,
> Whose crueltie nothing can refrayn.
> What vaileth trouth?
>
> (4)

What is interesting, given this context, is how Dunbar modernizes the poem. The refrain, repeated twice (as befits the rondeau style), begins with the nominative plural personal pronoun, which does not specify any body of persons as its referent. The line appears at least as much involved in performing a function as in conveying meaning. It seems that the function of "we" is only to refer to the action of wearing the mask; the vagueness of the pronoun seems aimed at drawing our attention not to the wearer but to the mask. The immediacy of the polarity set up between subject and object here is striking. The mask is introduced as the possession of the subject, but as soon as it is introduced, it assumes another character; it assumes an aspect of consciousness: "We wear the mask that grins and lies." The mask is introduced not merely as a metaphor but as a conduit of language as well as gesture.

As the poem proceeds, the polarity between subject and object and between self and mask become relationships of identity. It is no longer certain where the self ends and the mask begins: "With torn and bleeding hearts we smile / And mouth with myriad subtleties." The poem oscillates between polarity and identity of subject and object, and it is this oscillation that gives the poem its tension. In the final lines, the speaker has surrendered to a tragic condition, that of having to remain behind the mask. But the last lines reveal something unusual about the mask. It is that the world is unaware that the speaker and those for whom he is speaking are even wearing a mask. Although it is certainly valid to read the passage from which the lines quoted above are taken as having to do with specific historical circumstances—the "guile" which brought about the "nadir" of African American life—it is hard to escape the astonishing fact that the mask presented here consists of gesture and language; through gesture and language this mask hides not only the self but also the fact that it is, indeed, a mask. At the same time, it is clear that the speaker is aware not only that he is wearing a mask but also of the functions the mask is being deployed to perform. The speaker is aware that he is deploying the mask as a performative object—an inanimate object imbued with consciousness—and this self-consciousness makes the poem more than simply a lyric using a symbol that is chiefly representational. By the time the line containing the word "mask" is repeated a third time it has already become a cliché and is being self-consciously articulated as such.

The issue of language and its constitutive capacity is a concern that runs throughout Dunbar's poetry, existing as an element of his dialect verse just as strongly as it exists in a poem like "We Wear the Mask." All the other elements I've attempted to identify here in the "pure" English poems—the use of the cliché, the emptying-out of language, the self-conscious use of the symbol, and the anxious gap between subject and object—also appear in Dunbar's dialect poetry. Although in the dialect poems, readers too often find difficulty in seeing the distinctive aesthetic elements at work, these elements do exist in both styles and are among the characteristics that make Dunbar's work a precursor to the linguistic concerns that modernist poets take up in earnest just a few years after his death. That Dunbar's voice would not be a stranger to modern sensibilities can be seen in the way some of his poems continued to be a source for creative artists; in 1960, Abbey Lincoln recorded a modern jazz version of "When Malindy Sings" in an album that included a song with lyrics written by Langston Hughes. This fact, and the argument made here, can be taken as suggestive of Dunbar's importance to the linkage between the revolution in poetic language and the African American Imaginary—an important, if overlooked, part of the genealogy of modernism.

CHAPTER THREE

Minstrel

{ 1 }

IT IS USEFUL at this stage to remind ourselves of the characteristics of laughter as understood by Mikhail Bakhtin: its universality, "its indissoluble and essential relation to freedom" and its "relation to the people's unofficial truth" (*Rabelais and His World* 89, 90). The heyday of modernist culture in the 1920s was also the heyday of the silent film comedy, exemplified by the movies of Charlie Chaplin, Harold Lloyd, and Buster Keaton. Walter Benjamin offers the comment that Chaplin accomplished "in a more natural way" the same reaction in audiences that the Dadaists desired (250), but his examination of the rise of film and its relationship to the artistic enterprise does not offer an assessment of Chaplin's comedic art, or of comedic art as such. His comment nevertheless remains an important one, if only because the linkage he draws between Dadaism and Chaplin's work allows us to glimpse just how important the comedic is to the modernist enterprise.

To consider the importance of the comedic to modernism is, in a sense, to reconsider the relationship of popular culture to modernist aesthetics, seeing the former in a filial rather than a competitive relationship to the latter. Doing so runs the risk of prompting a further reconsideration, a theme throughout this study: that is, once the relationship of popular culture to modernist aesthetics is repositioned, then the further question of the relationship between African American culture and modernism comes to the fore. That is because within African American culture the relationship between these two poles is not as clear-cut as some modernist criticism has postulated for the aesthetic creations of the majority culture. To raise the question of the comedic also allows for consideration of another question, that of the relationship between modernism and African American culture as such; and to consider this relationship is at the same time to ask questions about how modernism came to have its particular "modern" caste. How do we recognize a work as "modernist"? One way of answering this question is to resort to the categories of radical subjectivity, multiple perspective, discontinuity, and so on (Everdell 346–60). As much as these categories may explain, or be used as signs that point to modernism, there is much they don't explain. Once the question of the comedic is posed, for instance, it is possible to inquire into other sources of modernist consciousness, into the shared cultural history and consciousness of modern society, and not only into the art of Chaplin but into such sources of that art as American minstrelsy.

One of the characteristics of late minstrelsy and early vaudeville, as African American artists performed it, was the use of humor as a means of conveying "unofficial truth." To do so, the old minstrel stereotypes had to be transformed and imbued with a new agency, one that embodied a distinctly modern form of humor, emerging in the twentieth century, in which agency and self-consciousness combined with the parodic to produce a new kind of comic hero.

To search for this comic hero of a new type involves a discussion about pairs, twins, doubleness, illusion, parody, minstrels, and tramps. It involves an inquiry into how this comedic type emerged in American comedy in the early years of the twentieth century in the work of the African American comedian Bert Williams. Williams first came to prominence, in 1898, as one half of a comedy team, Williams and Walker. His partner, George Walker, left the stage in 1908, after contracting tuberculosis, and died in 1911, one year after Williams joined the Ziegfeld Follies. Williams was the only African American star of this musical review, which also starred such comedians and singers as Eddie Cantor, W. C. Fields, and Sophie Tucker (Riis, *Just before Jazz* 43–47).

This exploration also involves a look at some affinities between the characters in *Waiting for Godot*, by Samuel Beckett, and certain characters and characteristics of American, and particularly African American, minstrelsy and vaudeville. Although I make no claims about influence and causality between African American vaudeville, on the one hand, and Vladimir, Estragon, Pozzo and Lucky, and The Boy, on the other, I am interested in seeking out affinities. In particular, I want to explore the question of familiarity: how is it that we recognize the characters in *Godot* so readily? At the same time, what is distinct about these comic clowns? Part of the answer has to do with the contributions Williams made to modernizing the tramp, or the vagrant, as a comic figure.

Involved here is a further exploration of the role of the African American Imaginary in the construction of the modernist imagination. If such affinities can be seen in earlier manifestations of modernism, is it also possible that they are implicated in later examples of literary modernism? It is one thing to assert that African American culture and its presence were intricately involved in the development of jazz age artworks; it is, perhaps, quite another to think about this presence as a part of the identity of modernism as a whole. If this is the case, then the argument for a view of modernism that sees modernism as an essentially white, "very masculine affair" (Macey 259) is perhaps a distorted understanding of a literary and cultural movement which, because it embraced and expressed the sense of the culture as a whole, had among its sources and exemplars hitherto underacknowledged artists, methods, and influences. In particular, placing both Williams and Beckett within the same discussion can allow us to understand how central the African American Imaginary is to the modernist project.

{ 2 }

Thomas L. Riis cites two teams and one individual singer as central figures in early twentieth-century African American stage entertainment: besides Williams and Walker, there are the Cole and Johnson Brothers and Ernest Hogan. "The shows of Williams and Walker, Cole and Johnson, and Hogan, constitute the principal, although not the only, contributions to black American musical theater from 1898 to 1911" (Riis 46). Bob Cole, J. Rosamond Johnson, and (often) James Weldon Johnson made up one of the most successful songwriting teams in the country in the first decade of the twentieth century. Ernest Hogan, who billed himself "The Unbleached American," was a key figure in the transition from old-style minstrelsy to vaudeville. To these must be added the team of Flournoy Miller and Aubrey Lyles, "the most influential black comedy team in the early century" (Watkins 159). All these figures were involved in the nearly fifteen-year presence of African American musical production in New York in the century's early years. Their shows—*Clorindy, or the Cakewalk* (1898), *The Sons of Ham* (1900), *In Dahomey* (1903), *Abyssina* (1906), *The Shoo-Fly Regiment* (1907), and *Bandanna Land* (1908), among others—were all Broadway hits (Riis, *Just before Jazz* 194–95).

Among these performers, Hogan might be considered a transitional figure between minstrelsy and vaudeville. He emerged as a nationally known performer during the coon song era of the 1890s, which he is credited with starting with his 1896 hit "All Coons Look Alike to Me"—a title the songwriter spent the rest of his life apologizing for. The song from this style that has lasted the longest is "Won't You Come Home, Bill Bailey" (Fletcher 138).

Hogan was also famous as a facial contortionist. "His mobile face was capable of laughter-provoking expressions that were irresistible," wrote James Weldon Johnson (*Black Manhattan* 103). But most audiences today would probably consider Hogan's type of humor tasteless, since it reportedly relied on racist stereotypes for its effectiveness. Yet Jessie Redmon Fauset, the Harlem Renaissance novelist and literary editor of the *Crisis* magazine from 1919 to 1926, had a high regard for him. Hogan, she writes, added something new to the minstrel tradition: he "changed the tradition of the merely funny, rather silly 'end man' into a character with a definite plot in a rather loosely constructed but none the less well outlined story." She adds: "The method was still humorous, but less broadly, less exclusively. A little of the hard luck of the Negro began to creep in. If he was a buffoon, he was a buffoon wearing his rue. A slight, very slight quality of the Harlequin began to attach to him. He was a clown making light of his troubles but he was a wounded, sore-beset clown" ("The Gift of Laughter" 162). She asserts that Hogan raised the status of the "end man," one of the pair of actors whose comic dialogue traditionally opened minstrel shows, by giving him depth of character. As Wittke puts it:

> The endmen furnished the comedy of the show, and according to all accounts, from the beginning of minstrelsy to its decline as a form of professional theatricals, they were universally successful in keeping their audiences in an uproar, by their grimacing while the balladists were performing, by their own comic songs sung to the accompaniment of various clever or grotesque dance steps, which sometimes became indescribably eccentric gyrations, and by their rapid-fire jokes. (141)

For Fauset, the distinction Hogan brought to his art had to do with the realism and pathos he gave to his characterizations. When the "hard luck" of black people's condition emerged as a part of the minstrel routine, it was the beginning of a transition in the history of American comedic stage performance. What oldtime minstrel enthusiasts like Wittke regard as the "decline" of the art form can also be seen, from a different angle, as black artists' appropriation for different ends of a theatrical form based on "Negro imitators." It becomes, in fact, the emergence of a self-conscious African American comedy.

In both the Williams and Walker and the Miller and Lyles teams, the transition that started with Hogan went a few steps further. For one thing, the comic clown was transformed from a plantation sharecropper to a city dweller. Sometimes he was an urban tramp; sometimes he was a naïve newcomer to the city; sometimes, as Barbara L. Webb points out, he was a dandy. What is important is the transformation—during the transition period from the minstrel to the vaudeville era (eras which overlapped as well)—of this African American comic character. When Williams and Walker performed as a duo act, Walker played the "prancing dandy" to Williams's "shiftless darky" caricature. "Williams would come onto the stage in tattered clothes, shambling, ill at ease, a forlorn, wide-eyed expression on his face, which was corked to appear much darker than Walker's," writes Mel Watkins. "Inevitably, Walker preyed on Williams's naïveté and supposed ignorance" (175).

Webb draws on the literary and the theatrical traditions of the dandy to provide some insight into the character Walker played: "Walker emphasized the dandy's point of view," she writes. "He sought to fuse everyday life and performance in a way that staked out a dandyist claim for the dignity and humanity of African Americans" (15). The duality the two performers presented, then, not only parodied the stereotypes inherited from minstrelsy but also presented a pair of new figures that sought to transcend the bounds of the stereotype by signifying a more "universal" and humanist character. In these routines, Williams and Walker's dual urban characters represented the fortunes and misfortunes of urban life, thereby making something new out of the minstrel stereotype. Webb observes that newspaper reviewer comments on Walker's elegant dress reflected the notion that he was transcending the received stereotypes. The descriptions, she writes, "indicate that neither blacks nor whites perceived Walker's dress as strictly, or even primarily, comic"; rather, the writers "all show an awareness of being in the presence of an *actual* rather than parodied well-dressed black man" (16; original emphasis). One result was that Williams's onstage persona was also increasingly seen as a performative role rather than a mimetic one. The effect was, in part, to raise his status as an artist in the eyes of his audience—perhaps one explanation for the increasing success of his phonograph records in the first two decades of the twentieth century.

The influence of Miller and Lyles on American comedy has yet to be fully quantified. They were the dialogue writers for the 1921 Broadway musical *Shuffle Along*, which is considered a key catalyzing event of the Harlem Renaissance (Krasner 240). Ann Douglas characterizes the show as a "free-form mock homage" to minstrelsy (378). Miller and Lyles, whose own act consisted of conversation of an almost surrealistic character, influenced both film and television comedy for decades, including the early Amos and Andy radio performers; indeed, Flournoy Miller worked as a writer for both the radio and television versions of *Amos and Andy*. "In 1908, Miller and Lyles began experimenting with two characters who, although similar to the familiar minstrel stereotype, had an assertiveness, an urban flair, and just enough trickster's cunning to set them apart," writes Watkins (169). The most indelible residue of their performance was their "Indefinite Talk" act, which Miller revived with his later partner, Johnny Lee, in the film *Stormy Weather*. Arthur Knight explains the practice this way:

> Indefinite talk is a mixture of an authoritative tone and obscure content cre-
> ated by the dialogue partners chronically cutting one another off. When the
> partners are not interrupting one another, their sentences alternate between
> abstractions (usually because their pronouns have no clear referent), questions
> (that go unanswered), and hyperbolic pronouncements (which are immedi-
> ately deflated). Along with precise gestures and timing, some punning and
> malapropisms, the deformations of dialect, and a schism between character
> and tone, what most makes indefinite talk unique (and funny) is that the in-
> definite talkers always understand one another. (110)

One striking aspect of this description is its similarity to the 1911 description by Howard W. Odum of rural African American folksongs, especially
those linguistic operations that render the sentences abstract. The omission
of pronouns in particular and the fact that the two speakers "always understand each other" (a point made explicitly by Miller in *Stormy Weather*)
seem to give the audience the impression that it is eavesdropping on a sort
of secret communication.

This sense of insider talk would have a long and deep history in African
American performance practice, which by no means died with the old-style
minstrel and blues performances. It reached its height in the "scat" singing
of jazz artists, starting with Louis Armstrong's "Heebie Jeebies" recording
of 1928, and continuing through the post–World War II period, when scat
became a staple of John Birks "Dizzy" Gillespie and other modern bebop
and jazz musicians. There, the practice would become allied with the
growth of the sensibility associated with the term "hipster"; but it would
also be perfected (and to some extent brought close to mainstream culture)
by singers such as Sarah Vaughn, Ella Fitzgerald, Mel Tormé, Anita O'Day,
Betty Carter, and the trio known as Lambert, Hendricks and Ross. The

nonsense syllable singing of the scat singers was one side of a verbal performance practice that had its roots in such scenes as one by Miller and Lee in *Stormy Weather.*

In that scene, Miller and Lee come onstage in an old beat-up jalopy which backfires before it stutters to a stop, steam jetting out of the radiator. The car is falling apart. Each man, made up in blackface, wears white gloves and light-colored top hat and tails. During the dialogue, each man is shouting:

> MILLER: What's wrong with it? Where'd you have it fixed?
> LEE: I just had it worked on!
> MILLER: Well, who worked on it?
> LEE: The man that's around . . . around—
> MILLER: He ain't no good. The man you want is the man—
> LEE: I had him! He's the one that ruined it.
> MILLER: Well, I see you got plenty of water, but it's out of gas.
> LEE: No, 'tain't that. I think maybe it's—
>   *(Lee leans on fender, which falls off the car, loudly.)*
> MILLER: Oh, it couldn't be that.
> LEE: Well, ain't much wrong with it.
> MILLER: What you need is one of them new gadgets. You know the kind
>   that you buy—
> LEE: I bought some.
> MILLER: Oh, not them. I mean the kind what fastens where they fits . . .
>   a whole dozen'll cost about—
> LEE: That's too much money. I can't afford it. I got to get some that don't
>   cost no more—
> MILLER : You can't get 'em that cheap.
> LEE: Well, we can get the car fixed up good maybe for around a—
>   *(Goes over to car, another piece falls off.)*
> MILLER: No . . . What you need *(leans on car, car collapses)* is a new car.
> LEE: Yeah.
>
>   *(Stormy Weather*; excerpts qtd. in Knight 110–19)

One source of the humor in this dialogue is the way the two speakers base their discourse on the use of fragments. In some cases, the fragments are produced by one speaker's dropping of nouns, pronouns, phrases, or clauses ("I got to get some that cost no more—"), only to have the second speaker respond as if he had heard the lost words ("You can't get 'em that cheap"), when in fact they were never uttered.

These absences also recall the speech disorders identified by Roman Jakobson in his discussion of speech aphasia. Speakers in a dialogue often ask for confirmation of meaning from each other: "Do you know what I mean?" The clarification is the way the "lost" elements in a sentence are often conveyed from one person to another. Aphasics, however, cannot name such an element. "Such an aphasic can switch neither from a word to its synonyms or circumlocutions nor to its *heteronyms* (equivalent expressions in other languages)," writes Jakobson (104; original emphasis).

In thinking about the fragmentation of language in modernist artistic discourse, it is also useful to remember that fragmented language was characteristic of minstrelsy, or, as Houston A. Baker notes: "The minstrel mask is a governing object in a ritual of nonsense" (21). For Baker, the use of nonsense is a means by which African American performers mastered, with parody and mockery, those elements of minstrelsy whose degrading, racialized stereotypes reinforced the legal environment of violence and oppression in which African Americans lived. At the same time, we can see these comedians making a distinction from the old, self-deprecating humor that characterized minstrelsy. The comic duo of Miller and Lee was a direct descendant of Ernest Hogan, and the pair's presentation is suffused with the "hard luck of the Negro" that Fauset identified in the older comedian. The basic theme here is poverty and the inability of one speaker (Lee) to get a fair deal in repairing his car. The field in which this comedy routine takes place is filled with signs pointing to urban life: the car, the dandyish clothes worn by Miller and Lee, and conversation that centers on money and commodities. The humor is self-reflective without being self-deprecating, yet if anyone is the object of this humorous routine, it is the "new," urbanized Negro.

{ 3 }

If Ernest Hogan was one of the first to begin to complicate the minstrel character's simple presentation by adding "a little of the hard luck of the Negro" to his characterization, Bert Williams seems to have brought to this character to a new level of complexity. His primary solo stage character, which won him international fame, came not just with a bag of comic tricks but with a philosophy as well. Williams not only modernized the minstrel but created, out of the degraded figure of the minstrel "darky," a modern, and modernizing, character.

It is almost impossible to consider the art and career of Bert Williams without noting the terribly racist conditions under which he worked. Even in the atmosphere of New York and big-city vaudeville, the segregation and violence that characterized this period of African American life was pervasive. W. C. Handy's reminiscences are suffused with stories of such violence, of the lynchings and near-lynchings of performers traveling through the South. He tells the story of Louis Wright, trombonist with the Georgia Minstrels, who was lynched in Missouri after besting a white mob in a snowball fight:

> That night a mob came back-stage to the theatre. They had come to lynch Louis. In his alarm the sharp-tempered boy drew a gun and fired into the crowd. The mob scattered promptly, but they did not turn from their purpose. They reassembled in the railroad yards, near the special car of the minstrel company. This time their number was augmented by officers. When the minstrels arrived, the whole company was arrested and thrown into jail. Many of them were brutally flogged during the questioning that followed, but no squeal was forthcoming. In time, however, Louis Wright was recognized. The law gave him to the mob, and in almost less time than it takes to tell it they had done their work. He was lynched, his tongue cut out and his body shipped to his mother in Chicago in a pine box. (Handy, *Father of the Blues* 43)

Racist segregation in the entertainment world was commonplace even in the northern cities. Buster Keaton recalled that "when Negroes were allowed in white saloons at all, they were restricted to the end of the bar farthest from the door." As part of the family act the Four Keatons, young Buster played a Boston theater with Williams in 1909. Years later he told a story about his father offering to buy Williams a drink in such a saloon, near the theater:

> "Bert," said Pops, "Come up here and have a drink with me." Bert looked nervously from one white face at the bar to another, and replied, "Think I better stay down here, Mr. Joe."
>
> "All right," said Pops, picking up his glass, "then I'll have to come down there to you." (Qtd. in E. Smith 113)

Blacks weren't allowed to sit in the audiences in many theaters. When Williams first appeared with the Ziegfeld Follies in 1910, Ann Charters reports, the comedian insisted that his contract state that "at no time would he be on stage with any of the female members of the company." This was, presumably, in order to forestall any fears of miscegenation, which was a major rallying cry of American racists. Charters adds that "Ziegfeld promised that the follies would never include Southern cities in its annual tours; this was promised as a favor to Williams, who Ziegfeld knew never appeared below the Mason-Dixon line" (115). Eric Ledell Smith quotes Williams to the effect that these terms were part of a verbal agreement the performer had with Ziegfeld. "There never has been any contract between us," Williams said of his work with Ziegfeld; theirs was, he added, "just a gentleman's agreement" (qtd. in E. Smith 132). That racism had a profound effect on Williams is widely known. "Bert Williams was the funniest man I ever saw and the saddest man I ever knew," recalled his friend W. C. Fields. In a moving tribute to his fellow comedian, Fields spoke of Williams's "deep undercurrent of pathos" (qtd. in Rowland 128).

This attitude seems to characterize most biographical and critical readings of Williams as well. Both Ann Charters and Eric Ledell Smith detail the conditions under which Williams worked, and the stress and exhaustion that hastened the pneumonia that killed him in 1922 at forty-seven years of age. Among the very few critical writings on Williams's art, most also emphasize these racist conditions. "Misfortune and Caricature" is how David Krasner titles his essay on Williams. Citing Freud on caricature and unmasking, he adds: "In blackface, the alleged pretenses of African Americans were exposed. Through the malapropian, deceitful and pompous caricatures personified by Miller and Lyles, and the fatalistic, naïve, and set-upon caricature of Williams, the 'unmasking' of their alleged superficialities manifested the supposed true image and revealed the so-called real traits of African Americans. Caricature thus assisted in 'exposing' pretenses for amusement" (268–69).

Although Krasner acknowledges the praise Williams got from African American community leaders such as Booker T. Washington, he cites approvingly the condemnation the comedian received from periodicals such as A. Philip Randolph's *The Messenger* and from Marcus Garvey's *Negro World* (Krasner 270). Williams was considered by his contemporaries however, not simply a pioneer but a great artist, and it is this consideration that is missing from evaluations such as Krasner's, which focus on the negative side of Williams's caricature. Most such comments on Williams focus on his relationship to the racist caricature his work was said to exemplify. Writers such as Krasner seem content to read Williams as operating within the legal limits set by the world of legal and institutional racism at the turn of the twentieth century. These critics don't seem invested in interrogating whether it is possible that Williams, though working from within the racist stereotype, may have at the same time performed it in such a way that it worked against the stereotype's apparent message.

Here it is useful to recall the work of Homi K. Bhabha, who thinks of the stereotype as a kind of fetish and focuses on its characteristic ambivalence. He reminds us that the stereotype is the "major discursive strategy" of modern racial domination, and that it is "a form of knowledge and identification that vacillates between what is 'in place,' already known, and something that must be anxiously repeated." Bhabha warns against seeing the stereotype as "offering, at any one time, a secure point of identification." Rather, the double nature of the stereotype offers an image that is at the same time an "other" and one that appears to be "entirely knowable and visible." When considering the antiblack stereotype embedded in American minstrelsy, this doubling can be seen as a site of degradation, on the one hand, and of fantasy, on the other. "The objective of colonial discourse," Bhabha reminds us, "is to construe the colonized as a population of degenerate types on the basis of racial origin, in order to justify conquest and to establish systems of administration and instruction" (66–71).

The maintenance of the idea of the colonized as "degenerate" is necessary as both an ideological and a psychological support for colonial discourse. In the early twentieth century U.S. entertainment industry, the parade of degenerate stereotypes of the African American was all but ubiquitous. James Weldon Johnson's well-known complaint about Negro dialect, that "it is an instrument with but two full stops, humor and pathos" (*The Book of American Negro Poetry* xl), illustrates the limits of this end of the stereotype dyad. It is in considering the other side of this dyad, the site of fantasy, that we can begin to unlock the element that made an entertainer like Williams such a pivotal figure. The side of the dualism embodied in the stereotype that appears familiar—"entirely knowable and visible"—is also, in Williams, the side in which the artist's own agency comes into play.

One of the problems recent critics of Williams have in interpreting his art derives from their sources. Most rely on descriptions of stage performances and on photographs of Williams in blackface makeup and outrageous costumes. But Williams's significance, both in his own time and in ours, derives from an additional source that is rarely studied. Williams was, for the first quarter of the twentieth century, the most prolific black American recording artist. He recorded about eighty songs between 1901 and his death, and these songs deserve closer study.

His most famous song was "Nobody," written with lyricist Alex Rogers. He introduced the song in 1905 and used it in *Bandanna Land*. It became his encore at nearly every appearance. Ann Charters recreates a typical Williams performance of the song:

> Usually his appearance on stage was announced by a spotlight that caught the tentative wiggling of gloved fingers against the closed plush curtains. Hesitantly the hand followed the fingers, then an arm, a shoulder, and finally, with awkward reluctance, a tall man in a shabby dress suit pushed through the curtains and walked slowly to the front of the stage. The applause started before he reached the footlights, but the face behind the mask of blackface remained downcast. As if resigned to some inevitable and unending stroke of bad fortune, he shrugged his shoulders. With exaggerated care he searched his ragged coat pocket, pulled out a small leather notebook, and slowly turned the pages of the book until he found what he was looking for. (Charters 8)

He would then begin, Charters adds, "to half-sing, half-recite" the song. In this reconstruction, "Nobody" is both song and text. Williams very often used literature, and the notion of the literary, in his act. One of his recordings, "Never Mo'," is a parody of Edgar Allen Poe's poem "The Raven." Charters shows how Williams again uses the stereotype against itself. The appearance of the illiterate "darky" who finds his verse in a notebook is precisely the sort of character that gives audiences both the comfort of the stereotype and the discomfort of the unknown. If the stereotyped blackface clown also has access to the "talking book" (to borrow Henry Louis Gates Jr.'s phrase), then how comforting is the stereotype? In a sense, by using the gesture of the notebook, by his employment of the gesture of reading, Williams renders absurd the very stereotype he performs.

In the 1913 recording he made for Columbia, with an orchestral arrangement by Will Vodery (Rowland 67),[1] "Nobody" begins with a fanfare, followed by a mournful, almost tuneless motif, as Williams recites:

> When life seems full of clouds and rain
> And I am full of nothin' and pain,
> Who soothes my thumping, bumping brain?
> Nobody!

As the song begins, the speaker is beset with illness and bad weather. He is "full of nothin, and pain," plagued not only from outside but from inside as well. The phrase is paradoxical, yet revealing. To be "full of nothing" suggests a consciousness of one's place in the world beyond the purely sensuous being that inhabited the antiblack, racist-stereotyped "darky." This is not simply sadness; this is alienation. Here, from within the scene of fetishism that Homi Bhabha ascribes to the stereotype, the fantasy enacts its opposite, "for the stereotype is at once a substitute and a shadow," writes Bhabha (82). The whole of minstrelsy was, in a sense, an enactment of the (white) fantasy of slave happiness and fulfillment, while it simultaneously harbored a narrative side that contradicted that fantasy. But here, in a performer presenting the sign of the stereotype—the African American blackface comedian—comes a conscious negation of the fantasy, with an appeal signifying a condition that has a paradoxical, and modern, appeal: "full of nothing, and pain."

In the following verse, nature's indifference is joined by human callousness: "Who says 'Here's twenty-five cents, go ahead and get something to eat?'" The figure that emerges lives in a modern, urban environment. The song's famous chorus follows:

> I ain't never done nothin' to Nobody;
> I ain't never got nothin' from Nobody, no time:
> And until I get somethin' from somebody sometime,
> I'll never do nothin' for Nobody, no time.
>
> (Qtd. in Charters 137)

In the published versions of the song, "Nobody" is capitalized, and in the recordings the word is stressed in such a way that it does double duty, as both pronoun and proper noun. The speaker, "full of nothing," has "done nothin' to Nobody." This "Nobody" suggests a figure that Frederick R. Karl identifies as the "new man" of modernism, "disaffected, effete or aesthetic, outside social coordinates, himself coordinate of emptiness, often a 'nil' man. He is a person for whom the outside world, however defined, has ceased to function, for whom it has become a dark place" (173–74). Karl's prototypes for this figure are Mallarmé and, significantly, Nietzsche, whose books Williams is reported to have had in his library. In this light, Nietzsche's comment, which he attributes to Silenus, seems to express a condition that is suggested by Williams's song: "not to be born, not to be, to be *nothing*" (22).

W. E. B. Du Bois expresses this idea in another way when he writes about the "veil" of color and of double consciousness. There is a sense in which the image of the veil, in *Souls of Black Folk*, anticipates the idea of invisibility as it would be developed half a century later by Ralph Ellison. The veil hides the speaking self, who cannot be seen but yet is at the same time familiar and of the same world as those on the other side of the veil. The idea is introduced in the first words of Du Bois's first chapter as a function of a conversation:

> Between me and the other world there is ever an unasked question: unasked by some through feelings of delicacy; by others through the difficulty of rightly framing it. All nevertheless flutter around it. They approach me in a half-hesitant sort of way, eye me curiously or compassionately, and then, instead of saying directly, How does it feel to be a problem? they say, I know an excellent colored man in my town; or, I fought at Mechanicsville; or, Do not these Southern outrages make your blood boil? At these I smile, or am interested, or reduce the boiling to a simmer, as the occasion may require. To the real question, How does it feel to be a problem? I answer seldom a word. (9–10)

For Du Bois, the persona of the African American is already an exemplar of the modern figure, the "nil man," the one who is seen by the world outside the veil as something other. To be sure, it can be argued that to be a problem is not "to be nothing," but that depends on what is meant by "problem." Du Bois remembers how the consciousness he is referring to here first thrust itself upon him: he attempted to exchange a visiting card with a schoolmate: when the girl "refused my card—refused it peremptorily, with a glance," he realized that he was "shut out from their world by a vast veil" (10). Although Du Bois poses the issue of the status of African Americans as both a *metaphorical* and an *ontological* one, he never loses sight of the fact that it was also a *legal* one; all three of these meet at the nexus of "problem" and "veil." And his schoolmate's refusal—assertive, abrupt, "with a glance"—with its rejection of even the simplest social intercourse, attempts to render Du Bois a nonperson.

It is here that we can see how Du Bois's veil became the subject of one of the most famous songs in the United States in the years preceding the First World War.

> When summer comes all cool and clear,
> And my friends see me drawing near,
> Who says "Come in and have some beer?"
> Nobody!
> (Williams, "Nobody," 1913 version;
> qtd. in Charters 135–36)

There is a sense in which Williams's approach to his material—and the way he carved out and fashioned a self from within that material—recalls Steven Greenblatt's description of Sir Thomas Wyatt's method of self-fashioning. "For all his impulse to negate," Greenblatt writes, "Wyatt cannot fashion himself in opposition to power and the conventions power deploys; on the contrary, those conventions are precisely what constitute Wyatt's self-fashioning" (120). The modernist self-fashioning of Bert Williams took place from within the conventions handed to him by American minstrelsy. From within those conventions he was able to create a modern character by invoking them and grafting them onto an urban (as opposed to a rural) persona. It was a persona with an introspective, instead of a simply humorous, consciousness, a character whose pathos and humor began to transcend minstrelsy, turning the sign of the minstrel into the modern tramp by making of that tramp a modern form of sensory and aesthetic communication, a symbol.

{ 4 }

Before the early twentieth century, the male itinerant, vagabond figure—the tramp—was generally considered an antiurban personage. His earliest literary ancestor is the Fool, but in the United States in the nineteenth century he emerges as strikingly different from the traditional Fool. He is a romantic figure whose cosmology is perhaps most idealized in the voice Walt Whitman assumes in "Song of the Open Road." This poem, which John D. Seelye calls "the manifesto of American bohemianism" (540), is also an example of how the nineteenth-century tramp was romanticized:

> Afoot and light-hearted I take to the open road,
> Healthy, free, the world before me,
> The long brown path before me leading wherever I choose.
> . . .
> I inhale great draughts of space,
> The east and the west are mine, and the north and the south are
> mine.
>
> (149, 151)

Whitman's tramp is an anti-urban figure, one who values the open, endless road, which, as he well knows, is rapidly passing away. The open road, "the efflux of the soul" (153), is to him the very embodiment of freedom. The persona of Whitman's poem is not a downtrodden tramp but a free vagabond. He is not at odds with the society that surrounds him but, in fact, sees himself as the embodiment of that society's highest ideals. In this sense, we can distinguish him from the Fool, whose satire is aimed at criticizing authority. Whitman's vagabond is self-sufficient, and yet there is in his soul a great yearning for a companionship that seems just out of reach:

> Allons! whoever you are come travel with me!
> Traveling with me you find what never tires.
> (154)

Though Whitman is as much a poet of the city as he is of the open road,[2] here his traveler contrasts the "impassive surfaces" (150) of the city to the road as a site of ecstasy:

> The efflux of the soul is happiness, here is happiness,
> I think it pervades the open air, waiting at all times,
> Now it flows unto us, we are rightly charged.
> (153)

This model of the tramp as rural wanderer was one that inspired urban bohemia well into the twentieth century (see Dell 176–89), even though this figure was being made obsolete as society rushed toward modern complexity. We can see this transition in Whitman's language, which presents lists of objects or gestures and emotions that together appear to suppress a coherent argument. Not only do the resulting fragments seem to represent the free spirit of the vagabond; in their insistent tug away from a stable, believable representation of its subject and his quest, the poem suggests a transition in an understanding of the role of the vagabond. When Michel Foucault writes that "at the beginning of the nineteenth century, the law of discourse having been detached from representation, the being of language itself became, as it were, fragmented" (*Order of Things* 306), he is suggesting how poetic language came to rely increasingly on abstraction, to be increasingly used by philosophers and poets (here he is talking about Nietzsche and Mallarmé) for its materiality, and increasingly became the subject of both poetry and philosophy. For Whitman, the persona on the open road appears in transition: still a part of society, but just barely; still able to represent a point of view, but barely.

The rhetoric of lists instead of argument in Whitman's poetry is an example of this transition toward fragmentation of poetic language, just as his vagabond, no longer the Fool of medieval and postmedieval literature, is an emblem, as it were, of a transition toward a new kind of figure that was to become embodied in the modernist figure of the tramp. This transition can also be expressed in historical terms. With the mass migration to the cities came a transformation of the idea of the tramp. Whitman's heroic bohemian figure gave way to its urban counterpart, the vagabond who was no longer at one with nature. This new vagabond was distinguished both by social isolation and by an oppositional relationship to society. In popular culture representations, this figure was often nameless and always without property. It was within the context of late nineteenth-century industrial society with its attendant labor wars that the modern, urban vagabond arose. One early manifestation of this new, urban vagabond was his rise as a heroic figure in the cosmology of the Industrial Workers of the World (IWW). It was in this atmosphere that Bert Williams began his career.

The migration of African Americans out of the South after 1875 added to the transformation of both the real world tramp and the romanticized vagabond. The Negro vagrant was subject to both legal and extralegal censure, but he was also the object of stereotype. Tom Fletcher notes that black traveling performers were a big part of the emergence of a distinctly African American entertainment milieu and that these performers, traveling as both individuals and in groups such as Maharry's Minstrels, formed part of the background out of which Bert Williams emerged. It is interesting, in this light, to see representations of Williams as they appeared in the poetry of American modernism. Hart Crane mentions Williams in "The Bridge," a poem that is, in part, concerned with modern life and alienation:

> Stick your patent name on a signboard
> brother—all over—going west—young man
> Tintex—Japalac—Certain-teed Overalls ads
> and lands sakes! under the new playbill ripped
> in the guaranteed corner—see Bert Williams what?
> (*Poems of Hart Crane* 57)

Williams appears here amid a network of signs showing the new urbanism of the twentieth century: among billboards advertising fabric dye, varnish, and overalls is a handbill advertising a performance by Williams.[3] In the preceding chapter I wrote that the language of modern advertising drew from a real and presumed African American vernacular syntax, and Crane here reproduces that syntax—not as African American "dialect" but as advertising speech.

Crane's hoboes are tied to the railroad and to other emblems of urban life. He employs an amalgam of signs similar to those that William Carlos Williams suggests when he writes, in a not too dissimilar context, that "the pure products of America / go crazy—" (*Imaginations* 131). He, too, was referring to the modern form of vagabondage. Both poets connected their vagabonds not just with industrial capitalism but with advertising, the "pure product" of that capitalism.

Jessie Fauset saw in Williams what critics such as Krasner appear to have missed: his symbolism. Her tribute to the comedian is titled "The Symbolism of Bert Williams," and she approached the comedian's art from the point of view of the aesthetic that seemed to catalyze his work:

> By a strange and amazing contradiction this *Comedian* symbolized that deep, ineluctable strain of melancholy, which no Negro in a mixed civilization ever lacks. He was supposed to make the world laugh and so he did but not by the welling over of his own spontaneous subjective joy, but by the humorously objective presentation of his personal woes and sorrows. His *rôle* was always that of the poor, shunted, cheated, out-of-luck Negro and he fostered and deliberately trained his genius toward the delineation of this type because his mental as well as his artistic sense told him that here was a true racial vein ("Symbolism" 255).

Emphasizing the role played by Williams, which he perfected in the late 1890s, Fauset suggests that the key to his art is the projection and universalizing of "his personal woes and sorrows." It is also true, however, that Williams, from the very beginning, created this character as a symbol. As Fauset and others have pointed out, Williams, who was born in the Bahamas and grew up (from about the age of twelve) in California (E. Smith 1–10), had to learn African American culture.[4] In this respect he had a certain characteristic in common with white Americans who played minstrelsy in blackface, but Williams's own part-African ancestry (his grandfather was Danish) helped him see and learn about African American culture from a position of closer social intimacy than his white theatrical colleagues could achieve.

{ 5 }

We are in familiar territory, then, when we hear Estragon's first words in *Waiting for Godot*: "Nothing to be done." The despair that's traded between the two major characters in that play seems almost an echo. The conventions of the play are familiar as well: they are both tramps. Throughout the first act, Estragon has trouble with his feet, with his boots. He has an odor. He sleeps in a ditch. He is cranky. Vladimir, by comparison, is more introspective. He is patient. He is the one who reminds Estragon (and the audience) of the purpose of the pair's vigil. The most extensive episode of physical intimacy between them is an elaborate comic charade involving three hats, at the end of which Vladimir rejects his own hat in favor of Lucky's, which he wears until the end of the play. All this also seems familiar to us, well-known theatrical tropes from the vaudeville stage.

Critics as wide ranging as Frederick J. Hoffman, Hugh Kenner, and John Bradby have commented on Beckett's debt to popular culture, especially his enthusiasm for the English and Irish music halls and the circus. Beckett's relationship to African American culture should also be acknowledged, however, in order to facilitate a more rounded reading of his work. As Alan Warren Friedman has shown, Beckett became knowledgeable about several aspects of African American life and culture when he contributed nineteen translations, comprising more than 63,000 words, to Nancy Cunard's *Negro*. They include studies of jazz and of Louis Armstrong; historical and cultural articles on Brazil, Haiti, Guadeloupe, Madagascar, and the Congo; the Surrealist manifesto "Murderous Humanitarianism"; and Rene Crevel's "The Negress in the Brothel."

It is useful to remember that the Paris of the 1930s was the Paris to which African American musicians and other artists flocked in order to find a freedom that was unavailable to them in the United States. It was the Paris in which Josephine Baker was a major star, to be sure, but it was also a place where lesser-known musicians, writers, visual artists, and performers joined with those of many other nationalities in making that city the world center of the arts.

Beckett was personally acquainted with at least one of these musicians, Henry Crowder, a pianist who arrived in Paris in the late 1920s with violinist Eddie South and his band, the Alabamians. Crowder was also the lover of Nancy Cunard. Cunard published Beckett's first separately issued work, the poem "Whoroscope" (1930). James Knowlson cites at least one episode when Beckett and the couple socialized together in one of the city's jazz clubs (120–21).

It is not necessary to draw direct links between Beckett's later work and these translations in order to acknowledge the writer's familiarity with African American popular culture and with the idea of stereotype. Several of Beckett's translations address the later point, in particular "Sambo with-

out Tears," by Georges Sadoul, in which the author surveys the racism of
French children's papers "that are calculated to turn their readers into perfect imperialists" (Cunard 349). Sadoul gives an example of the stereotype
as a means, as Bhabha reminds us, of refashioning the colonized as "a population of degenerate types on the basis of racial origin," a refashioning that
provides a means of justifying conquest and creating a system of administration and instruction (Bhabha 70). One way of reading *Waiting for Godot*,
then, can be founded on a reconsideration of how Beckett addresses these
issues of stereotype and degradation, in what might be seen as a barely de-
racialized presentation of these tropes.

The play centers on the behaviors of three pairs: Vladimir and Estragon;
Pozzo and Lucky; the goatherd boy and his offstage brother. The setting is
a country road, but the two main characters, Vladimir and Estragon, are not
on a journey. They are there simply to wait. The play reverses the motif of
freedom that the road represents in other literature. When Bakhtin writes
about the "chronotope of the road," he suggests that the road is a metaphor
for discovery and searching, but nothing of the kind is at work here ("Forms
of Time and Chronotope in the Novel," 243–45). These characters are on no
voyage, take no external action. The enactment of the play largely consists,
as David Bradby has suggested, of play itself. The two tramps in this "tragi-
comedy in two acts" (as Beckett subtitles the work) replay old comedic routines, but these routines veer more toward pathos than comedy.

There are several ways in which this play echoes its roots in minstrelsy. It
seems obvious that Vladimir and Estragon suggest the "end men" of the minstrel performance. They spend the first part of each of the play's two acts
mainly trading one-line statements, many of which take the form of absurd
paradoxes or insults:

ESTRAGON: What is it?
VLADIMIR: I don't know. A willow.
ESTRAGON: Where are the leaves?
VLADIMIR: It must be dead.
ESTRAGON: No more weeping.
VLADIMIR: Or perhaps it's not the season.
ESTRAGON: Looks to me more like a bush.
VLADIMIR: A shrub.
ESTRAGON: A bush.
VLADIMIR: A—.What are you insinuating? That we've come to the wrong
    place?
ESTRAGON: He should be here. (10)

This exchange recalls the "Indefinite Talk" routine of Miller and Lyles (and Lee), which became a standard of duo comic teams during the early twentieth century. It also recalls, as Bradby and others have pointed out, the music hall routines of English, Irish, and American theater, all of which owe some of their origins to American minstrelsy.[5] Indefinite Talk appears to be an early ancestor of the widespread "cross talk" routines of vaudeville, which became a staple of film comedy beginning in the 1930s. Miller and Lyles's version, each partner speaks to the other with a form of address that suggests intimacy, but neither partner quite connects logically with the other; it is a form of paired malapropism. The fact that the dialogue is carried out in fragments not only heightens the comic effect but also serves to give it a sense of unreality. This fragmentary language, language in which objects are present in the conversation but cannot be named, becomes in the hands of Miller and Lyles a sign of irony and of comedy. In the world of *Waiting for Godot*, the absences produced by the fragments are emblematic of a world in which neither Vladimir nor Estragon can even name the single living thing in their environment outside of themselves: "What is it? / I don't know. A willow. / Where are the leaves? / It must be dead."

It is an effect that certainly would have appealed to artists who, like Beckett, were a part of the Surrealist milieu of 1930s France. In *Waiting for Godot* the dialogue resembles a normal conversation more closely than does that of Miller and Lyles, in keeping with Beckett's overall fidelity to a naturalist approach in his play, and yet the true subject of the conversation (who is Godot? why are they waiting?) remains elusive. In each act, this sort of banter leads up to the entrance of Pozzo and Lucky, the master-slave duo who provide the second structural component drawn from minstrelsy, the olio. Mel Watkins describes this part, as it occurred in nineteenth-century American minstrelsy:

> In the second part of the show—the olio, or variety segment—the comedy highlight was the stump speaker, a lone comic who stood and delivered a discourse that ranged from pure nonsense to supposedly serious lectures on some social or philosophical issue. The comic, usually one of the end men, spoke in a black version of the familiar vernacular dialect of the Yankee or Frontier type. Often he satirized Emancipation, women's suffrage, education, or some other current political or scientific topic. Malaprop reigned supreme; although important issues were often addressed, the focus here was purely on humor. (92)

In *Godot*, this role is played, in the first act, by Lucky, and in the second, by Vladimir. Malaprop is a distinguishing feature of the modernist use of language, ranging from the suggestiveness favored by Symbolist writers to the automatic writing favored by the Surrealists. The idea is not simply to supply the absurdities and paradoxes that produce laughter—the ludicrous as "a subdivision of the ugly" (Aristotle 59), or the comic degradation that Freud speaks about in his analysis of caricature (*Jokes and Their Relation to the Unconscious* 200–201); it is an attempt to reveal the hidden unconsciousness behind reality. Beckett, however, was attuned to both the high artistic and the "low" comedic properties of malapropism and unites these qualities in Lucky's speech.

> Given the existence as uttered forth in the public
> works of Puncher and Wattmann of a personal
> God quaquaquaqua with white beard
> quaquaquaqua outside time without extension
> who from the heights of divine apathia divine
> athambia divine aphasia loves us dearly with
> some exceptions for reasons unknown but time
> will tell and suffers like the divine Miranda with
> those who for reasons unknown but time will tell.... (28)

The speech, with its apparent references to religion, to Beckett's own work, to bodily functions, and to Nancy Cunard ("in view of the labors of Fartov and Belcher left / unfinished for reasons unknown of Testew and / Cunard left unfinished." [28–29]), seems to suggest several ideas but to explain none of them. It comprises, as Lois Gordon points out, "a series of clauses that lack resolution" (76) and is very similar to the kind of speeches Watkins and others write about in describing the stump speeches in minstrel shows. As stump speaker, Lucky recalls a similar speech in *Huckleberry Finn*, in which Mark Twain satirizes Hamlet's soliloquy. That novel also owes much to minstrelsy in its structure and its use of humor. In both Lucky's speech and the Duke's apparent parody in Twain's novel, malapropisms form a basic component of the monologue. Each text is presented as a learned speech but is uttered by someone who is signified by the text as a comic character performing an absurd function. In addition, while Twain is satirizing the Shakespearean revival of the American Elizabethans of the nineteenth century, Beckett appears to be satirizing modernism and its uses of tradition in the twentieth, including the modernist's atheism.[6]

Pozzo and Lucky, too, as master and slave, can be seen as a parody of a minstrel motif. In minstrelsy, ridicule was often aimed at the idea of freedom for blacks. All aspects of the freedom to be exercised by blacks were lampooned, from simple everyday transactions to voting and holding office.[7] Beckett here reverses the stereotype by ridiculing the idea of slavery and lordship. In Beckett's rendering, slave and master are equally objects of humor, with the slave acting out a ritual of knowledge production in which his response to his master's directive to "think" is, in fact, to speak. This parody, writes Bradby,

> is the shape of a mind that shrinks, pines and dies as a result of the failure of the world, as perceived, to meet the demands of the inquiring mind. Where academic discourse claims to discern order, logic and even progress, the "Think" resembles a lecture as it might be given in a bad dream. The monologue enacts a struggle between an attempt to impose a structure of scientific research and philosophical discourse on experience, which is constantly disrupted by the breaking through of phrases (such as "abode of stones") suggesting brute natural forces quite indifferent to human logic or consciousness. (34)

It is possible to read this conflict as one involving identity. By "thinking" aloud, Lucky subverts the "natural" position of the slave, which is that of silence. If colonialism "repeatedly exercises its authority through the figures of farce" (Bhabha 85), then so do other modes of power. Lucky, like the minstrels Hogan, Williams, and Miller and Lyles, is parodying the authority of knowledge, which exercises its power by speaking "over the heads," as it were, of its audience. Lucky's speech, composed as it is of fragments and disjointed phrases whose overall architecture and subject is suggested but never stated, is over the heads of all who hear him. At least Lucky's primary audience, however, seems to be in on the joke. When the speech is finished, Estragon responds, "Avenged!" (30).

Beckett repeatedly returned to the use of minstrel tropes in his work. It is necessary to consider, briefly, only a late play of his in order to see how the relationship between the playwright and the older theatrical form continued to be a productive one for him. One striking element of *Not I* (1972) is how the play is staged as a kind of satire on blackface theatrics. Here are the stage directions, as written by Beckett:

> Stage in darkness, but for MOUTH, upstage audience right, about 8 feet above stage level, faintly lit from closeup and below, rest of face in shadow. Invisible microphone.

AUDITOR, downstage audience left, tall standing figure, sex undeter-
minable, enveloped from head to foot in loose black djellaba, with hood, fully
faintly lit, standing on invisible podium about 4 feet high shown by attitude
alone to be facing diagonally across stage intent on MOUTH, dead still
throughout but for four brief movements where indicated. . . .

As house lights down MOUTH's voice unintelligible behind curtain.
House lights out. Voice continues unintelligible behind curtain, 10 seconds.
With rise of curtain ad-libbing from text as required leading when curtain
fully up and sufficient into . . . (*Collected Shorter Plays* 216)

At this point a woman's voice, the MOUTH, begins her monologue.
The illuminated mouth is contrasted, in these directions, to its darkened
environment and can be seen as an ironic restaging of the blackface comedic
performance. Here the blackened face provides the audience with a familiar ground on which to accept a performance that consists entirely of a
monologue.

The other figure, dressed in a garment associated with Muslim and former
colonial populations, serves as a kind of interlocutor. The silence of this interlocutor, however, in no way diminishes the minstrel association of the duo,
the pair, whose interaction is essential to the dynamics of the performance.

The play is a monologue, given in a voice that delivers its message in fragments. In fact, much of the dialogue is little more than a set of clichés seem-
ingly piled on top of each other. These utterances, is about three or four
words each, are separated by ellipses:

> . . . . out . . . into this world . . . this world . . . tiny little thing . . . before its time
> . . . in a godfor—. . . what? . . girl? . . yes . . . tiny little girl . . . into this . . . out
> into this . . . before her time . . . godforsaken hole called . . . (216; ellipses as
> in original)

The autobiography told by the voice that is MOUTH is one that starts,
stops, begins again, interrupts itself with rhetorical questions. It is a discourse
consisting of introjections, exclamations, prepositional phrases, and other
fragments of sentences. Here the linguistic operations that have become commonplace in modernist verbal art are taken to their limit and reflect back on
the viewer (and reader of the text) as a kind of jabberwocky. The dropping of
pronouns and conjunctions, the absence and suppression of context, are
marked by the graphic elliptical sign of three (sometimes four) dots.

As in other literary forms where such operations are at work, the audience
is left to supply its own context; a reasonable assumption may exist that the

speaker is talking in a "secret" language, whose meaning she knows. In this way, Beckett's play appears to belong to a lineage that includes songs and comedic routines of late minstrelsy and the blues, or the routines of performers Flournoy Miller, Aubrey Lyles, and Johnny Lee. The assumption of a secret language is promoted precisely because the suppressed material is so obviously suppressed, and because the speaker seems to understand herself. This form of interiority gives the appearance of a speaker who is talking to herself, yet by virtue of the fact that the talk is performative, the secrecy of the language also appears communicative. Interiority is a feature that *Not I* shares with a large array of linguistic practices, formally performative ones as well as those that take place in everyday cultural practice. These practices include the dialects and vernacular forms associated with minorities such as African Americans, as well as with cultural subgroups (hipsters, rappers) which are direct spinoffs form African American culture.

In this sense, *Not I*, and much of Beckett's work, derives its power, at least in part, from utilizing those elements of American-style poetics identified by Denis Donoghue, in which the verse is animated by the apparent syntactic autonomy of its phrases. This could be termed the poetics of the cliché. It is part of another secret history, the outlines of which are a major subject of this study: the elements identified by Donoghue, and utilized to such effect by Beckett, echo many of the elements of African American poetics as they were developed in the performing and literary practices of black American poets and entertainers. The secret history of modernism is its intricate relationship to African American artistic practices. It is in this sense that the work of Beckett can be said, at least in the uses of language outlined here, to be indebted to the African American tradition.

To return, finally, to the comedic: the syntactic disruption of Beckett's play is also a comedic gesture: its apparently random interruptions of discourse appear intended to get a laugh, even as they also portray a tragic situation. The white mouth peeping out of the shadows directly signifies on the old American tradition of minstrelsy. The vision is at first disturbing to those who know this tradition, yet once the mouth begins to speak, the jangled syntax seems to displace the signification. We may be reminded of a minstrel show, but we are not, finally, in such a show. We are in a thoroughly modern work in which the psychological decline of a consciousness is on display. But how far away are we, really, from minstrelsy—from the traditional sources of American-style comedy—in *Not I*?

At the same time, it might be productive to inquire into the reasons why the relationship between minstrelsy and its conventions, on the one hand, and the dramatic art of Beckett, on the other, has not occupied a larger space than it has so far in the critical discourse. One reason may be found in the nature of that critical discourse itself. The idea of an ontological tension in the relationship between the popular arts, such as minstrelsy and vaudeville, on the one hand, and modernism on the other, has been a staple of modernist criticism. This idea needs to be interrogated—if we are to more fully understand the aesthetic sources of much of modernist literature and culture—with the aim also of clarifying the relationship between African American writing and modernism.

CHAPTER FOUR

Vaudeville

{ 1 }

THE USE OF THE TERM "vaudeville" as a metaphor for the modernist project is one that goes back to the beginnings of modernism itself. Music hall performers and dancers inspired the English Decadent and Symbolist poets, and Arthur Symons, in his collection *London Nights* (1895), is considered to have created a classic expression of the connection the precursors of modernism (who thought of themselves as modernist) made between their art and the emergent variety, or vaudeville, theater, as he demonstrates here, in the "Prologue" to the collection:

> My life is like a music-hall,
> Where, in the impotence of rage,
> Chained by enchantment to my stall,
> I see myself upon the stage
> Dance to amuse a music-hall.
> (*Selected Writings* 38)

As Linda Dowling remarks, Symons treated the music hall "in the spirit of art" (233).[1] The word vaudeville, which in the late nineteenth century began to be used to refer to a particular genre of theater performance, came to be identified as well with a style of making art, characterized by the mixing of genres with the aim of emphasizing their varietal character. One particular feature of this genre was the assembling of various parts of the performance in what appeared to be random order. James Weldon Johnson described one early vaudeville performance, *The Octoroons* (1895) this way: "It was billed, 'A Musical Farce,' but it was made up of a first part, a middle part, and a finale, neither one having any sequential connexion with the others" (*Black Manhattan* 96; original spelling). Robert W. Snyder has described the structure of these performances. "To an outsider, the sequence of acts looked as random as the scenes glimpsed from a trolley car on a busy city street," he writes; however, the selections "were actually based on established principles of vaudeville" (66). Those principles, as described by George Gottlieb, a booker for the Palace Theater, and as summarized by Snyder, divided the vaudeville performance into nine parts: first, a "dumb act" involving dancers or trick animals, followed by "anything more interesting than the first act," such as a singer; third, a comic; fourth, another two singers, one lesser known than the other. Then there is an intermission, followed by the last four acts, which consist, again, of miscellaneous performers, including mimes; comics presenting skits; and, of course, the big star, who is followed by "the closing act, preferably a visual number—trick animals or trapeze artists—that sent the audience home pleased" (Snyder 66–67).

The lack of developmental or sequential connection between the various parts of the show is crucial to understanding what differentiated vaudeville from other forms of comedic stage performance. The lack of an overarching, determinative narrative was a modernizing characteristic of the form. It prefigured the disruption of narrative and sequential architecture that became a hallmark of modernist art.

Among those who understood this were the original publicists of the book *Cane* by Jean Toomer. The description they wrote on the dust jacket of the first edition called it "a vaudeville out of the South." Presumably, the authors of this description had some confidence that their audience would understand the term as it applied to the book. Here is the dust jacket copy, as quoted by Michael Soto:

> This book is a vaudeville out of the South. Its acts are sketches, short stories, one long drama and a few poems. The curtain rises (Part One) upon the folk life of Southern Negroes, their simple tragedies, their wistfulness, their waywardness, their superstitions, and their crude joy in life. Part Two is the more complex and modern brown life of Washington. Jazz rhythms all but supplant the folk tunes—one simple narrative weaves its plaintive way, and is almost lost amid the complications of the city. Part three (a single drama) Georgia again. But this is not a brief tale of peasant sorrow. It is a moving and sustained tragedy of spiritual suffering.
>
> There can be no cumulative and consistent movement and, of course, no central plot to such a book. But if it be accepted as a unit of spiritual experience, then one can find in Cane a beginning, a progression, a complication, and an end. It is too complex a volume to find its parallel in the Negro musical comedies so popular on Broadway. Cane is black vaudeville. It is black super-vaudeville out of the South. (Qtd. in Soto 169–70)

The linkage established here between jazz, vaudeville, and certain characteristics of a modernist literary work ("no cumulative and consistent movement," "no central plot," "a unit of spiritual experience") is one that was commonly drawn by those attempting to understand literary modernism in the 1920s. In fact, the linkage between "high" modernism and the art forms of which vaudeville was a part was, if not a commonplace, at least widely and importantly used as a hermeneutic tool by prominent early critics of modernism. Among these were Clive Bell and Gilbert Seldes, both of whom identified literary modernism as a movement belonging to the same impulse that gave rise to jazz. Bell, in his essay "Plus de Jazz" (1921) goes so far as to say that T. S. Eliot "is about the best of our living poets, and, like Stravinsky, he is as much a product of the Jazz movement as so good an artist can be of any," and he describes modernist literature in terms of its perceived affinities to jazz: "In literature Jazz manifests itself both formally and in content. Formally its distinctive characteristic is the familiar one—syncopation. It has given us a ragtime literature which flouts traditional rhythms and sequences and grammar and logic. In verse its products—rhythms which are often indistinguishable from prose rhythms and collocations of words to which sometimes is assignable no exact intellectual significance—are by now familiar to all who read" (223). Here the revolution in poetic language that was heralded by modernism is described in terms of its relationship to jazz; in particular, the metaphor for the linguistic disruptions and jaggedness of modernist poetry is syncopation, which is a distinctive characteristic of African American music.

Seldes, whose association with the *Dial* magazine made him one of the major arbiters of modernist literary taste in the 1920s, took pains to draw these same connections. Referring to the work of James Joyce, he writes, "If he is jazz, then Mr. Joyce's sense of form, his tremendous intellectual grasp of his aesthetic problem, and his solution to that problem, are more proof than is required of the case for jazz" (106); he adds, "Similarly for Mr. Eliot." Seldes makes this case in his essay "Toujours Jazz," first published in the *Dial* in August 1923 and reprinted the next year in *The Seven Lively Arts*. In this essay, Seldes argues that the popular arts and what has come to be known as "high" modernism have a shared sensibility.[2] It is important to note that both critics contextualized literary modernism in terms of the aesthetic values of African American expressive culture, especially ragtime and jazz, rather than the other way around: "The fact that jazz is our current mode of expression, has reference to our time and the way we think and talk, is interesting; but if jazz music weren't itself good the subject would be more suitable for a sociologist than for an admirer of the gay arts," Seldes writes. "Fortunately, the music and the way it is played are both of great interest, both have qualities which cannot be despised; and the cry that jazz is the enthusiastic disorganization of music is as extravagant as the prophecy that if we do not stop 'jazzing' we will go down, as a nation, into ruin" (Seldes 83).

Many significant ideas are at work here. First there is the idea that jazz is "our current mode of expression," which suggests that Seldes sees the music, as a mode of expression, as a starting point for understanding modern artistic expression generally. It is a point of departure for understanding how "we think and talk." He continues, however, that it is the music itself, seen not simply as a cultural form of reference but as a distinct art form in its own right, that allows both jazz and Seldes's claims for it to become the means of defining and understanding modernism generally. Perhaps the most interesting aspect of the essay is that point which has come under the most criticism: Seldes is faulted by Michael North for his alleged ignorance of African American musicians and for extolling white ones such as Paul Whiteman and Darius Milhaud. But the significance of Seldes's accomplishment here is often overlooked: he shows just how deeply the "jazz" sensibility has affected Western music, thereby permanently transforming twentieth-century Western musical culture. "The free use of syncopation," he writes, "has led our good composers of ragtime and jazz to discoveries in rhythm and to a mastery of complications which one finds only in the greatest masters of serious music" (88). He then quotes Henry Edward Krehbiel, who compared the music of Hector Berlioz and that of the drummers from Dahomey who performed at the 1893 Chicago World's Fair: Berlioz, writes Krehbiel, "produced nothing to compare in artistic interest" with the Dahomian drummers, whom he calls "savages." Seldes then adds: "I am fully aware of the difference between savage and sophisticated, between folk and popular music; yet I cannot help believing that this entire statement, including the Berlioz whom I greatly admire, could be applied to Paul Whiteman playing *Pack Up Your Sins* or his incredible mingling of *A Stairway to Paradise* with a sort of *Beale Street Blues*" (88–89).

The focus by such sensitive critics as North on the racist language used by Bell, or on the alleged ignorance of the African American roots of jazz on the part of Seldes (*Reading* 144–47), seems to miss the overall significance of these essays for their authors, who were attempting, among other things, to find a way of communicating to a broad audience just how modernist culture worked.[3] The criticism seems to elide the very milieu in which these discussions of the meaning of the term "the jazz age" are taking place. North's suggestion that because Seldes refers to the white bandleader

Paul Whiteman as his major model of a jazz composer, he thereby compromises his interpretive authority and authenticity, glosses over several points. For one thing, Seldes is careful to cite African American singers, songwriters, and bandleaders (especially Florence Mills, Henry Creamer and Turner Layton, and James Reese Europe) as well as white ones. It must also not be forgotten that recordings by African American dance bands were still relatively rare in the early 1920s, when Bell's and Seldes's essays first appeared.[4]

As if to demonstrate the claims made by Bell and Seldes, T. S. Eliot began his exploration of the possibilities of poetic drama, in 1923, with a farce drawing directly from the minstrel tradition, racist mythology, and the creative work of at least one African American poet. *Sweeney Agonistes* has long been recognized as Eliot's introductory foray into poetic drama and his major public engagement with the African American Imaginary. In 1935, F. O Matthiessen situated the play in just this fashion: "Eliot subtitled his first brief scenes 'fragments of an Aristophanic melodrama,' but the source of the verse spoken by Sweeney and his friends was much nearer at hand," for Eliot "was trying to utilize vaudeville rhythms for reasons that he had recently articulated in his appreciation of Marie Lloyd as 'the greatest music-hall artist of her time.'" Matthiessen adds, "The songs in Eliot's play, 'Under the bamboo tree' and 'My little island girl,' found their stimulus in American jazz, as did the syncopation of the dialogue" (158–59).

Eliot wrote his eulogy for Lloyd, the English music hall performer, in November 1922, and it was published the next month in *Dial*.[5] He was interested in Lloyd as a "popular" performer. Popularity "in her case," he writes, was "something more than success. It is evidence of the extent to which she represented and expressed that part of the English nation which has perhaps the greatest vitality and interest." Eliot cites a report of Lloyd's funeral and then comments on her work as a performer. What most interests him is her connection with and her ability to express the lives and sensibilities of the working class: "To appreciate for instance the last turn in which Marie Lloyd appeared, one ought to know already exactly what objects a middle-aged woman of the charwoman class would carry in her bag; exactly how she would go through her bag in search of something; and exactly the tone of voice in which she would enumerate the objects she found in it. This was only part of the acting in Marie Lloyd's last song, I'm One of the Ruins That Cromwell Knocked Abaht a Bit" ("Marie Lloyd" 659, 661).

The combination of vaudeville and working-class culture that interested Eliot became the foundation on which he would build *Sweeney Agonistes*. The play evokes both the minstrel show and paranoid white colonial fantasies associated with cannibalism ("I'll carry you off / to a cannibal isle," Sweeney says to Doris, "I'll gobble you up" [*Complete Poems* 79–80]), and closes with a set of chanting lines in a meditation on death and loneliness ("And you wait for a knock and the turning of a lock for you know the hangman's waiting for you. / And perhaps you're alive / And perhaps you're dead / Hoo ha ha" [*Complete Poems* 85]). Rachel Blau DuPlessis shows how this fantasia is embedded within a "construction of whiteness," but her observations about the formal qualities of *Sweeney Agonistes* are also of interest to the present discussion: "As a fusion of genres 'Sweeney Agonistes' is rich, compounding melodrama, tabloid talk, working-class sentimental poetry, true crime confession, bartender's parable, religious ritual, and Gilbert and Sullivan operetta—as well as minstrel and vaudeville" (683).

The play combines the cross-talk style of dialogue of the comedic duet (though it doesn't quite rise to the level of parataxis one finds in Miller and Lyles's "Indefinite Talk" routines) with allusions to the end men's performance of minstrel shows and a recasting of a coon song–era composition cowritten by James Weldon Johnson ("Under the Bamboo Tree") into a brief, two-act play.[6] In her description of Eliot's melodrama, DuPlessis shows just how deeply involved modernism was with popular culture. This involvement deepened further throughout the interwar years and provoked a critical reaction that had broad implications for the construction not only of the modernist canon but also of our society's cultural memory of what modernism as such was as a creative endeavor and artistic movement.

Just as it is important to recall how involved Eliot was with popular forms, it is also important to recall that this contextualization was a part of the way *Cane* was first discussed. *Cane* was published by Boni and Liveright, the same house that published Eliot's *The Waste Land* in 1922 and, later, other canonical texts of modernist literature—such as *Personae* by Ezra Pound and *White Buildings* by Hart Crane in 1926—and this fact suggests the place of Toomer's work at the center of modernist literature. Yet the canonization process that has taken place renders *Cane* as different and, to some extent, marginal in relationship to the others in this company. In addition, the fact that at least some of the earliest critics of modernism saw the modernist project in terms of its relationship to African American expressive culture has been lost to the process of canonization that modernism underwent in the second half of the twentieth century.

How did this happen? Although a detailed examination of the history of modernist criticism is out of place here, examining some of the ideas that have come down to us can help us further understand not only the relationship of modernism to the African American Imaginary but also what might be called the critical displacement that faced *Cane* and, by implication, much of the rest of the African American literature produced during the modernist era.

{ 2 }

It seems that the further the historical moment of modernism recedes, the more urgent becomes the exploration of questions about its genre, genealogy, and canon. This is so for many reasons, at least one of them being our need to better understand the history and culture that are presumed to be the immediate antecedents of our own. At the same time there is a strong current—by no means limited to what might be called "conservative" criticism—which seems to suggest that these are settled questions. Even as these questions are raised, the first reactions to them can still be heard, suggesting that the major task for literary criticism now is to examine the details.

It is remarkable how these ideas continue to inform much of our understanding of literary modernism, and it remains of interest how impervious the received wisdom on these questions seems to be to the challenge posed by new claims on the categories of canon, genre, and genealogy. How this could be so is as important a question as why it should be so. A large part of literary studies seems to remain within a discursive field bounded by a set of assumptions about literary modernity that differ little from those set out at the time these questions were first posed, and presumably answered, in the mid-twentieth century. Examples are abundant, but a cursory look at just one contemporary definition of literary modernism will suffice to make the point.

Definitions of modernism abound.[7] Of greater interest is how this vast literature is summarized, and what such a summary can tell us about how we understand the modernist project. One such summary, appearing in a reference work published at the beginning of the twenty-first century, can serve as a guide for an inquiry into the idea of modernism itself. David Macey, in the *Penguin Dictionary of Critical Theory*, under the heading "Modernism" (257–59) writes us that the word "is widely used to describe a variety of tendencies within the European, and especially Anglo-American, literature of the early twentieth century" (257). "Modernism is in fact a surprisingly elusive term," he adds, "not least in that there are so many national variations to its meaning" (258). He defines the word in terms of the famous names associated with the movement—Joyce, Stein, Eliot, Stevens, Pound—and attempts to situate modernism firmly as an Anglo-American phenomenon by arguing that the word as it is used in French, Italian, and Spanish refers to cultural phenomena that are distinct from those it refers to in Great Britain and North America. He also identifies modernism with some of the same characteristics William Everdell does: stream of consciousness, free verse, abstraction. And, citing Clement Greenberg, he points to the artist's focus on the medium as the material for art-making as a characteristic of modernism. In a second reference to Greenberg, Macey says of the latter's argument "that the abstraction of modernism is the only real defence against the kitsch of mass culture" (259). On this point, he adds that "the aesthetic introversion that leads to the accusation of elitism and the distrust of popular culture are perhaps symptomatic of the darker side of modernism typified by Eliot's anti-Semitic remarks in *After Strange Gods* or Pound's apologias for Italian Fascism" (259).

What follows is a rhetorical gesture that can serve to illustrate the major concern of this discussion. It is the only mention in Macey's entry of the literary and cultural output of nonwhite artists; at the same time, it seems to situate those artists within a framework that is itself canonical the context of modernist criticism: "Despite the presence in the modernist canon of Woolf and Stein, modernism often appears to be a very masculine affair, but Scott's *Gender of Modernism* anthology (1990) does much to correct the gender imbalance. Sara Blair's suggestion (1999) that the Harlem Renaissance should figure in any serious discussion of modernism is also to be welcomed" (259).

The most interesting aspects of this definition are those elements that are most familiar: canon-building by naming what might be called modernism's Big Six (Eliot, Woolf, Pound, Stein, Stevens, and Joyce); the subsequent claim of modernism's Anglo-American provenance; the definition that focuses on artistic technique and the artist's concentration on the materiality of the artwork as both the means and object of art-making; and the counterposing of high against low culture, of the avant-garde against kitsch, abstraction against mass culture, modernism against popular culture. These dualities have governed the consensus about literary modernism since at least the late 1930s. Macey's deployment of them is particularly telling because one aspect of its characterization of them, we are told, is the growth in influence of right-wing political ideology on some of the leading modernist writers. This influence is remarked upon without any evaluation concerning how it could have come about.

It is not here, however, that the definition reveals the fissure that is of most concern. What is of real interest is the way in which gender and "race" are deployed within this definition. "Modernism appears to be a very masculine affair" is an idea that has been widely challenged, as Macey points out, but the idea that the Harlem Renaissance would "be welcomed" within any discussion of modernism is remarked upon without elaboration. What is the effect of this rhetoric? By using the consensus view of the ontology of modernism, and then parenthetically adding the questions of gender and of African American culture, Macey appears to accomplish two things. He allows the consensus view to stand unchallenged and, by the device of the parenthetical nod, rhetorically places any would-be challengers to this view (gender and "race") at the margins of the discussion.

Macey's definition can stand, then, as a kind of metaphor for a whole set of critical concerns, including those that have so far occupied this book. There have been several responses to this consensus view. One of them has been to engage in the project of historical recovery, such as that suggested in the paragraph quoted above. Gender studies have gone a long way toward reconstructing a canon of modernist literature in which the list of important women writers goes beyond Woolf and Stein. Yet the consensus view can still be deployed, even in a book as useful and comprehensive—when it comes to identifying trends, thinkers and ideas of contemporary theory—as the *Penguin Dictionary*. Modernism "often appears" to be a masculine affair, despite the importance of writers ranging from H.D. and Marianne Moore to Zora Neale Hurston and Djuna Barnes. Recovery, then, seems to have its limits. Barnes may be marginal to Macey's definition, and yet her novel *Nightwood* received from T. S. Eliot (who wrote an introduction to the book) the praise "that it is so good a novel that only sensibilities trained on poetry can wholly appreciate it" (xii). Eliot's act of legitimization may seem patronizing and old-fashioned, yet curiously, it does not signal to a critic writing several decades later the need to revise his own authoritative "masculine affair" theory of modernism.

Another response to this rhetoric of marginalization has been the construction of a counter-canon with its own set of definitions. Here, again referring to the literary movement cited in the *Penguin Dictionary*, we find advocates of those writers associated with the "Harlem" school of the 1920s resorting to a new vocabulary. Hence, we have the terms "Afro Modernist Aesthetics" (Mark A. Sanders), "Afrocentric Modernism" (Lorenzo Thomas), "African American Modernism" (Michael Coyle), and the two terms "Afro Modernity" and "black modernism" (Houston A. Baker Jr.).

One consequence of such an overdetermined use of qualifiers is the suggestion that these texts and writers were somehow marginal to the modernist project itself. It is a view that is certainly shared by consensus builders like the compiler of the *Penguin Dictionary* but one that does not necessarily accord with the facts. To claim an "Afro" modernism is to appear to agree not only that the writers under discussion were overlooked in their lifetimes but that their works had no discernible impact on the culture beyond a small, select circle. This is true, of course, for many of the writers whose works were recovered by feminist and African American literary specialists in the latter part of the twentieth century; the idea should be interrogated, however, when it is meant to ascribe a condition of "marginality" to such writers as Gertrude Stein or Langston Hughes. Stein was famous enough to be a popular cultural reference in the movies: at one point in the 1935 film *Top Hat*, Dale Tremont (Ginger Rogers) responds to a character who reads her a telegram that he finds incomprehensible by saying, "sounds like Gertrude Stein."[8] For his part, Hughes was for decades the most widely read African American writer in any genre, with a body of work that ranged from poetry and fiction to libretti for the Broadway stage. One of the founders of the "New Critics" school of modernist criticism, Cleanth Brooks, in a telling remark, called both Genevieve Taggard and Hughes guilty of "sentimentality" (*Modern Poetry and the Tradition* 50–51), which he considered a cardinal sin. On the other hand, James Edward Smethurst (93–115) has argued the case for seeing Hughes as a modernist poet whose use of an African American vernacular voice was a distinguishing element of his modernist style. The question remains, however: how productive is it to read a poet like Hughes as one whose work must be considered solely from within an African American tradition?

While not disputing the claim that the category of "Afro Modernism" and its related terms are useful for purposes of recovering lost texts, assigning the place of such texts within the black literary tradition, and articulating an African American poetics, it must be said that the claims made under such categorizations seem to demand very little of the broader English language literary tradition as such. Those operations that set up a distinct canon, as valuable as they are, do not ask whether such a canon, or the texts within it, have any affect on the composition of that canon which is generally ascribed to the "majority" culture. Given the richness and complexity of African American literature, how can the maintenance, for example, of a definition of modernism that makes the Harlem Renaissance a parenthetical category be allowed to stand? In a word, the claims of those critics who are establishing a distinct African American literary tradition seem to be too modest. What is the source of this modesty? One way of looking at this question is to inquire into what qualities the modernist consensus and its Afro Modernist counterpart may have in common.

Among the distinguishing features of the Afro Modernist discourse is its attention to the question of identity and to the use by black writers of elements from popular culture. In the criticism that focuses on African American writers of the modernist period, these two features are given pride of place, and are part of what seems to be what is meant when critics of African American literature claim, along with Houston A. Baker Jr., that "African and Afro-Americans—through conscious and unconscious designs of various Western 'modernisms'—have little in common with Joycean or Eliotic projects. Further, it seems to me that the very *histories* that are assumed in the chronologies of British, Anglo-American, and Irish modernisms are radically opposed to any adequate and accurate account of the history of Afro-American modernism, especially the *discursive* history of such modernism" (xvi; original emphasis). Baker's sense of the discursive history of Afro-American modernism certainly includes the engagement by such discourses with issues of the racialized self and with popular culture, in particular the blues and jazz. It is, however, the very distinctions drawn by these critics when writing about black literature and modernism that place them in what seems to be a discursive intimacy with the consensus view. Both groups seem to presume the nonracialized universality of the modernist speaking subject, and both seem to agree that the fissure between "high" and "low" culture, the distinction between avant-garde and kitsch, is one of the distinguishing characteristics of "Joycean or Eliotic projects." Both groups appear to believe that part of the anxiety that produced modernism in the first place was what Macey calls high modernism's "distrust of popu-

lar culture," and that therefore black writers who write in a modernist mode
must be considered as separate and distinct precisely because they exhibit
less of this distrust.

The consensus views about universal identity and the fissure between
modernism and popular culture have their own history, and that history is
in large measure identical with the history of modernist criticism itself. In
other words, there is the distinct possibility that modernism, as it emerged
in the first decades of the twentieth century and as it was understood by
artists and critics alike, was not at all a "very male affair," and certainly not
an all-white project. One has only to read the earliest issues of *Poetry* magazine to see how many of the earliest free verse practitioners were women;
the most famous of them all, Amy Lowell, was one of the best-known American poets of the early twentieth century.[9] An important American literary
critic and champion of the new poetry was William Stanley Braithwaite
(1878–1962), who wrote a widely read newspaper column on modern
poetry in the *Boston Evening Transcript* and edited an annual series of poetry
anthologies that for nearly two decades influenced popular taste in modern
poetry in the United States.[10] These facts would seem to suggest a reality
that preceded the consensus view, an alternative reality that has only recently
begun to receive attention once again. Curiously, however, the attention
very often seems to come from within a discourse that signifies itself as coming from the margins, thereby reenacting the very moves that created the
consensus in the first place.

Figuring out how literary criticism in general, and modernist literary criticism in particular, came to this state of affairs would require writing a history of that criticism, a task that is outside the scope of this study. Although
it is true that the emergence of "practical criticism" of the English school
(I. A. Richards, F. R. Leavis, and William Empson) in the late 1920s (and the
publication of Richards's book of that name in 1929) is generally acknowledged as a critical juncture in the development of formalist criticism, what
is less understood is how its emergence would lead to the displacement of the
African American Imaginary from the critical and aesthetic understanding
of modernism. It might be said that even raising the issue in this way is
provocative. However, it is useful to remember Cary Nelson's observation
that "we no longer know" the history of American poetry of the first half of
the twentieth century. He adds "most of us, moreover, do not know that the
knowledge is gone" (4). Nelson's point is much like the one I am making,
and, indeed, his book can be seen as an important forbear of this one. He

argues that literary history and criticism have repressed the memory of the poetry written by women, those on the political left, and the racialized minorities. Such repression, suggests Nelson, has distorted our understanding and appreciation of the history of American poetry as such, including that of the canonical avant-garde, and of the canonical mainstream. Although the same might be said for the development of modernist criticism, it might be useful, in lieu of attempting a historical reconstruction, to speculate on how the emergence of formalism was implicated in the displacement of the African American Imaginary from our understanding of modernism.

{ 3 }

The charge of sentimentality that Brooks levies against Taggard and Hughes comes at the end of a long discussion drawing on the poetics of John Donne and the Metaphysical poets to mount an argument that opposes poetic truth to propaganda (39–53); a charge of the latter is made against the poets who contributed to the left-wing literary anthology *Proletarian Literature in the United States*, edited by Granville Hicks, and other writers associated with the Communist left and the popular front.[11] The issues Brooks is concerned with have to do with elevating the value of metaphor and irony in poetry, in opposition to a "scientific" (and propagandistic) poetry. At the same time, the issues he raised were part of a larger debate, one which is itself implicated in the displacement of texts by African American and many women authors from the canon of modernism. This displacement was a major result of the rise of formalist literary criticism in the 1930s. Its history is well documented, and need not be repeated here.[12]

Much discussion about the rise of formalist criticism identifies this displacement with the political struggles of the 1930s, and comments such as those of Brooks in *Modern Poetry and the Tradition* give ample ground for such a view. Little attention has been given, however, to how the rise of formalism affected black writers and writing. John Fekete has pointed to the racially reactionary ideas of some critics, especially the defenses of slavery and the Confederacy undertaken by John Crowe Ransom and Allen Tate in the 1930s (233).[13] Even though Aldon Lynn Nielsen (*Reading Race* 108–13) and Michael Bérubé (62–206) have detailed the impact of the writings of Tate and Karl Shapiro on the critical reception of the poetry of Melvin Tolson, it seems that more can be said on this score. For one thing, both Fekete and Bérebé appear to treat the displacement and marginalization of

African American writers and black culture as a commonly understood and accepted fact of literary history. This rhetorical naturalization of the marginal status of black writing seems difficult to comprehend when we consider the publication history of a text such as *Cane*, or the apparent need of a critic of Brooks's stature to engage in an act of critical dismissal of an artist as well known as Hughes. On the other hand, if the displacement of black writing is considered as a historical act, one undertaken as a deliberate critical move, then perhaps the relationship between black writing and modernism can come into a different focus than has hitherto been the case.

One problem in reconsidering how this displacement came about is that most of the relevant discussions have focused on political questions, making it difficult to see the aesthetic issues involved. A quotation from Clement Greenberg can serve as an illustration of this problem. In a parenthetical comment in the essay "The Late Thirties in New York," he writes that "some day it will have to be told how 'anti-Stalinism,' which started out more or less as 'Trotskyism,' turned into art for art's sake, and thereby cleared the way, heroically, for what was to come" (230). This comment, together with the essay in which it is embedded, seems at first glance a straightforward political statement, yet the phrase "turned into art for art's sake" is suggestive of more than politics. It suggests an aesthetic positioning with regard to the place and time that the essay claims to recall; it is a positioning in which politics "turned into" art, thereby stimulating a "heroic" age. This heroic age that Greenberg identifies can be seen a little more prosaically as the age in which, as Karen O'Kane suggests, the Nashville group of former Southern Agrarians joined with a group of left-wing critics (who were beginning to abandon their former leftism) under the aegis of the Rockefeller Foundation to create the institution of modern literary criticism. This story, as O'Kane tells it, is somewhat different from the way this turn is often described.

Paul Lauter has charted the exclusion of African American and women writers from poetry anthologies and from the college curriculum in the decades of the 1920s through the 1960s, but he cites two important anthologies that did include black writers: Alfred Kreymborg's *Lyric America* (1930) and Louis Untermeyer's *Modern American Poetry*, which went through six editions between 1919 and 1942. Lauter relates how the fortunes of African American poets fared in this anthology: "Untermeyer's editing exemplifies the rise and fall of interest in black writers. His first two editions (1919 and 1921) contained poems by Dunbar, joined in the 1925 version by Countee Cullen, James Weldon Johnson, Claude McKay, and Alex Rogers, and then later by Langston Hughes, and Jean Toomer. By the 1942 sixth edition, however, only Dunbar, Johnson, Cullen and Hughes remained; the seventh edition witnessed the elimination of Dunbar (25).

What happened? "Three important factors may be responsible," writes Lauter. These include "the professionalization of the teaching of literature, the development of an aesthetic theory that privileged certain texts, and the historiographic organization of the body of literature into conventional 'periods' and 'themes'" (27). The explanation is striking in its projection of these developments as having apparently come about "naturally," as it were, and stands in some contrast to the agentive explanation that Greenberg gives. O'Kane offers a more motivated explanation as well when she recounts how the New York critics associated with the *Partisan Review* came into an alliance with the "Nashville group" in a project that produced, among other things, Cleanth Brooks and Robert Penn Warren's textbook *Understanding Poetry*. Each of these stories might be open to an interpretation showing the dominance of formalist criticism from the mid-twentieth century as a phenomenon that came from an opportunistic alliance between a group of Marxist New York intellectuals and another group made up primarily of defenders of slavery, the Confederacy, and racial segregation in the South.

One trouble with this interpretation is that it underestimates the degree to which the writers associated with the *Partisan Review*, as it was newly reorganized in 1938, had already severed any association they had once had with African American writers. As James Smethurst points out, this magazine, which "as a publication of the JRC [John Reed Club] and the Communist Left, from 1934 to 1936 published and reviewed works by African American authors." These included Langston Hughes, Richard Wright, Arna Bontemps, and Sterling Brown. The magazine suspended publication in 1936, but "after a hiatus of eighteen months, *Partisan Review* reappeared in December 1937 as a journal of what came to be known as the 'anti-Stalinist left.'" Smethurst then adds:

> From that point, as far as I can tell, nothing written by an African–American author appeared in the journal until James Baldwin's "Everybody's Protest Novel," a patricidal assault on Richard Wright and the Communist Left via *Uncle Tom's Cabin*, in June 1949. During the same period, no African Americans were included on the masthead of *Partisan Review* and only three reviews of books by African-American authors (a review of Wright's *Uncle Tom's*

Children in 1938, a brief review of *Native Son* in a survey of current fiction in 1941, and a longer review of *Black Boy* in 1945) were published. (222)

Strictly speaking, Smethurst is mistaken on one point. In its June 1948 issue the journal did publish "A Portrait of the Hipster" by Anatole Broyard, an African American who was passing for white. His article was an examination of a social type that was characteristically ascribed to African Americans and would become an iconic symbol of the African American Imaginary in the post–World War II years.[14] On the other hand, Smethurst's observation highlights the fact that for ten years, the only African American writer to appear in the "anti-Stalinist left" edition of the *Partisan Review* was one who denied being black, one who pretended to be a white person examining and explaining an aspect of black culture for a (presumably) white audience. This sort of "racial masquerade" in reverse (to borrow, again, a phrase from Michael North [*Dialect of Modernism* 77–99]) is ironic, given that a distinguishing characteristic of modernism in the years between the world wars was the impact of the African American Imaginary on modernist literary culture. The turn away from this influence by the intellectuals around *Partisan Review* was part of a larger cultural development whose impact on American literary culture would be felt for a generation. The terms that governed this development have largely been articulated as political ones, but it is the case that aesthetic issues were involved as well. There is no particular reason why a means of teaching and interpreting literature that focuses on close textual readings should, in and of itself, exclude black writers, yet this is precisely what happened. It did not happen naturally, however, but was in part the result of an aesthetic strategy which, when recalled as the "turn to art for art's sake," appears to obscure more than it reveals.

{ 4 }

One place to look for the rupture that helped displace African American writing and culture from modernism is another article by Greenberg, one published in *Partisan Review* after that journal's revival and revamping as a critical voice of "high" modernism. Greenberg's "Avant-Garde and Kitsch" opens with a claim that is itself a kind of rhetorical enactment of the displacement that I have been attempting to identify: "One and the same civilization produces simultaneously two such very different things as a poem by T. S. Eliot and a Tin Pan Alley song, or a painting by Braque and a

Saturday Evening Post cover. All four are on the order of culture, and ostensibly, products of the same culture and products of the same society. Here, however, their connection seems to end" (3).

This essay is widely taken as a kind of aesthetic manifesto of the postwar avant-garde in painting, but in its original place of publication, it was also an argument for an interpretation of modernist culture generally. Its opening pair of binaries and its polemical tone point to an unidentified opponent who, apparently, does not agree with the author's opinion. The terms under discussion are presented in a way that seems obvious. We presumably "know" who "T. S. Eliot," and "Braque" are, just as we "know" what a "Tin Pan Alley song," or a "*Saturday Evening Post* cover" is; and just as we "know" what they are, we also "know" that they are ontologically different from each other. They may belong to the same society, but "here, however, their connection seems to end." Yet the supposed obviousness of these terms should not be so easily accepted. They are worthy of interrogation within the context of this book, in part because Greenberg's essay stands at a critical juncture in the history of modern culture. It stands at the dividing line in recent cultural memory when—to repeat Cary Nelson's formulation—the history of American poetry (and, by extension, of American culture) that "we no longer know" began to be submerged to the point of becoming a kind of secret history, a body of knowledge so secret that most of us "do not know that the knowledge is gone." One way of identifying this "secret" history is to follow the revisionary histories of the interwar period that have emerged in the last few years. Along with Nelson and Smethurst, Michael Denning, Ann Douglas, Lewis A. Erenberg, Walter Kalaidjian, Nina Miller, and others have given us a much more complicated view of the workings of modernist culture than that argued in the opening lines of Greenberg's essay.

Before considering the implications of this history for the argument I am advancing, it will be useful to explore in more depth the argument made in "Avant-Garde and Kitsch," because, as Greenberg himself says, the questions he raises are aimed at examining "the relationship between aesthetic experience as met by the specific—not generalized—individual, and the social and historical contexts in which that experience takes place" (3). Greenberg has already located these "social and historical contexts" as residing across a line of difference where "one and the same civilization" can produce the binaries he identifies. The beginning of the essay is a historical review of the emergence of the avant-garde, and what is significant, given the character of the binaries he proposes, is that this history is exclusively one of late nineteenth-

and early twentieth-century European culture. This is all the more remarkable because his argument begins with a characterization that applies to both
European and U.S. artists and artworks. The avant-garde, he writes, arose in
the mid-nineteenth century, deriving in part from "a superior consciousness
of history—more precisely, the appearance of a new kind of criticism of
society, an historical criticism"; and "the birth of the avant-garde coincided
chronologically—and geographically, too—with the first bold development
of scientific revolutionary thought in Europe" (4).

By identifying the avant-garde and its sources as strictly European,
Greenberg revives an old inferiority complex that has lived at the heart of
American criticism since revolutionary days. At the same time, he elides the
question of whether any American sources of the avant-garde can be found;
the idea that began this chapter, that vaudeville (or its musical headquarters,
Tin Pan Alley) can in some way be a metaphor for modernism, is thus elided
as well. One advantage he gains is his ability to claim that the "purity" of
abstract art derives from the artists' concentration on the artwork's materiality as the sole source of value. "The avant-garde poet or artist tries in effect
to imitate God by creating something valid solely on its own terms, in the
way nature itself is valid, in the way a landscape—not its picture—is aesthetically valid; something *given*, increate, independent of meanings, similars,
or originals," he writes (6; original emphasis). "Avant-garde culture is the imitation of imitating" (8). For Greenberg, what the avant-garde artist imitated were the materials of the work of art. This is a fundamental part of his
argument, because he believes that when artists seek to use new—even
abstract—means of making art that are also involved with the popular, such
art is no longer avant-garde; such art is kitsch.

It is immediately apparent that Greenberg elides the most obvious impact of African and African American culture on modern culture as such:
the impact of black vernacular speech, the African sources of Cubism, and
other African sources of abstract visual art. Commentators on his essay have
often concentrated on its political dimension, and such a concentration is
justified.[15] For Greenberg, kitsch is tied not only to popular culture in the
United States but to totalitarian political power abroad as well. He goes to
great lengths to describe the affinities for kitsch of both the Nazi and Soviet
states. He argues that the rise both of the avant-garde and of kitsch, are themselves symptoms of the world crisis that also brought about the economic
crisis and the rise of Nazi and Soviet totalitarianisms.[16] The economic crisis,
he says, caused a split between the avant-garde culture and its primary

sponsors and patrons, the ruling classes: "The masses have always remained more or less indifferent to culture in the process of development. But today such culture is being abandoned by those to whom it actually belongs—our ruling class" (8).

In Greenberg's formulation, kitsch appears as a site of tension, almost of paranoia. It is an encroaching, haunting presence that exists alongside modernism; indeed, he even proposes that kitsch *arose* alongside modernism, suggesting a filial (but *oppositional*, as opposed to constitutive) relationship between the two. Both avant-garde and kitsch are products of modern society; each is, in a sense, a reaction to modern society. Where avant-garde stands for purity, however, kitsch stands for pollution and is, in fact, a source of pollution. It is, he says, "ersatz culture," which is "destined for those who, insenible to the values of genuine culture, are hungry nevertheless for the diversion that only culture of some sort can provide." Those who enjoy this "debased" culture, however, are, Greenberg suggests, victims of debasement brought about by their affection for kitsch. As a fake culture, kitsch is also a dishonest culture; it is "mechanical and operates by formulas. Kitsch is vicarious experience and faked sensations. Kitsch changes according to style, but remains always the same. Kitsch is the epitome of all that is spurious in the life of our times. Kitsch pretends to demand nothing of its customers except their money—not even their time" (10).

This extraordinary passage, which resounds with all the energy of a ritual chant, provides a set of values by which the reader would presumably be able to determine what products are kitsch. Andreas Huyssen (56–57) argues for an affinity between Greenberg's anxieties about mass culture and those of Theodor Adorno. It is true that both thinkers identify such phenomena as Hollywood films with these anxieties. (Greenberg adds the *New Yorker* magazine, the funny papers, and the *Saturday Evening Post* to his list.) It is important, though, to draw a distinction between the two. Greenberg is writing from within a modernist culture in which the relationship between "high" and "low" culture is already more complicated than he lets on; and it is to the silences embedded within his critique that attention must be paid if we are to see what is really at stake in this essay.

"Avant-garde and Kitsch" is almost silent about two major cultural events of its time: the rise of swing music, and the forms and movement associated with the Popular Front. In some senses, as Michael Denning and Lewis A. Erenberg suggest, both swing music and popular culture were part of the same cultural formation that dominated U.S. society in the interwar years.

These cultural milieus increasingly blended the linguistic and artistic innovations of the avant-garde with the instruments of popular culture in the
service of a populist-oriented art. This mixing of genres and styles had become pervasive by the late 1930s and could be seen in such forms as swing
bands and motion pictures, as well as in the poetry of such writers as
Hughes, Taggard, and Kenneth Fearing. These writers had used popular
forms such as vernacular speech, music, advertising, and other elements of
popular culture as sources of allusive reference, just as Eliot had done during the previous decade. It was, in a sense, this 1930s modernism, which did
not shrink from identifying with the African American Imaginary, which
was one of Greenberg's major targets in "Avant-garde and Kitsch." In a word,
when he talks about kitsch, Greenberg is talking, at least in part, about
African American culture and its impact on modern culture generally. His
attempt to draw a line between "T. S. Eliot" and "a Tin Pan Alley song" can
be read, then, as an attempt to reconstruct modernism on a basis that
eschewed the mixing of genres and the populism that had been characteristic of modernist literature and cultural forms during the interwar period
and especially characteristic of American modernism during this period.[17]

What seems to be at stake for Greenberg in making this attempt is the
legitimacy of the modernist project. Part of the rise of kitsch, and the dan-
ger it represents to high culture, comes, he suggests, from the fact that the
avant-garde has lost the sense of its audience. "The avant-garde itself," he
writes, "is becoming more and more timid every day that passes. Academi-
cism and commercialism are appearing in the strangest places. This can
mean only one thing: that the avant-garde is becoming unsure of the audience it depends on—the rich and the cultivated" (9). At least one aim of
Greenberg's essay, then, seems to be to restore the relationship between "the
rich and the cultivated" and the avant-garde artist. That is exactly what happened with the visual arts, beginning in the early years of World War II and
extending throughout the postwar years. This opposition to the culture of
the Popular Front formed the basis for the alliance between the New York
writers associated with *Partisan Review* and those associated with the
Fugitive group in Nashville. This alliance, which was to dominate intellectual discourse in the United States for a generation or more after World War
II, had the effect of nearly erasing one of the singular achievements of
modern art during the interwar years: the ascendancy of African American
art and culture to a place of respect and influence within the culture of modernism as such.

This is a very different modernist culture from that envisioned and pro-
moted by "Avant-garde and Kitsch." Its heroes include modernist poets who
write Broadway shows and detective fiction (Langston Hughes and Kenneth
Fearing); who valorize the products of kitsch as sources of creativity (the
Eliot of "Sweeney Agonistes); and who begin to inject the visual abstraction
that had been the hallmark of the avant-garde into popular culture generally
(Stuart Davis and Jacob Lawrence). The conservative turn signaled by
"Avant-garde and Kitsch" would not only bury the modernist aesthetic that
I have been describing but would, in effect, create a fissure in the way modernism was understood in critical discourse, a split whose resonance remains
with us today in the split and splintered narratives that seek to explain the
modernist past. This is especially true when we look at texts by African
American writers that appeared during the interwar years. To insist that
these texts can best be understood either as "Afro Modernist" or as symptomatic of the failed hopes for a multiracial modernism that were defeated by
the limitations imposed by a racially polarized society comes very close to
reading literary and cultural history through the eyes of the conservatism
inherited from the Faustian alliance between a group of post-Marxist New
York critics and a group of post-Confederate Nashville ones.

We can perhaps see this as the case by taking a look at the life of one such
text. Jean Toomer's *Cane* offers an opportunity to rethink questions of
canonicity and history with regard to modernism, if for no other reason
than that it stands at the boundary of all the categories that I have been
discussing.

{ 5 }

If we consider *Cane* both from a historical standpoint and in terms of its
genre as a literary text, it is surprising that it is less regarded as a central text
of literary modernism than appears justified. Indeed, the most important
defenders of *Cane*'s modernism seem to be those who write from the standpoint of also defending it as a central text of the African American tradition
(Gates, *Figures in Black* 196–234). *Cane* went through two printings, in
1923 and 1927, before disappearing from view, and in its first five years of
existence had sales comparable to Hart Crane's *White Buildings* (also published by Boni and Liveright), which sold five hundred copies within the
first three years of publication.[18] That each book sold fewer than one thousand copies of its first printing is less important than what the existence of

both books within the same milieu (and market) suggest about *Cane's* place in the avant-garde. Yet there remain literary historians who problematize *Cane's* place in literary history by seeming to suggest that the ambition its author had for the book should be read as a symptom of failure.

For Michael North, *Cane's* importance lies in the idea that "it distills a dilemma that faced the Americanist Avant-garde and the Harlem writers at the same time." That dilemma, he writes, had to do with irreconcilable artistic agendas: "Whether it was the avant-garde, trying to make modernism into a dialect so as to challenge the cultural supremacy of the English, or the Harlem writers, trying to make dialect into a modern literature so as to avoid the primitivizing pressures of the past, the central problem of reconciling competing linguistic motives remained. In the end, perhaps it was simply this dilemma that that two groups shared and nothing else" (*Dialect of Modernism* 174). It is usually unproductive for a critic who is attentive to the details of American culture to underestimate how powerful, pervasive, and ubiquitous racism is in that culture. To the extent that North draws our attention to the fact of this racism in his examination of the relationship between Toomer and the white members of the literary avant-garde, he allows us to better understand some of the underlying issues at play in this relationship.

Such a reading has its limitations, however. By using a binary that echoes the one proposed by Greenberg (e.g., North's "avant-garde," and "Harlem writers," versus Greenberg's "T. S. Eliot" and "a Tin Pan Alley song"), North presents readers with a problem: how can *Cane* best be interpreted? In this passage he appears to suggest that the text belongs to the Harlem writers and not to the avant-garde, but his argument is not so simple. The passage comes at the end of a chapter in which North narrates a literary history shared by Toomer and William Carlos Williams in the 1920s American avant-garde. It is a narrative based on a pair of ideas. The first is that despite its interest in African and Meso-American culture, the (presumably all white) American avant-garde "proved ill-prepared to include within its conception of the new American writing any examples that actually stretched the old categories of race and ethnicity." Second, Toomer's increasing alienation from a legal system of racial categorization forcing him to identify solely as an African American demonstrates "the fundamental asymmetry of the American racial situation, in which Williams was free to define himself, even if it meant defining himself vicariously as black, while Toomer was not" (North 150). In his examination of what he calls the avant-garde's "contradiction of racial cross-identification and racial hatred" (161), North is at pains to draw the conclusion that the distinct and differing relationship to language that black writers and white writers had during this period created a circumstance in which each group was engaged in competing, if not contradictory, aesthetic projects.

Part of the argument North mounts for this point of view involves comparing *Cane* with Williams's *Spring and All*. It is a surprising move in that he is, in a sense, comparing two works which, while they share some formal affinities, are unlike in one significant aspect. Although it was published in Dijon, France, by Robert McAlmon in the fall of 1923 in an edition of three hundred, *Spring and All* is a book that in effect does not exist as a contemporary of *Cane*. Paul Mariani explains: "Almost no one saw Williams' book in the original edition. The Paris booksellers weren't interested in limited editions, McAlmon was to explain, and most of the copies that were sent to America were simply confiscated by American customs officials as foreign stuff and therefore probably salacious and destructive of American morals. In effect, *Spring and All* all but disappeared as a cohesive text until its republication nearly ten years after Williams' death" (*William Carlos Williams* 209). Some of the poems in *Spring and All* (without the accompanying prose) appeared, in 1923, in a pamphlet called *Go-Go*, published by Monroe Wheeler, and a few in the little magazine *Succession* and elsewhere. Some of the poems were published in an edition of the poet's complete collected poems in 1934 (Williams, *Collected Poems* 1: 500–505). But the full edition of *Spring and All* would have to await the 1970 publication of *Imaginations* before it could be read by the general public. As the poet himself said of the 1923 edition of the book, "Nobody ever saw it—it had no circulation at all" (*I Wanted to Write a Poem* 36).

Although North does briefly acknowledge the virtual nonexistence of *Spring and All* by calling it "a work that, if it had had any readers, would have seemed the very epitome" of the avant-garde's desired style of "plain American" writing (147), he doesn't clarify the point. He places his examination of Williams's text near the beginning of the chapter and, because he is writing a literary history, gives the impression of a social and historical equality between *Spring and All* and *Cane*. It is a curious critical move. By elevating Williams's virtually nonexistent text to the discursive (and historical) level of Toomer's text, which was well known and highly regarded in its own time, and then by ascribing to Williams's text an advantage denied Toomer, North seems to reproduce the very condition of "the fundamental asymmetry of the American racial situation" that he criticizes the American avant-garde for not overcoming. The formal qualities that *Spring and All* possesses, which North lists, include qualities that readers—in particular, readers of the literature of the American avant-garde—could have seen in Toomer: "generic indeterminacy," "formal jaggedness," and "the breathless incompletion of its style" (152). In fact, attentive readers of the books of the leading New York avant-garde publisher of the early 1920s would come to identify these qualities with Boni and Liveright's T. S. Eliot and Jean Toomer, and they are qualities that readers and the marketers of the avant-garde would have identified with vaudeville, and with jazz.

It is useful, in this connection, to call attention to certain sections of *Spring and All* which readers would have seen not in the complete book but as at least one of them appeared in the most prominent little magazine of the avant-garde. Poem XVII of *Spring and All*, "Shoot It Jimmy," is widely discussed by critics who are interested in the relationship between Williams and African Americans, and between the poet and jazz music. North points out that this section "includes some of the most extremely demotic lines in the whole sequence" (153). The poem originally appeared, slightly altered, in the *Dial* in August 1923 (Williams, *Collected Poems* 216, 504). It consists of free-verse couplets:

> Our orchestra
> is the cat's nuts—

Some, presumably including the editors of the *Dial*, might read this couplet as sexual innuendo, but such readers might be unaware of the vernacular meaning of the word "cat," which had already entered the language as a synonym for a wise and aware person (usually male).[19] Indeed, Langston Hughes published a poem a few years later, "The Cat and the Saxophone (2 a.m.)" (Hughes, *Collected Poems* 89), which can be seen as signifying on the Williams poem.

Both poets engage in demotic language, and their poems both revolve around verses from the same jazz song. Williams closes his with the lines

> Nobody
> Nobody else
>
> but me—
> They cant copy it

This verse resembles lyrics from "Everybody Loves My Baby." Since that song was published and recorded in 1924, the year after his poem was published, it is not clear whether Williams was actually quoting it, but it is possible that the song was being sung in New York cabarets long before it was copyrighted so that Williams may have heard it in live performance.

It is very likely that Langston Hughes did hear the song in live performance, as well as on record. The Red Onion Jazz Babies, a band led by New Orleans composer-pianist Clarence Williams and including Louis Armstrong and Sidney Bechet, recorded the song twice on November 6, 1924, each time with a different singer: Eva Taylor (Clarence Williams's wife) and Alberta Hunter. (Louis Armstrong appears on both recordings.) It is possible that Alberta Hunter sang the song four days later, at an NAACP benefit in Harlem, where the entertainers included singer Florence Mills, dancer Bill "Bojangles" Robinson, a band led by Noble Sissle, and Fletcher Henderson's orchestra (with Louis Armstrong as the featured trumpet soloist). Langston Hughes was in the audience (Hunter; Rampersad 96–97).

Both Williams and Hughes employ multiple voices. In Williams's poem there are two or perhaps three voices, each discussing the uniqueness of jazz music, as is expressed by the poem's final line. Hughes ups the ante by creating a poem of some five voices, including the voice that is singing (in all capital letters) the song's lyrics:

> EVERYBODY
> Half-pint,—
> Gin?
> No, make it
> LOVES MY BABY
> corn. You like
> liquor,
> don't you, honey?
> BUT MY BABY
> Sure. Kiss me,
> DON'T LOVE NOBODY
> daddy.
> BUT ME.
> Say!
>
> (*Collected Poems* 89)

North argues that the "Nobody" of the Williams poem refers to Bert Williams's song. "It is not at all unlikely," he writes, "that William Carlos Williams would have quoted the title and refrain of Bert Williams's song in his poem on jazz" (154). The phrase "Nobody but me" does not appear in Bert Williams's song; nevertheless, the supposition that the poet is quoting the recently deceased ragtime-era master (North points out that Bert Williams died in 1922) rather than the contemporary Eva Taylor or Alberta Hunter, allows North to suggest that the resulting "Shoot It Jimmy" pivots on an act that resembles bad faith. Not only does North appear to assume that the poem's reference to "Nobody" comes from Bert Williams's song; he refers to Gilbert Seldes, whose essay "Toujours Jazz," with its reference to Paul Whiteman, appears in the same issue of the *Dial* as Williams's poem. "If this is true, however, then the whole poem simply consumes itself," writes North. "If the white Williams is putting himself in the role of the black Williams, making a play on surnames quite the reverse of Seldes's, then the proud boast 'They can't copy it' becomes ironic nonsense." The word "nobody," North adds, "curls up on itself" in a way that has the poet using the word in blackface; a blackface that inverts Bert Williams's grievance to put "African Americans in a seamless trap: they are nothing whenever they try to say anything but that they are nothing" (154). North adds: "How is it that a term that makes a black man invisible and impotent can, when used in blackface, as it were, make for a white poet's assertion of difference and originality? The difference that made jazz appealing in the first place has been replaced here by a perfect simulacrum of itself" (154–55).

One answer to these questions is that the poet Williams might be engaged, here, in a subtle game of racial passing. Lisa Sánchez González claims Williams as a member of the Puerto Rican "Boricua" diaspora in the United States. She reminds us that his mother "was born in Mayagüez, a city on Puerto Rica's western coast, sometime during the mid-nineteenth century. Her mother's family had been in Puerto Rico for countless generations, while her father's family were apparently immigrants from the West Indies (probably of Dutch extraction)" (42). She goes on to quote the poet's own enigmatic assessment of his family history: "Nothing is known of our family beyond the last three generations and not all of that—other than vague rumors, enticing, irritating, scandalous—racially doubtful in certain cases" (55). In her own reading of the poet's *In the American Grain* (1925), Sánchez González points out how Williams elides the presence of African

Americans in his account of American history; but more important, for my purposes, is how she describes the poet's racial identity: "Williams was a figure forced into the U.S. binarism of racial identifications that ironically made him the (nonwhite male) Other of the (Black male) Other. But instead of unraveling these contradictory subjective dialectics, Williams sublimates them by exploiting the (nonwhite female) Other of the (nonwhite male) Other of the (Black male) Other, creating a subjective syntax that confounds rather than compounds the now commonsense Hegelian approach to subjectivity" (53).

There is a sense, then, in which Williams and Toomer were each responding to a situation in which they found themselves but had had no influence over creating. How were they to negotiate multiple racial identities in a world that disallows such multiplicity? The ventriloquism practiced by Williams was one way for a (legally white) Puerto Rican (a "Boricua") poet to surrender to the binarism, and to pass for white while performing "blackness." For Toomer, the stakes were different. To be forced to make a choice among racialized binaries would have meant that he had to choose against himself. Those who argue, as Arna Bontemps did in 1972, that Toomer "gave up his racial identity" ("The Awakening" 39) seem not to take seriously the idea that multiracial identities are possible in a multiracial society. For Toomer the solution was not, finally, to pass for black but to isolate himself as much as possible from the social and literary worlds that would force such a choice upon him. For Williams, passing for white, though it allowed him access to all the social privileges of whiteness, nevertheless brought with it a racial anxiety that he was never to shake off. It is useful in this connection to note that the comment, quoted above, about his "racially doubtful" family was published in 1959.

For differing reasons, then, the significance of the lyrics to "Everybody Loves My Baby" was not lost on either William Carlos Williams or Langston Hughes. "Everybody Loves My Baby" was a major signpost of the jazz age sensibility, one in which the word "nobody" transcended the boundaries it had adhered to in late-minstrel and ragtime-era discourse. African Americans, in this new song, were individuals, creating an individual art and an individualized aesthetic sensibility. The distinction of this fact was surely not lost on the poet Williams, who was probably aware of the sense of the phrase "they can't copy it" as jazz musicians used it: to signal that the new music they created couldn't be easily copied and commercialized by mainstream culture. However mistaken they may have been on this point, the struggle to create an art form in which this phrase would be perennially true was one of the motive forces behind the modernist (including the jazz) sensibility. This sensibility was also something that the poet Williams was trying to capture in "Shoot It Jimmy."

Another aspect of the significance of "Everybody Loves My Baby" has to do with the fact that it was a love song. I return to this point shortly, but here it is sufficient to point out that one characteristic of the New Negro sensibility as it entered the 1920s was the assertion of equal social status in matters of the heart. (Songs asserting the individual right to love replaced the comic love songs of the ragtime era. A companion song to "Everybody Loves My Baby" was "I'm a Little Blackbird," also recorded by Eva Taylor with Clarence Williams, which includes the lines "I'm a little jazzbo looking for a rainbow too / Building fairy castles same as all the white folks do.") This claim can be seen as both an existential assertion and a political one, for the right to individual choice in love had been denied or constricted by white supremacy since the slave era. Hughes was certainly recognizing this fact by embedding "Everybody Loves My Baby" into a poetic record of a couple engaging in a sexual negotiation. If Williams was in fact alluding to that song, then he can be seen as acknowledging the presence of the New Negro sensibility and its value to his own work. Yet it must be conceded that this recognition produced anxieties similar to those shared by other white modernist writers. Aldon Lynn Nielsen writes about the primitivism, "romantic racism," and "aesthetic slumming" practiced by white American modernist poets. In examining Williams's work, Nielsen finds that he "shared with Pound the tendency to employ blacks as objects of local color, as he shared with Stein and so many other modernists an intense and highly romanticized interest in the purported sexuality of black people." In a comment on "Shoot It Jimmy," however, Nielsen acknowledges that Williams "nevertheless was inspired by the rhythms and energies of jazz and wanted them for his own" (*Reading Race* 51–52, 72, 80). Although these conflicting and contradictory impulses are commonplaces within modernism, as Nielsen demonstrates, they also reflect the importance of the African American Imaginary to the modernist project. Perhaps it would be too strong to say that modernist writers couldn't help engaging this Imaginary, but it is certainly not too strong to suggest that this engagement was constitutive of the modernist identity.

At the same time, the tendency to see the role of African American artists as passive bystanders or otherwise disengaged from modernism, by virtue of

the results of an aesthetic or a social contradiction that is deemed irreconcilable, strains our understanding of modernism as a pluralistic cultural phenomenon and moment. Consider the following observation from Michael
North about Toomer, Williams, and the American avant-garde: "If anything,
Toomer was more solidly ensconced within this group than was Williams"
(149). At the same time, North can argue for the relative marginalization of
Toomer from this group. That marginalization, argues North, is a reflection
of a contradiction he sees within *Cane* itself: a conflict that consists of the
work's existence as a formally experimental work of literature, on the one
hand, and one in which the author sought to express something of the social
dimension of African American life, on the other. "The formal task that
Toomer set for himself," writes North, "was to use the tools of modernism in
such a way as to draw from them something more socially responsible than
he found in the imagists," and Toomer also wanted to "use traditional forms
in a way that would not conduce to the sort of primitivism he loathed" in
such writers as Sherwood Anderson and Waldo Frank (173–74).

  This problem of needing to create a work of art using experimental language *and* needing to express ideas concerning the social conditions of the
historical life world embodied in the text is seen by North as reflecting the
"competing linguistic motives" dividing the white and black writers of the
1920s. This divide has similarities with the one proposed by Greenberg, in-
sofar as each divide somehow proposes a fissure between white and black
writers and culture that is embedded in the natural state of each group. Once
this happens, it becomes even more difficult to ask questions concerning
how these divisions came into being in the first place. In the case of *Cane*,
asking these questions becomes even more urgent, since it was clearly a
central text of the 1920s American avant-garde, despite the racialized social
conditions under which it was produced, just as it was a central text of the
New Negro, or Harlem, Renaissance. That the latter movement became, as
it were, the keeper of *Cane*'s reputation as it languished in a literary limbo
for four decades should not divert attention from the larger questions concerning how this displacement, and by extension the displacement of many
African American writers from the literary canon, came about.

{ 6 }

To argue that *Cane*'s stature in the canon of literary modernism has been displaced by a criticism that has diminished part of the identity of modernism

itself is not quite the same thing as arguing for a consideration that places *Cane* in a central place in the modernist canon. It is true that the critical recovery of Toomer's work, in particular the recovery that has been undertaken by African American literary criticism, has claimed it as a central text of the African American literary tradition, and to the extent that such claims base themselves on recovering (or discovering) an African American modernism, the text has been considered a central text of such modernism. Any claim for *Cane* as a central text of literary modernism as such could rest on another set of claims: that African American literature is itself a central strain of literary modernism. This claim may be on its way to becoming a commonplace, but it has not yet become so, as I hope I demonstrated above in the discussion of David Macey's definition of modernism. To claim *Cane* as a text that is central to the modernist canon may require a reading that allows us to see, in this work, the identity of modernism itself. As a work consisting of the mixture and interplay of genres, *Cane* may claim a long and distinguished genealogy that includes works as diverse as the early American almanac; a novel like *Clotel; or, The President's Daughter*, by William Wells Brown; *Darkwater*, by W. E. B. Du Bois; and *Winesburg, Ohio*, by Sherwood Anderson. At the same time, the establishment of *Cane* as an avant-garde text is accomplished not just by its proximity to other texts but by its own form and identity.

The first story in *Cane* announces itself with a poetic epigram that echoes the blues. This firmly places it within a stylistic framework that immediately raises the question of genre, and of the instability of genres. The allusion to the blues in "Karintha" is signaled by the repeated refrain "when the sun goes down," which had already entered popular culture as an utterance with blues connotations. This is just one of several references to black music in *Cane*. Nathaniel Mackey cites the allusions to the spirituals and, in the poem "Cotton Song," to the African American work song (236–40). Mackey does not, however, refer to the echo of the first line of "The St. Louis Blues" ("I hate to see the evenin' sun go down") that can be found in "Karintha." This echo also anticipates the well-known blues lyric "I hate to see the evenin' sun go down" which would be recorded later in the 1920s and in the 1930s by Leroy Carr, Leadbelly, and others.

> Her skin is like dusk on the eastern horizon,
> O cant you see it, O cant you see it,
> Her skin is like dusk on the eastern horizon
> ... When the sun goes down.
>
> (Toomer 3)

The story itself is one of male lust, a young woman's sexual initiation, and the death of her baby. The main tension of the story is, as Monica Michlin points out, sexual: the integration of the allusion to the song lyric into the text ("Men had always wanted her, this Karintha, even as a child, Karintha carrying beauty, perfect as dusk when the sun goes down" [Toomer 3]) turns the lyric in which the allusion is embedded, writes Michlin, from a song of praise "into one of sexual domination and reification." The story's syntax, she adds, "makes Karintha an object, not a subject, of what should be *her* story" (99; original emphasis). The hints of male pedophilic desire in the text, Michlin writes, only sharpens the sense that Karintha is simply an object of sexual desire: "Even if one takes it to be an organic image, the reduction of the human to the organic is disturbing, although it is part of Toomer's half-primitivistic, half mystical strategy to use the same words ('a growing thing') for Karintha's body, her soul, and later (implicitly) for the unwanted baby" (99).

The story oscillates between a praise song for Karintha's sexual independence and a narrative that objectifies her body, and the tension has given rise to numerous interpretations that focus on one side or the other of the story's duality. Yet it is the tension itself that seems to be the story's subject, a tension that is not resolved by an ending that circles back to the beginning, with Karintha as an adult described in nearly the same terms as she was at the beginning: "Karintha is a woman. Men do not know that the soul of her was a growing thing ripened too soon. They will bring their money; they will die not having found it out ... Karintha at twenty, carrying beauty, perfect as dusk when the sun goes down. Karintha ..." (4; ellipses as in original). "Karintha" is one of the early texts that exemplified the then-new blues sensibility as it was emerging from the African American communities of the time. Although the earliest blues singers and performers were often itinerant male performers, by the time "Karintha" and *Cane* were published, the blues had become identified in the public consciousness as a vehicle of expression for women artists. Most of the popular blues performers were women. The first woman to record blues songs, Mamie Smith ("Crazy Blues," 1920), started a development during which dozens of women performers made blues records, many of which sold in the thousands (Davis xii; Harrison 43–62). Throughout the 1920s the blues was widely understood as a form of expression dominated by African American women. That these singers, most prominently Bessie Smith (who recorded 160 songs in the decade after 1923), were considered a part of the modernist aesthetic by literary contemporaries is apparent not only in the influence they had on black writers such as Toomer and others of the Harlem Renaissance but in their influence, whether direct or residual, on a wider range of literary culture. When a young white Mississippi poet named Charles Henri Ford wanted to start an avant-garde literary magazine in 1929, he called it *Blues*. Kay Boyle, William Carlos Williams, Louis Zukofsky, and Kenneth Rexroth, among others, contributed to it (Denning 211–12).

These blues performers and blues songs distinguished themselves by their unique approach to poetic language, as well as by their new approach to the position of women in both private and public spheres. As already noted, blues lyrics share many of the qualities that were identified with the renovation of poetic language that characterized modernist verse. It has only recently been noted, however, that these lyrics were also an important reflection of the new, modern consciousness among women, of which the feminist movement of the time was only one manifestation. The significance of women's blues as a modernist expression among women—and thereby amid society as such—lay in part in the music's approach to individual sexuality. "The classic blues women sang of female aspirations for happiness and frequently associated these aspirations with sexual desire," writes Angela Y. Davis, "but they rarely ignored the attendant ambiguities and contradictions" (23). In addition to the complex approach to sexuality and individual love that was the subject of much of the blues, these songs were also notable, writes Davis, for the way they disestablished the social boundaries that kept women confined to the domestic sphere: "The blues as a genre never acknowledges the discursive and ideological boundaries separating the private sphere from the public" (25). These two aspects of the blues seem to inform "Karintha." If the story is understood within the context of the blues, as (to use musicians' parlance) a riff on the blues, then the contradictions articulated within it become that much more comprehensible. Far from creating a tension that undermines the piece, as Michlin and others have suggested, these contradictions appear to be held in precarious balance, and it is this balance that gives the story its edgy, modernist feeling.

Another thematic tension within "Karintha" is that between the urban and rural selves. Much attention has been given to the exploration of the rural setting in *Cane*, and this attention seems to imply that the text's attention to rural Georgia is an almost hermetic one. But the rural settings can also be seen as harboring within that theme another one in which the city is regarded as a means of escape, almost as a utopian alternative to the harsh rural landscape that is foregrounded in the text. This tension can be found throughout *Cane*, yet it seems to have elicited little comment from critical readers. In "Karintha," for example, the city appears as the place young men travel to, only to return with gifts intended to impress Karintha: "Young men to the big cities and run on the road. Young men go away to college. They all want to bring her money" (Toomer 4). The railroad and the city are both symbols of modernity, and of escape. In "Becky," the story of a woman who is socially isolated as a "white woman who had two Negro sons," the railroad serves as a symbol not only of modernity but also of a world that is quickly rendering the rural life obsolete, while Becky herself seems to be an icon for both racial alienation and rural isolation. "Six trains each day rumbled past and shook the ground under her cabin. Fords, and horse- and mule-drawn buggies went back and forth along the road. Trainmen, and passengers who'd heard about her, threw out papers and food. Threw out little crumpled slips of paper scribbled with prayers, as they passed her eye-shaped piece of sandy ground" (Toomer 7). Throughout the stories and poems set in rural Georgia the instruments of modernity intrude, as crude interruptions in the pastoral environment. These instruments can be the railroad, an automobile, or a factory such as the sawmill in "Carma": "The sun is hammered to a band of gold. Pine-needles, like mazda, are brilliantly aglow. No rain has come to take the rustle from the falling sweet-gum leaves. Over in the forest, across the swamp, a sawmill blows its closing whistle" (Toomer 12).

These eruptions and intrusions of modernity have been seen not as evidence of a text that is evoking a world in transition but as evidence of its lack of engagement with that world. Barbara Foley argues that "Toomer offered a somewhat superficial portraiture of the economic life of the sharecropping and working class blacks" of rural Georgia in the early 1920s. She adds that *Cane*'s evocation of the sawmill factories in the poems "Georgia Dusk" and "Song of the Sun" serve only lyrical rather than mimetic purposes. "In both poems," Foley writes, "Toomer's lush lyricism is achieved only through a fetishization of labor processes. The mill whistle that summons men to and from their labor takes shape as a natural phenomenon; low wages, layoffs, and debt peonage are invisible" ("In the Land of Cotton" 182–83).

The term "fetishism," in this connection, seems to be derived from Karl Marx, who wrote that commodities appear to us as, in a sense, simple objects in which the social relations that produced them have disappeared;

such relations are, to use Foley's word, "invisible."[20] It is in this sense that the sawmills (and, perhaps, the railroads) are fetishized in *Cane*; if so, however, what is accomplished in the text by such fetishization? It is true that the sawmill and other icons of modernity appear as if out of nowhere; yet what is remarkable is that they also appear as fleeting images, almost without a life of their own. It is not until "Blood Burning Moon" that a factory becomes the center of any action in *Cane*, and then it is as the site of a lynching. Each of the story's three parts is punctuated by the following verse:

> Red nigger moon. Sinner!
> Blood-burning moon. Sinner!
> Come out that fact'ry door.
> (Toomer 37)

By fetishizing the labor processes, *Cane* simultaneously offers a picture of a world in transition. Rather than giving simply a picture of a pastoral South that is passing away, *Cane* at the same time shows, through glimpses, icons, and symbols, the modern world that is already encroaching on the southern landscape. It is this attempt to present both worlds at the same time that constitutes another major stylistic tension within the first section of the book.

This dynamic presentation of both old and new worlds recalls Henri Bergson's conceptions of time and duration. Bergson explains that we experience time, or duration, in two ways. First, a "homogeneous" experience corresponds to our conscious experience of time as a phenomenon consisting of sequential events, what he calls "the numerical multiplicity of conscious states." Second, at the same time, we experience what he calls a "qualitative multiplicity": "a self in which *succeeding each other* means *melting into one another and forming an organic whole*" (128; original emphasis). This idea, which Bergson first published in 1889, would become the foundation for modernism's "stream of consciousness," the conception made famous by James Joyce.[21] Toomer's use of time to signal the distinction between the present pastoral setting, which is in the process of passing away, and the future urban one is related to the stream; but the dynamism with which he locates both past and present within the lyrical and narrative present of the text suggests that what Foley calls the "fetishization of labor processes" at work in *Cane* can also be seen as a form of symbolic critique of a world in which the pastoral landscape, in which both loving and lynching take place, is shared by machines (railroads, factories) that contain both promise and tragedy. This duality of promise and tragedy is yet another opposition within which the tensions of *Cane* unfold.

In "Blood Burning Moon" the factory in which Tom Burwell is burned alive by a lynch mob is an abandoned prewar, cotton factory (Toomer, 28–35). It appears to have some relationship to the illusions Burwell expresses earlier in the story: his hopes to have a farm leased to him by the town's large landowner; and his initial disbelief in the sexual interest the landowner's son, Bob Stone, has for Louisa, the woman Burwell is courting. The verse quoted above, from which this story's title derives, is repeated three times, a number that can signify misfortune.[22] The violence that concludes the tale, in which Burwell slits Stone's throat and is subsequently lynched in the abandoned factory, seems to bring to a climax the tensions between the pastoral environment and the encroaching machine age that have animated the first section of *Cane*; but the repetition of the verse at the end creates more ambiguity than the finality of Burwell's lynching would seem to give to the story.

If the text shows a pastoral beauty of the South canceled by violence, then the second section of *Cane*, with its stories and lyrics set in northern cities, develops the tensions of the first section in reverse. The urban sections introduce a heroic figure that resembles another character typical of modernist texts: the aesthete. Toomer's urban figures sometimes evoke a southern past that, if not paradisal, at least summons an idealized memory—for example, Dan Moore's internal monologue about the old man who sits on a chair outside Muriel's house: "Saw the first horse-cars, the first Oldsmobile. And he was born in slavery. I did see his eyes. Never miss eyes. But they were bloodshot and watery. It hurt to look at them. It hurts to look in most people's eyes. He saw Grant and Lincoln. He saw Walt—old man, did you see Walt Whitman? Did you see Walt Whitman! Strange force that draws me to him" (Toomer 67–68).

It may be stretching the point to claim that several of the characters in *Cane*—Dan Moore, Rhobert, Ralph Kabnis, and the lyric and narrative voice of the text as such—are all manifestations of an aesthetic personality and of that modernist character called the aesthete. It is important to note, however, that these characters all seem to center their attention on the sensuous and the aesthetic, and that the lyric voice in the poems, whatever subject appears on the surface, always seems to circle back to the aesthetic as a major source of concern:

My body is opaque to the soul.
Driven of the spirit, long have I sought to temper it unto the spirit's
    longing,
But my mind, too, is opaque to the soul.

(Toomer 70)

Like many of the verses in *Cane*, this one echoes Walt Whitman, especially some of the ideas found in "Song of Myself," and the concerns of the verse (called "Prayer," in *Cane*) are those of the relationship between the corporeal and the spiritual. Those who see Toomer's conversion to the spiritual practices of Georges Gurdjieff and, later, to the Quaker religion as evidence of a retreat from modernism seem to forget just how much these and others practices were part of the modernist search for spiritual knowledge outside of traditional Western religions. It is just this search that inspired, for instance, some of the most powerful poems of William Butler Yeats. The speaker in the verse quoted above shares with Whitman the idea that transcendence can be sought in the temporal world, through the body. Yet the search in this realm is, perhaps inevitably, a failure, and this failure is the subject of the poem:

> O Spirits of whom my soul is but a little finger,
> Direct it to the lid of its flesh-eye.
> I am weak with much giving.
> I am weak with the desire to give more.
>
> . . . .
>
> My voice could not carry to you did you dwell in stars,
> O Spirits of whom my soul is but a little finger . . .

(Toomer 70)

The diction here is reminiscent of Whitman and Yeats, and recalls the mood of some of the poems of Rainer Maria Rilke. The verse evokes the sense of a modern yearning and skepticism that seems to haunt much modernist poetry. It is this skepticism that we find in Paul's last speech, in "Bona and Paul," despite its apparent bravura: "My thoughts were matches thrown into a dark window. And all the while the Gardens were purple like a bed of roses would be at dusk. I came back to tell you, brother, that white faces are petals of roses. That dark faces are petals of dusk. That I am going out and gather petals" (Toomer 80). That Paul turns away at the end of this speech to find that Bona, one of the "petals of roses" he is seeking to gather, has disappeared seems emblematic of a major theme at work in *Cane*: the subject of loss and the unavailability of any redeeming remedy for such loss. The idea that loss is a common human condition pervades much modernist literature and is certainly one of the major themes of modern American lyric art—in particular, the blues and the African American–influenced popular song.

Consideration of the surface bravura of Paul's speech also uncovers one of the major problems facing critics of African American literature. Henry Louis Gates Jr. has written that many consider works by black authors to be transparent in their meaning. Gates writes about the "trope of blackness" being signified by "an absence, the sheer absence of invisibility." Borrowing a phrase from Barbara Johnson, he defines this trope of blackness as being the "already read text." In this sense, he adds, *Cane* and its author are the "'blackest' text and author of all" (*Figures in Black* 200). That this trope is a problem is demonstrated by the degree to which criticisms of *Cane* are dependent on historical and biographical factors for their explications. This fact is at least in part due to the challenge posed to social norms by Toomer's refusal to acquiesce to demands that he perform "race" within the socially constructed boundaries and binaries that the term embodies in modern U.S. society. "It should not prove surprising," writes Gates, "that much of the published Toomer criticism is, in some sense or other, biographical or pseudo–psychological" (*Figures in Black* 211). Even readings that proclaim themselves as textual often fall back on negotiating the anxiety provoked by the author's own racial nonconformity. Such readings very often find themselves at a loss when faced with the fate of Ralph Kabnis, who, after being panic-stricken by an unpredictable, beautiful but violent environment, finds himself in a cellar, dressed in a "gaudy ball costume" (Toomer 106), overwhelmed by the thought that he, Kabnis, is the embodiment of "sin": "The whole world is a conspiracy t sin, especially in America, an against me. I'm th victim of their sin. I'm what sin is," he says (116, original punctuation and syntax). In a sense, the "sin" is the mixed text, the vaudeville text, that is Kabnis, and *Cane*; it is the artist who cannot find his place in a society that rejects such mixtures out of hand. In the end, Kabnis "trudges" (117) out of the cellar, presumably to take his place as a laborer in the workshop upstairs.

If the concerns of *Cane* have, because of the "already read" trope of blackness, kept this text at the margins of critical considerations about the central texts of modernism, then it should be no surprise that African American literature as such should be similarly kept at those margins—perhaps for no other reason than that the universalistic claims of black literature are not so read by those who look for such claims from literature. If the alienation expressed by the lyric voice and demonstrated by the characters in *Cane* is judged according to conformist values in which "racial" concerns are, by definition, not universal, then it follows that the split in critical consciousness that allows for the (often unremarked) displacement of African American culture and writing can also be seen as normative. Yet the problems posed by a consideration of *Cane*'s relationship to the central concerns of modernism should be a challenge to such normative readings. The same problems can be said to arise when one examines many texts of the African American tradition, especially those that are contemporaneous with *Cane* and those that followed in its wake. When Langston Hughes wrote a few years later, in "The Negro Artist and the Racial Mountain," that black artists should be looking toward Bessie Smith, Paul Robeson, Aaron Douglas, and Jean Toomer as models to follow in their artistic practice (95), he was not posing a problem simply for black artists. He was posing an aesthetic problem that faced all modern artists, one which, despite the attempted reconstruction by later critics of what modernism meant, remained a central problem for American (and not *just* American) artists throughout our modern era.

Conclusion

{ 1 }

İT CONTINUES TO SURPRISE me that the argument put forth in this book still has to be made at this rather late date in our cultural history. Yet daily immersion in contemporary cultural discourse continues to drive home the point that we do not yet really know the importance of African American culture to the history of our culture as a whole. This may seem an odd claim, since artifacts of black culture are common in the modern world, especially in the United States. The truth of my assertion is easy enough to demonstrate, though, by considering the following illustration.

It is a commonplace to assert that as far as contemporary culture is concerned, the authority, integrity, and power of African American music are no longer in doubt. One comes across plenty of evidence supporting this notion, and sometimes it appears in the most unlikely places. For instance, physicist Lee Smolin, in the middle of an omnibus review in a leading American literary journal discussing several books about the life and work of Albert Einstein, offers this paragraph: "It is true that many mathematicians and physicists do their best work when young. But in Einstein's later work we see something much more extreme than the usual falling off. It is as if Thelonious Monk or John Coltrane turned into an obscure twelve-tone composer. How did the greatest physicist since Newton turn into a failed player of mathematical games? All the biographers ask this question; none gives an answer that seems remotely plausible to me as a working scientist" (80).

Here the equivalence the writer draws between Monk or Coltrane, on the one hand, and Einstein, on the other, is taken for granted. The writer assumes the assent of his readers on this matter, as well as the elevation of the two musicians' work above one of the twentieth century's most highly regarded styles of European music. One might say that this signals the musical taste of one individual, but I would argue that it signals more than that, and that what it signals is quite germane to the argument I have been making.

Before connecting Smolin's comment with my own argument, however, I want to point out just how unremarkable that comment is—as if, perhaps it is not too flippant to say, on the question of the importance of African American music the twentieth-century culture wars are over, and black culture has won. Yet this example suggests something else about contemporary culture. African American musical artists such as Monk and Coltrane

149

are nearly universally accepted for their great contributions to music, and it could hardly be otherwise, given how much music in all genres has been shaped by their innovations. Quite nearly the same thing can be said about late twentieth-century black literature. Since Toni Morrison won the Nobel Prize, the status of the African American writer as an integral part of contemporary culture, both inside and outside the academy, is, if not assured, at least no longer controversial.

The same cannot quite be argued for the era and for some of the figures discussed in this book. Although it is probably unremarkable that in many secondary and higher education classrooms, and in many salonlike book discussion groups, examinations of contemporary fiction are likely to include (indeed, it could be said, must include) a discussion of Morrison and other African American writers, it is also true that a classroom that studies modernist literature could, even at the dawn of the twenty-first century, conclude a semester without looking at one work by an African American author. The point is that black literary culture of earlier eras simply does not have the cultural authority that Smolin so routinely attaches to the musical culture of Monk and Coltrane, or the authority that is today attached to some of the more famous musicians of earlier eras, such as Louis Armstrong and Duke Ellington. It is important to note, though, that such authority ascribed to African American musical artists is itself of relatively recent origin; one would be hard pressed to find such comparisons as Smolin's in the serious press even a couple of decades ago. Yet such comparisons are now increasingly common. As far as African American literature is concerned, however, black writers—especially those of the eras I write about here—are usually classed with other black writers and not generally understood as having cultural authority with regard to the society as a whole.

This book is an attempt to counter that situation. The claim I have made, that we do not yet really know our history when it comes to the impact of black culture upon it, should provoke scholars and others to ask new questions about how the culture that is the immediate ancestor of the world in which we now live was produced. Several scholars have asked those questions over the last several decades, and I am indebted to their works. Others continue to ask such questions, yet the research is far from comprehensive, or even adequate.

There is a lot at stake in raising these questions. To do so honestly and rigorously means that we might come to understand the cultural masks we use to explain reality to ourselves as just that, masks; that the polite fictions rendering American culture as a series of neighboring cultures hiding behind masks of legalized racism and racial identification are, in the end, fictions that in the name of domination have hidden our culture from ourselves.

One obstacle to a deeper understanding of the interrelationship between African American culture and the larger culture has been the dominance of what might be called the "marginality" narrative. This narrative starts from the assumption that racialized minorities in the United States have produced a culture that has little in common with that of the majority, that its concerns are fundamentally different, even ontologically so. Yet there is nothing more central to twentieth-century American—and, indeed, world—culture than "The St. Louis Blues." As I have already pointed out, that song's importance can hardly be overestimated. An example of cultural synthesis itself, the song and the body of work it helped usher into the world can be said to stand in a similar relationship to world culture in the twentieth century as the symphony that concludes with the "Ode to Joy" had to nineteenth-century European culture.

{ 2 }

Throughout this book I have argued that an understanding of the catalytic role of black music is essential to an understanding of the new developments in modernist poetry in the last years of the nineteenth century and the early years of the twentieth. I have also argued that the importance of African American poetry and poetic language is an overlooked factor in our understanding of the emergence of modernist poetic language as such. That these ideas are not more widely discussed in the literature on modernism stands in sharp contrast to the evidence, especially as it appears not only in the work of modernist poets themselves but in some important memoirs of the participants in the movement as well. To cite just one example: in his memoir, the poet Kenneth Rexroth recounts his brief stay, in early 1924, in an apartment house on Grove Street in New York's Greenwich Village. Rexroth lived in a basement apartment. Among the building's other tenants was Hart Crane:

> The week I moved in Crane was busy writing one of his best poems. At that period he was writing everything to what he considered jazz—in this case Bert Williams' "The Moon Shines on the Moonshine." On his phonograph he had one of those old tin contrivances which picked up the needle and sent it back to the beginning of the record with a loud squeak. Hour after hour, day and

night, I could hear coming through the ceiling "So still de night, in de ole distillery, de moon shines white on de ole machinery." It wasn't jazz, but it produced "Whitely, while benzine rinsings of the moon dissolve . . ." (Rexroth
332; original ellipsis)

Rexroth misremembers the song's verse slightly. It really goes "How sad and
still tonight / By the old distillery / And how the cobwebs cob / In the old
machinery" (B. Williams, "The Moon Shines on the Moonshine"). His
joining of Williams and Crane, however, is an evocative example of the kind
of associations I have been making. Both the song Williams sings and
Crane's "Lachrymae Christi" share words and images that seem close to one
another—"machinery," "still," "nights"—and in Williams, the "mahogany is
dusty," while in Crane, "swart / Thorns freshen the year's / First blood" (19).
None of this matters much, until we are reminded by Paul Mariani that
"Lachrymae Christi" is not only Latin for Christ's tears but "was also the
name of a delicate white wine" (*Broken Tower* 150). Williams's song is unusual in that its two choruses are not identical; the last line of the first, "Oh,
how the moon shines on the moonshine so merrily," is followed at the end
of the song with "Up where the moon shines on the moonshine so stillery,
so stillery." It is a song of ironic protest, if you will, against the prohibition
law; but it is also a song about sadness, regeneration, and hope.[1]

Readers of Crane's poem have found it obscure and difficult, and interpretations have ranged from those who find it incomprehensible to those
who seem intent on mustering a mythology, however fragile, within which
to contain it. For Joseph Riddel, this is both a poem about a love affair and
"Crane's most incoherent poem, stylistically his most outrageous" (487). He
reads elements of both sexual generation and sacrificial ritual in it. From this
point of departure, Riddel attempts to grapple with the imagery of the poem.
In the end, he admits, "the clarification of particular images or symbols, however, is no easy task, in part because the strategy of the poem is to distill a new
language, the language of primal force residual in the baser elements of the
world's words. One can only pick at the parts, describe the arrangements
and the possible relationships into which the parts coalesce" (489). Riddel
then points out, almost in passing, that "borage" ("Let sphinxes from the
ripe / Borage of death have cleared my tongue / Once and again") is both an
herb and "the source of a cordial wine." His reading of the poem's language
of violence often seems as difficult as the poem itself, and his attempt to unpack the poem's dense imagery leaves readers with little inkling of the life of
the poem itself.

For Warner Berthoff, the poem coheres into a statement of rebirth: every "densely unfolded sentence is keyed to a violent and continuous metamorphosis, or, by radical complementarity," he writes, "to a counterpoise of stasis and miraculous resolution" (71). At the same time, Berthoff seems to suggest that what may appear incoherent to others (he cites Riddell's examination of the poem), may, in fact, be linked to the poet's method of composition: "'Lachrymae Christi' only lacks, perhaps, the interposed narrative momentum of Crane's strongest work. It is almost wholly an apostrophe in form, a prayerful summoning of linked qualities and impressions that seem, in the end, less cumulative and self-enacting than merely assembled" (72–73).

Indeed, both these readings, as intriguing and illuminating as they are, seem to reveal a deep discomfort on the part of the critics with Crane's method of composition. To say that the poem consists of "linked qualities and impressions," or that its strategy is to "distill a new language, the language of primal force residual in the baser elements of the world's words," is to suggest the methodologies of both symbolism and imagism. Poets who practiced these styles, as well as those who followed the Cubist style—exemplified most famously in English by Gertrude Stein—hoped to be able to write a poetry consisting entirely of symbols, or images, without the interference, if you will, of what Berthoff calls the "interposed narrative momentum" (72). This is perhaps what Rexroth meant when he (who in his youth wrote poems in the Cubist style) called "Lachrymae Christi" one of Crane's "best poems."

What are we to make, then, of the other claim Rexroth makes, that "The Moon Shines On the Moonshine" "produced" Crane's poem? Before succumbing to the urge to dismiss this claim as an offhand comment, we may find it useful to remember that the song and the poem share similar concerns with, as I have already noted, despair and rebirth. Here are the first verse and chorus. Bert Williams recorded the song in the same year, 1919, that he premiered it in the Follies:

> The mahogany is dusty,
> All the pipes are very rusty,
> And the good old fashioned "musty,"
> Doesn't musty any more.
> All the stuff got bum and bummer,
> From the middle of the summer,
> Now the bar is "on the hummer,"
> And "For Rent" is on the door.

How sad and still tonight,
By the old distillery.
And how the cobwebs cob,
In the old machinery.
But in the mountaintops,
Far from the eyes of cops,
O how the moon shines on the moonshine so merrily.
(DeWitt; Williams, "The Moon Shines on the Moonshine")

Perhaps the first thing to notice is what looks like odd, unusual vocabulary: "And the good old fashioned 'musty' / Doesn't musty any more"; "Now the bar is 'on the hummer.'" The use of common words like "musty," and "hummer" in this context renders the lyric obscure, until we recall that one of the oldest uses of "musty" in the language is, according to the OED, "of or relating to must or new wine; made with must; (of wine or beer) not yet fermented, in a state of newness." Furthermore, one of the OED's definitions of "hummer" is "false or mistaken arrest." "All the stuff got bum and bummer" is also somewhat obscure, until we consider that one of the definitions offered by the OED is "of poor, wretched, or miserable quality." And "stuff," meaning bootlegged or illegal whisky, was, according to Harold Wentworth and Stuart Berg Flexner, in common use in early Prohibition-era days (526). This lament about the dwindling availability and quality of legal alcohol in the months before Prohibition went into effect, then, ends in a chorus that celebrates the newly illegal "stuff."

How this excursion into the vocabulary of an old Prohibition-era drinking song might help us read Crane's poem becomes evident when we consider that one of the strategies of "Lachrymae Christi" is also the use of obscure vocabulary, much of it related to alcohol; however, it is also of interest that Crane seems to recontextualize his words. Take, for example, these lines:

Twanged red perfidies of spring
Are trillion on the hill.

(19)

These lines can be read most easily as a reference to the crowds that surrounded the crucified Christ; yet it is also the case that "twang" in one of its meanings was an Australian slang term for opium, and that "trill" can "of tears, water, a stream" (OED). Like the benzene (Crane's is an archaic spelling) of the poem's opening line, it seems as if the dense imagery of the poem has many allusions to illegal intoxicants, and the poem can be read as an intertwined helix that both concerns the emergence of Prohibition and constitutes a meditation on death and resurrection, using the image and story of Christ as its foundation. In this, we might find at least two points of linkage with the song Williams sings. The first is, of course, thematic. The other, though, might be compositional, in that the poem deploys both common words conveying double meanings, and obscure words whose meanings are commonplace. Both poem and song engage in similar strategies, and one might, then, think of the poem as a kind of response to the song in a more complex way than may be apparent at first.

{ 3 }

In Rexroth's remarkable memoir about the early years of modernism, the poet gives many examples of the sorts of associations I have been making about the relationship of black culture to the larger one in the early days of the twentieth century. Rexroth was born in 1905 in South Bend, Indiana, to well-to-do parents and spent his childhood in the small towns of the Midwest. He speaks of his childhood in Indiana, where the abolitionist traditions were still strong: "The towns of northern Indiana lying along the Michigan border had been the last stops on the Underground Railway. They had a good many Negro freedmen living in them. Elkhart became one of the centers of the Ku Klux Klan only fifteen years after that, but in my days there if you called a man a nigger in the street a white man would very likely walk up to you and knock you down. People today have no idea how living a thing the Abolitionist spirit was as late as 1914" (27).

As Rexroth suggests and as I argue, in the northern part of the United States, including sections like the small-town Middle America that Rexroth grew up in, African Americans were not as segregated as they would become after the First World War. Indeed, an attentive reading of the poet's memoir shows that they were often very much a part of their communities. Black people were also a part of the poet's life, including his aesthetic education and work as an artist, from his earliest years. He remembers hearing musicians from the Clef Club when he was a boy (xv), and he himself thought he had both American Indian and African American ancestors (7–8). He had an uncle who owned a barbershop in Columbus, Ohio, staffed by black barbers (5). Later, when the family moved to Battle Creek, Michigan, his parents entertained traveling African American speakers, including Josephine St. Pierre Ruffin, Mary Church Terrell, and Ida Wells Barnett (62).

Rexroth also lived in Toledo during part of his childhood, and spent a couple of summers living and working on a farm in Michigan that had been owned by his father. The farm's tenants consisted of two sisters and their elderly mother; they were all suffragettes and socialists. He writes about the family on the neighboring farm:

> On the next farm lived a family descended from pre–Civil War Negro freed-men. They had several children near my own age with whom I spent the happiest hours of those Toledo years. There was a picture of Harriet Tubman on the parlor wall and works by Frederick Douglass and John Langston on the shelves, along with the first poets of the Negro Renaissance and W. E. B. Du Bois's *The Souls of Black Folk*, and a thrilling book, *The Ethiopian Cicero*: a collection of speeches of Negro Senators, Congressmen, legislators, and governors from Reconstruction days, ending with their final speeches–"Some day we will return." (95–96)[2]

The aspect of this reminiscence that I want to draw readers' attention to has to do with the point I made in the introduction to this book, that the lives of African Americans and whites were not as separate in the early part of the twentieth century as they were to become later, and that it was entirely possible for a young modernist artist such as Rexroth to have had this kind of neighborly interaction with black people and thereby be introduced to African American literary culture. Throughout his memoir, Rexroth shows an easy familiarity with African American literary as well as musical culture. (Curiously, he shows almost no knowledge of black *visual* culture, despite the fact that Chicago, where he spent his late teens and early twenties and where some of the most thrilling episodes of *An Autobiographical Novel* take place, also harbored an active community of African American painters. Archibald Motley, in particular, was active in Chicago in the middle 1920s.)

Rexroth's intimate knowledge of black culture was hardly unique among white artists of his time, but where he is open about this knowledge, many others have offered only a (to me at least) puzzling silence. The poet talks about his work as co-secretary, in San Francisco, of the left-wing League of Struggle for Negro Rights, an organization that had, for a time, Langston Hughes as its president (Rexroth 422; Rampersad 217). Such connections were not simply social; Rexroth related that when he was reading poetry to jazz in Chicago in the 1920s, the only other poet who was attempting the same thing at the time was Hughes (Rexroth 168).

Not enough has been written concerning the stature of Langston Hughes in twentieth-century literature, and the reason for that has to do with my central argument. One might consider this book a kind of prelude to the book that needs to be written about Hughes, one that does not limit itself to explicating the poet's own (partially) self-made image as the "Poet of the Negro People" but begins to ask questions about Hughes's poetic project, taking as a starting point his involvement in African American culture but inquiring more broadly about his poetics. "Let us invent an idiom for the proper transposition of jazz into words!" wrote poet Hart Crane in a 1922 letter to Allen Tate. "Something clean, sparkling, elusive!" (Weber 89). One can argue whether Crane achieved this objective; but there is little question that one of the distinguishing characteristics of modernist poetry is that as a whole, it did do so, and the role of Hughes in this development, in the establishment of how a poem is understood to be modern, is a subject worthy of study.

{ 4 }

Aside from the work of uncovering the relationships and links between black culture and the majority culture in the making of modern culture as such, much work needs to be done in fleshing out some of the historical and aesthetic concerns broached in this study. That we lack a full picture of the breadth of modernist culture is evident by the lack of modern full-length studies of some of the figures written about in this book. This is especially true of the African American writers, but it is also true of others. Although we lack either a modern full-length biography or a sufficiently serious critical study of Paul Laurence Dunbar, he is not the only one. One wonders if more can be done on the work of Asian American writers such as Sadakichi Hartmann. More work needs to be done on such figures as James A. Bland and William Stanley Braithwaite. There are Harlem Renaissance figures— Jessie Redmon Fauset, James Weldon Johnson, Alice Moore Dunbar Nelson, Angelina Weld Grimké—who also need more attention. Further, investigations are needed into the influences and interactions between these artists and the larger society. For example, there have been a few essays on Braithwaite and the work he did in publishing the *Anthology of Magazine Verse*, but a full-length study could examine, in depth, its effect on the growth of modernist poetry.

The Braithwaite anthologies, as Lorenzo Thomas and Craig S. Abbott have pointed out, were an integral part of the growth of modern poetry in the second and third decades of the twentieth century, and Lisa Szefel's penetrating essay on Braithwaite's career shows that he was a significant literary celebrity in his day; it is hard to overestimate his importance to the poetry scene of those days. Abbot's work gives a taste of what is possible in examining these anthologies. And we might point, once again, to Hart Crane to get a glimpse of how poets felt about being asked to contribute to them. Here is Crane in a 1922 letter, written from Cleveland, to Gorham Munson in response to the rejection by the *Dial* of his poem "For the Marriage of Faustus and Helen" (it was subsequently accepted by *Broom*): "This wholesale 'fertilization' of America by such half-baked people as the Algonquin gang is one of the most depressing features of all, because it is without any sense of values. Ben Hecht and Eliot get equal honors in such company. But at any rate I can rival you in some ways. Where you have Untermeyer, I can trot out Braithwaite. A letter from Braithwaite came last week inviting or rather soliciting my 'Praise for an Urn' for the 1922 Anthology" (*Letters of Hart Crane* 104).

The poets who accompany Crane in the *Anthology* for 1922 include many of the best writers of the day: Maxwell Anderson, John Peale Bishop, Louise Brogan, Louise Bryant, Witter Bynner, E. E. Cummings, H.D., Max Eastman, Du Bose Heywood, Georgia Douglas Johnson, Amy Lowell, Claude McKay, Harriet Monroe, Edward Arlington Robinson, Leonora Speyer, Wallace Stevens, Sara Teasdale, Louis Untermeyer, John Hall Wheelock, Clement Wood, and Elinor Wylie, among others. And this partial list is typical of the contents of the anthologies Braithwaite edited. It is small wonder, then, that Crane was so enthusiastic at the prospect of appearing in the 1922 edition but curious how little attention this singular project in the history of American poetry has received. Although that attention is growing, the fact that no modern book-length study exists on Braithwaite and his work suggests just how open the prospects are for a re-examination of the literary history of modernism, one that focuses on the overlooked contributions of black Americans to the modernist project.

I have tried to support and join the conversation of those who want to oppose the approach to thinking about African American literary culture in terms that resemble what Milan Kundera calls, in a somewhat different context, "the provincialism of small nations." For Kundera, provincialism is "the inability (or the refusal) to see one's own culture in the *large context*"

(37; original emphasis). Small nations resist seeing their own culture in the large context, he writes, because they feel a certain inability to participate in that context:

> They hold world culture in high esteem but feel it to be something alien, a sky above their heads, distant, inaccessible, an ideal reality with little connection to the national literature. The small nation inculcates in its writer the conviction that he belongs to that place alone. To set his gaze beyond the boundary of the homeland, to join his colleagues in the supranational territory of art, is considered pretentious, disdainful of his own people. And since the small nations are often going through situations in which their survival is at stake, they readily manage to present their attitude as morally justified. (37–38)

The tendency is, as Kundera points out, to see the art of small nations as part of the history of nations rather than as part of the history of art. Thinking about the problem in this way helps to explain a central problem facing critics and scholars of African American literature: as I have pointed out, it is almost as if they are demanding too little from the culture at large. For a long time it was vitally necessary to demand and achieve simply the recognition of the right of black literature to exist. Now it is time to ask, and to answer, the question of what role that literature plays in the larger context of American literature. This book is one attempt to pose and answer such questions.

The problems that Kundera identifies are reminiscent of those faced by many scholars of African American literature: hence the term "African American modernism" and its variants. This term places works such as those examined here, like Jean Toomer's *Cane*, in the context of African American history rather than in the context of the history of modernism and modernist poetic language. *Cane*, however, belongs within the history of modernism just as properly as it does within the history of African American cultural and social history. My insistence that the position of *Cane* in the canon of modernism has been misunderstood derives in part from the distinction Kundera is making. I have attempted to open the question of the relationship of Toomer's book to the history of modernism, rather than only to the history of black culture. Similarly, in treating the work of Samuel Beckett, I have attempted to show how, by talking about its relationship to African American minstrelsy, our understanding of his work in relation to the history of art can be broadened. And what of the Harlem Renaissance? Besides its leading writers' place in the history of modern poetry, that literary movement also made important contributions to the development of the realist (and the so-called proletarian) novel, to the feminist novel and other literature by women, and to the detective novel. None of this is news to the scholars of the Harlem Renaissance (or to feminist literary scholars), but works from this movement are still not widely examined in terms of their relationship to their larger context.

At least some of the resistance to the ideas and methodology that I have attempted to promote comes, in part, from those who still insist on studying the literature written by black Americans in provincialist terms, in terms of the history of nations. Such terms were necessary at an earlier stage, when the works of many black writers lay unread and gathering dust in obscure archives. But though it would be premature to say that such a condition no longer exists, it is true that we are in a new situation with regard to the importance that scholarship places on the archival aspect of literary studies concerning texts authored by African Americans; now, the discovery of a "lost" text written by an African American can garner widespread publicity and prestigious publication. Such discoveries will continue to be made, further establishing the canon of African American—and American— literature. This work is vital and necessary. At the same time, will be difficult to see just how deep and widespread the influence of black culture has been on American (and for that matter, Western) culture, and on the history of literature itself, unless we unlock the culture from such provincialism. That can best be done, as this book has attempted to argue, by going beyond historicity to pose aesthetic questions as well.

NOTES

INTRODUCTION

1. Paul Laurence Dunbar lets us glimpse the decline of the ubiquity of the southern black barber in his 1901 novel *The Sport of the Gods.* Joe Hamilton, driven in disgrace from the white "Tonsorial Parlors" where he had been employed, tries to find work among the town's black barbers but is rejected. "You're a white man's bahbah," one black barbershop proprietor tells him (67).

2. This question is very much in the spirit of the same question as it was raised by Mary Helen Washington ("Disturbing the Peace") with regard to the discipline of American Studies. Indeed, the present book can be seen as an instance of taking up her call to explore this very idea.

3. On the occupations of the African American population of Philadelphia, see Du Bois, *Philadelphia Negro* 96–146; on caterers, see 32–39, and 119–21. For a study of occupations generally, with comparative data on African Americans and European immigrant groups, see Lieberson 292–360. For a discussion of *Philadelphia Negro* and of the "talented tenth," including data on its size, see Lewis, 179–210, 288–91, and 644 n 51.

4. One commercial, for a New York City clothing store, used the version recorded by Jimmy Rushing with the Dave Brubeck Trio. See BZ/Client Projects. Also see Brubeck and Rushing.

5. For a history of Black Swan records, see Suisman.

6. Cristanne Miller also identifies the "Hero" as a tour guide. The guide's gender is not mentioned, but in the parlance of the day the word "Negro," when used as a proper noun, was taken to be masculine and to signify a man (Webster's *Collegiate Dictionary,* 5th ed.).

7. This poem first appeared, in *Poetry* 40 (June 1932): 119–28, as the third part of a sequence titled "Part of a Poem, Part of a Novel, Part of a Play." See Schulman, 415.

1. HAUNTED

1. See Du Bois, *Souls of Black Folk* 154–64. "Deep River" was published in an art song arrangement by Harry T. Burleigh in 1916. "With 'Deep River' Burleigh created a new format, sometimes known as the art song spiritual," write Doris Evans McGinty and Wayne Shirley. By doing so, Burleigh "opened the door for the inclusion of the spiritual on vocal solo recitals" (108). Among those who recorded the song were Roland Hayes, Nettie Moore, John McCormack, and Paul Robeson.

2. In chapter 4 I take up some of these issues again, in an examination of the art of Bert Williams.

3. Butler herself has supplied us with this warning in *Gender Trouble* (xvi).

4. Dillard, in his survey of the research, does not mention Hurston's essay, which had just come back into print with the republication of Cunard's *Negro,* two years before the publication of Dillard's book.

5. All citations are from the Turtle Island edition.

6. Bodacious: an adjective meaning "complete, thorough, arrant," according to the Oxford English Dictionary (OED), which cites its first use as 1833 and regards it as a variant of an English dialect word. Major, who gives the definitions "extreme; exceedingly excessive; grand," dates its appearance in English from the 1680s and claims that its root word is *botesha*, from the Bantu language (50).

7. Hurston renders the poem in couplets, for reasons that are unclear. In Hughes's *Collected Poems*, it is rendered ijn quatrains. I have chosen to use the latter, since it is the authoritative source for this poem.

8. For an extensive musical analysis of the song, see Friedwald, 39–74.

9. The Gullah people are occupants of the Sea Islands off the coast of Georgia. These people have occupied a legendary status in African American culture because they have been able to retain much of their African culture, since they have been living in relative isolation since arriving on the islands in the seventeenth centure. See Apppiah and Gates.

2. LYRIC

1. I use the distinction between "verse" and "chorus" as it is understood by song writers and music historians. The "verse" is the introduction of the song, which usually carries dramatic and scene-setting content; the "chorus" is a kind of response to the situation or scene set by the "verse." This form seems to be related to the "call and response" form that emerged from African American sacred music (see L. Jones, *Blues People* 62).

2. The song, "Carry Me Back to Old Virginny," became a source of heated controversy in the late 1990s. In 1997 the Virginia state legislature, ceding to demands by African American constituents who were angry at the song's affectionate references to plantation life, voted to replace it. See Sacks 187.

3. The verse printed by Arna Bomtemps in his poetry anthology, *Golden Slippers*, differs somewhat from the original song lyrics. He regularized some spellings ("yer" becomes "you") and made others irregular ("And" becomes "An"). Bontemps's book remained in print for at least a quarter century after its initial publication and was one popular source for the lyrics of the song (Bontemps, *Golden Slippers* 118–21). While sticking to Bontemps's lineation, I have used, here, the 1879 lyrics as published by the music publisher John F. Perry of Boston. These are available at the Library of Congress American Memory website.

4. While I was preparing this chapter, this occurred twice in private conversations: with Amina S. Parker (September 4, 2003) in her account of her childhood memory of the song; and with Rachel Rubin (September 6, 2003), who began singing the song as a way of showing her familiarity with it.

5. On these characteristics of the utterance, see Bakhtin, "Problem" 79–81.

6. For a discussion of the history of the word "cliché," see Pickrel.

7. I place the term "Negro dialect" in quotation marks here to distinguish it from spoken speech and to point to its character as a stage and literary form. All subsequent uses of the term in this study should be understood as signifying this meaning.

8. On lynching, see Litwack; Patterson gives an insightful analysis of the symbolism behind the practice.

9. Cunningham writes that Dunbar would recite Poe at public literary gatherings. Bruce (*Black American Writing from the Nadir* 79) cites echoes of Blake in Dunbar's poetry.

10. There is no satisfactory critical edition of Dunbar's poetry. The same poem may differ in its line breaks in each of the texts used in this chapter. I am using selections from the various texts listed in the bibliography according to how the chosen poem best fits the discussion at hand.

11. It should be remembered that the poem appeared during the earliest days of mass advertising—before radio and television, to be sure, but certainly during the time when advertisements using songs began to appear as part of popular culture.

12. Dunbar's poem first appeared in *Majors and Minors* (1895). It is possible that he knew Wyatt's poem. The most recent edition of Wyatt then available was probably the Aldine edition of 1866. *Tottel's Miscellany*, where that poem first appeared, was also in print in the United States at that time, in editions published in 1854 (Little, Brown) and 1870 (Houghton Mifflin). I am indebted to James Smethurst for this information. Moreover, W. E. Simonds's study of Wyatt's three rondeaux appeared in 1891 in *Modern Language Notes*. Alice M. Dunbar contributed to this journal, though her article did not appear until 1909, some three years after Paul Laurence Dunbar's death.

3. MINSTREL

1. Williams recorded at least three versions of "Nobody" (Charters 149–51), two in 1906, one on a cylinder, the other on ten-inch disk, another in 1913. The verse quoted here is from the 1913 recordings. Charters offers the published sheet music of the song (135–37), which varies slightly from the recorded versions.

2. "Song of the Open Road" immediately precedes "Crossing Brooklyn Ferry" in the standard, or so-called "Death-Bed," edition of *Leaves of Grass*.

3. For an analysis of Crane's poem, see Berthoff, 100–102.

4. Various biographers differ on where Williams was born. Ann Charters and Mabel Rowland, for example, have his birthplace as Antigua. Eric Ledell Smith, however, refers to Williams's birth certificate of 12 November 1874, which gives the comedian's birthplace as Nassau, in the Bahamas (236).

5. On Godot and music hall theater techniques, see Bradby 38–40.

6. On Twain's satire and the Elizabethan revival, see Reardon.

7. One late example of this motif can be seen in the film *Rufus Jones for President* (1933), starring Ethel Waters and Sammy Davis Jr. in his first film role. See Watkins, 214.

4. VAUDEVILLE

1. On the relationship between the English music hall and the Symbolist poets, see Adlard; Faulk; J. Gordon; and Kermode, 127–40.

2. On Seldes's book, see North, *Reading* 1922, 140–72.

3. These criticisms may be especially unfair to Krehbiel, who, despite his use of the offensive "savages" (65), wrote a landmark book on black music, cited Booker T. Washington and W. E. B. Du Bois in the book's preface, and printed several songs arranged by Harry T. Burleigh.

4. At that time, Paul Whiteman was the most famous bandleader in the country, but his ascension to that post was in some ways accidental. James Reese Europe, the most

famous of the African American bandleaders, was murdered in 1919, and it was not until the mid-1920s that a black bandleader of his stature would again emerge, when Fletcher Henderson's band became the first nationally known black-led jazz orchestra of the era. See Charters and Kunstadt; Jacques. On Europe, see Badger.

5. For some reason, the date given in Eliot's *Selected Essays* (1935) is 1923. Quotations given here are from the essay as it appeared in the *Dial*.

6. Ronald Schuchard writes that when Eliot arrived in London in 1914, "he was already steeped in American vaudeville and minstrel shows"; in the later 1920s he would entertain friends such as I. A. Richards with the 1927 record "Two Black Crows," by the (white) American blackface comic duo Moran and Mack (104, 149).

7. Harry Levin has written a succinct essay covering the topic. For more extensive, book-length explorations, see Bradbury and McFarlane; Karl; and Everdell (363–65), who provides an extensive bibliography.

8. The telegram read by the character Alberto Beddini (Erik Rhodes), follows:

> Come ahead, stop.
> Stop being a sap, stop.
> You can even bring Alberto, stop.
> My husband is stopping at your hotel, stop.
> When do you start, stop.
>
> (*Top Hat*)

9. It is certainly true that by the mid-1920s, most of the contributors to *Poetry* magazine were women—104 in 1923, versus 51 men. See *Poetry: A Magazine of Verse*.

10. Braithwaite edited the *Anthology of Magazine Verse* annually from 1913 to 1929. See Butcher. Also see Szefel; and Thomas 45–73.

11. For a discussion of this book and the milieu from which it arose, see Denning 200–229.

12. See Wimsatt and Brooks. A more succinct, modern version can be found in Dickstein. Both Fekete and Lentricchia have written more critical studies of this subject.

13. Fekete quotes Ransom from "The Aesthetic of Regionalism" in *American Review* 2 (January 1934): 303: "The peculiar institution of slavery set this general area [the South] apart from the rest of the world, gave a spiritual continuity to its many regions, and strengthened them under the reinforcement of 'sectionalism.'" Fekete quotes Tate from his book *Stonewall Jackson: The Good Soldier* (1928, 39): "The institution of slavery was a positive good only in the sense that Calhoun said it was: it had become a necessary element in a stable society." (Tate also wrote a biography of Jefferson Davis, president of the Confederacy.)

14. Broyard became a leading *New York Times* book critic. See Gates, "The Passing of Anatole Broyard." On the concept of hip and hipsters, see Ross, 65–101; and Eversley.

15. See the debate in Frascina for some political implications of Greenberg's argument.

16. For a summary of the political environment in which Greenberg's essay was written, and the political issues at stake, see Guilbaut. Though not attempting to underestimate those issues here, my primary concern is how the rhetoric of "Avant-garde and Kitsch" seems to have signaled a shift in literary and cultural politics which, among other things, displaced black writers and culture from the place they had occupied in the modernist mainstream since the early 1920s.

17. Theodor Adorno, whose writings on popular culture are compared (by Huyssen, among others) with Greenberg's, valorized Arnold Schoenberg's music as the epitome of high art values. It is interesting, though, how Adorno (*Philosophy of Modern Music* 103, 120) in doing so, downplayed Schoenberg's late, tonal works, which the composer wrote after he moved to Los Angeles and became connected with Hollywood. The composer's relationship with film industry musicians is explored in Friedrich 31–59.

18. On the sales of *White Buildings*, see Mariani, *The Broken Tower* 325. Michael Soto writes (180) that *Cane* had sold 653 copies by mid-1928.

19. The OED has this figurative use of the word: "an expert, or one expertly appreciative of, jazz. *Slang* (orig. U.S.)" and follows with a reference from 1922 to John Alden Carpenter's ballet based on the comic strip *Krazy Kat*, by George Herriman; Carpenter called his ballet a "jazz pantomime" (qtd. in Seldes 321–45. 377–79). J. L. Dillard, however, writes that the word's meaning as "a person," "comes from the Wolof 'hipicat,' meaning 'an aware person'"; he says its first English literary usage occurred in 1902, in *The Black Cat Club* by James Corrothers (*Lexicon* 66, 67). Also see Corrothers, esp. 32–37.

20. See Marx, *Capital*, 72.

21. On Bergson and the stream of consciousness idea, see Kern 24–27; and Karl 235–39.

22. Folklorist Newbell Niles Puckett was told in the mid-1920s, by an informant from Keysville, Georgia, that odd numbers were considered "unlucky" (462, 599). Keysville is about forty-five miles east of Sparta, the town on which Toomer's fictional Georgia town of "Sempter" is based. See Foley, "Jean Toomer's Sparta."

CONCLUSION

1. "The Moon Shine On the Moonshine" is a vaudeville prohibition song, with music by Robert Hood Bowers and lyrics by Frances DeWitt. Williams first sang the song in the 1919 Ziegfeld Follies. The musical arrangement on the recording made that year is uncredited.

2. I have so far been unable to locate any book that fits Rexroth's description of *The Ethiopian Cicero*. I suspect that he is referring to *Masterpieces of Negro Eloquence*, a collection of speeches edited by Alice Moore Dunbar. That book contains the well-known January 29, 1901, farewell speech of Rep. George Henry White (R-NC) to the House of Representatives. After White, no African American was elected to Congress for nearly three decades. "This," said White, "is perhaps the Negroes' temporary farewell to the American Congress; but let me say, Phoenix-like he will rise up some day and come again" (Dunbar 241).

WORKS CITED

Abbott, Craig S. "Magazine Verse and Modernism: Braithwaite's Anthologies." *Journal of Modern Literature* 19 (1994): 151–59.

Adlard, John. "Poetry and the Stage Doors of the Nineties." *Review of English Literature* 7.4 (1966): 50–60.

Adorno, Theodor W. "On Lyric Poetry and Society." *Notes to Literature*. Vol. 1. New York: Columbia UP, 1991. 37–54.

———. *Philosophy of Modern Music*. 1948. Trans. Anne G. Mitchell and Wesley V. Blomster. New York: Seabury, 1980.

Allen, James, et al. *Without Sanctuary: Lynching Photography in America*. Santa Fe, N.M.: Twin Palms, 2000.

Anderson, Sherwood. *Winesburg, Ohio*. 1919. New York: Penguin, 1976.

Appiah, Kwame Anthony, and Henry Louis Gates Jr. "Gullah." *Africana: The Encyclopedia of the African and African American Experience*. 2nd ed. *Oxford African American Studies Center*. 27 March 2008. http://www.oxfordaasc.com/public/.

Aptheker, Herbert, ed. *A Documentary History of the Negro People in the United States*. 3 vols. New York: Citadel, 1968.

Aristotle. *Poetics*. Trans. S. H. Butcher. New York: Hill and Wang, 1961.

Armstrong, Louis. "Heebie Jeebies." Rec. 26 February 1926; "West End Blues." Rec. 28 July 1928; "Black and Blue." Rec. 22 July 1929. *Louis Armstrong: From the Original Okeh's*. King Jazz, 1993. 5 vols.

Badger, Reid. *A Life in Ragtime: A Biography of James Reese Europe*. New York: Oxford UP, 1995.

Baker, Houston A., Jr. *Modernism and the Harlem Renaissance*. Chicago: U of Chicago P, 1987.

Bakhtin, Mikhail. "The Problem of Speech Genres." *Speech Genres and Other Late Essays*. Trans. Vern W. McGee. Austin: U of Texas P., 1986. 60–102.

———. *Rabelais and His World*. Trans. Hélène Iswolsky. Bloomington: Indiana UP, 1984.

Bakhtin, M. M. [Mikhail Mikhailovich]. "Forms of Time and of the Chronotope in the Novel." *The Dialogic Imagination: Four Essays*. Austin: U of Texas P, 1992. 84–258.

Barnes, Djuna. *Nightwood*. 1937. New York: New Directions, 1961.

Beckett, Samuel. *Collected Shorter Plays*. New York: Grove, 1984.

———. *Waiting for Godot*. New York: Grove, 1954.

———. "Whoroscope." *Collected Poems in English and French*. New York: Grove, 1977. 1–7.

Behn, Aphra. *Oroonoko*. 1688. New York: Norton, 1973.

Bell, Clive. "Plus de Jazz." *Since Cézanne*. London: Chatto and Windus, 1922.

Benjamin, Walter. "The Work of Art in the Age of Mechanical Reproduction." *Illuminations*. Ed. Hannah Arendt. New York: Schocken, 1969. 217–51.

Bergson, Henri. *Time and Free Will: An Essay on the Immediate Data of Consciousness*. 1889. New York: Harper, 1960.

Berlin, Edward A. *Ragtime: A Musical and Cultural History*. Berkeley, U of California P, 1980.

Berthoff, Warner. *Hart Crane: A Re-Introduction*. Minneapolis: U of Minnesota P, 1989.

Bérubé, Michael. *Marginal Forces / Cultural Centers: Tolson, Pynchon, and the Politics of the Canon*. Ithaca: Cornell UP, 1992.

Bhabha, Homi. *The Location of Culture*. New York: Routledge, 1994.

Blair, Sara. "Modernism and the Politics of Culture." *The Cambridge Companion to Modernism*. Ed. Michael Levenson. Cambridge: Cambridge UP, 1999.

Blake, Eubie. "Baltimore Buzz; In Honeysuckle Time." Piano solo. Emerson 10434. Rec. July 1921. *Shuffle Along*. New World, 1976. NW 260.

Bland, James. "Carry Me Back to Old Virginny," "In the Morning by the Bright Light," "Oh dem Golden Slippers." 1879. Library of Congress American Memory, African-American Sheet Music, 1850–1920. http://memory.loc.gov/ammem/.

———. "Oh, Dem Golden Slippers." 1879. Bontemps, *Golden Slippers*. 118–21.

Blesh, Rudi, and Harriet Janis. *They All Played Ragtime*. 1950. 4th ed. New York: Oak, 1971.

Bloom, Harold. *Wallace Stevens: The Poems of Our Climate*. Ithaca: Cornell UP, 1976.

Blount, Marcellus. "The Preacherly Text: African American Poetry and Vernacular Performance." *PMLA* 107 (1992): 582–93.

Bontemps, Arna. "The Awakening: A Memoir." *The Harlem Renaissance Remembered*. Ed. Arna Bontemps. New York: Dodd, Mead, 1972. 1–26.

———, comp. *Golden Slippers: An Anthology of Negro Poetry for Young Readers*. New York: Harper & Row, 1941.

Bradbury, Malcolm, and James McFarlane, eds. *Modernism: 1890–1930*. London: Penguin, 1981.

Bradby, David. *Beckett: Waiting for Godot*. Cambridge: Cambridge UP, 2001.

Braithwaite, William Stanley, ed. *Anthology of Magazine Verse for 1922 and Yearbook of American Poetry*. Boston: Small, Maynard, 1923.

Brenkman, John. *Culture and Domination*. Ithaca: Cornell UP, 1987.

Brinnin, John Malcolm. *The Third Rose: Gertrude Stein and Her World*. 1959. Reading, Mass.: Addison-Wesley, 1987.

Brooks, Cleanth. *Modern Poetry and the Tradition*. 1939. New York: Oxford UP, 1965.

Brooks, Cleanth, and Robert Penn Warren. *Understanding Poetry*. 1938. 3rd ed. New York: Holt, Rinehart and Winston, 1960.

Brooks, Shelton. "The Darktown Strutters' Ball." Chicago: Will Rossiter, 1917. Library of Congress American Memory, African-American Sheet Music, 1850–1920. http://memory.loc.gov/ammem/.

———. "Some of These Days." *Thirty-Five Song Hits by Great Black Songwriters*. Ed. David A. Jasen. New York: Dover, 1998.

Brown, Sterling. *Negro Poetry and Drama and the Negro in American Fiction*. 1937. New York: Atheneum, 1968.

Brown, William Wells. *Clotel; or, The President's Daughter*. 1853. New York: Carol, 1995.

Broyard, Anatole. "A Portrait of the Hipster." *Partisan Review* 6 (June 1948): 721–27.

Brubeck, Dave, and Jimmy Rushing. *Brubeck and Rushing: The Dave Brubeck Quartet Featuring Jimmy Rushing*. Rec. 1960. Columbia, 1968.

Bruce, Dickson D. *Black American Writing from the Nadir: The Evolution of a Literary Tradition, 1877–1915*. Baton Rouge: Louisiana State UP, 1989.

———. "On Dunbar's 'Jingles in a Broken Tongue': Dunbar's Dialect Poetry and the Afro-American Tradition." *A Singer in the Dawn: Reinterpretations of Paul Laurence Dunbar*. Ed. Jay Martin. New York: Dodd, Mead, 1975. 94–113.

Butcher, Philip. *The William Stanley Braithwaite Reader*. Ann Arbor: U of Michigan P, 1972.

Butler, Judith. *Gender Trouble: Feminism and the Subversion of Identity*. 1990. New York: Routledge, 1999.

BZ/Client Projects. "A Partial Listing of Recent Projects." 28 January 2004. http://www.bzrights.com/projects.htm.

Charters, Ann. *Nobody: The Story of Bert Williams*. New York: Macmillan, 1970.

Charters, Samuel B., and Leonard Kunstadt. *Jazz: A History of the New York Scene.* 1962. New York: Da Capo, 1981.

Chesnutt, Charles. *The Marrow of Tradition*. 1901. New York: Penguin, 1993.

Clarke, Donald. *The Rise and Fall of Popular Music*. New York: St. Martin's, 1995.

Cook, Will Marion. *In Dahomey: The Music and Scripts of "In Dahomey."* Ed. Thomas L. Riis. Madison, Wis. A-R Editions, 1996.

Cornell, Drucilla. *At the Heart of Freedom: Feminism, Sex, and Equality*. Princeton: Princeton UP, 1998.

Corrothers, James David. *The Black Cat Club*. 1902. New York: AMS Press, 1972.

Courlander, Harold. *Negro Folk Music, U.S.A.* 1963. New York: Dover, 1992.

Coyle, Michael, ed. *Ezra Pound and African American Modernism*. Orono, Maine: National Poetry Foundation, 2001.

Crane, Hart. *The Letters of Hart Crane, 1916–1932*. Ed. Brom Weber. Berkeley: University of California Press, 1965.

———. *The Poems of Hart Crane*. Ed. Marc Simon. New York: Liveright, 1986.

Cunard, Nancy. "Negro" (1934). *Negro: An Anthology*. Ed. Hugh Ford. New York: Continuum, 1996.

Cunningham, Virginia. *Paul Laurence Dunbar and His Song*. 1947. New York: Biblo and Tannen, 1969.

Cutler, David M., Edward L. Glasser, and Jacob L. Vigdor. "The Rise and Decline of the American Ghetto." *Journal of Political Economy* 107 (June 1999): 455–506.

Damon, Maria. *The Dark End of the Street: Margins in American Vanguard Poetry*. Minneapolis: U of Minnesota P, 1993.

Davis, Angela Y. *Blues Legacies and Black Feminism: Gertrude 'Ma' Rainey, Bessie Smith, and Billie Holiday*. New York: Vintage, 1999.

Dell, Floyd. *Intellectual Vagabondage*. 1926. Chicago: Ivan R. Dee, 1990.

de Man, Paul. *The Rhetoric of Romanticism*. New York: Columbia University Press,1984.

———. *Romanticism and Contemporary Criticism: The Gauss Seminar and Other Papers*. Ed. E. S. Burt, Kevin Newmark, and Andrzej Warminski. Baltimore: Johns Hopkins UP, 1993.

Denning, Michael. *The Cultural Front: The Laboring of American Culture in the Twentieth Century*. New York: Verso, 1997.

De Witt, Frances (lyrics), and Robert Hood Bowers (music). "The Moon Shines On the Moonshine." New York: Shapiro, Bernstein. Sheet music. New York Public Library, Digital Gallery. http://digitalgallery.nypl.org/nypldigital/.

Dickstein, Morris. *Double Agent: The Critic and Society*. New York: Oxford UP, 1992.

Dillard, J. L. *Black English: Its History and Usage in the United States*. New York: Vintage Books, 1972.

———. *Lexicon of Black English*. New York: Seabury, 1977.

Donoghue, Denis. *Words Alone: The Poet T. S. Eliot*. New Haven: Yale UP, 2000.

Dormon, James H. "Shaping the Popular Image of Post-Reconstruction American Blacks:

The 'Coon Song' Phenomenon of the Gilded Age." *American Quarterly* 40 (1988): 450–71.

Douglas, Ann. *Terrible Honesty: Mongrel Manhattan in the 1920s.* New York: Noonday, 1995.

Dowling, Linda. *Language and Decadence in the Victorian Fin de Siècle.* Princeton: Princeton UP, 1986.

Doyle, Bertram Wilber. *The Etiquette of Race Relations in the South: A Study of Social Control.* 1937. Port Washington, N.Y.: Kennikat Press, 1968.

Doyle, Laura. "The Flat, the Round, and Gertrude Stein: Race and the Shape of Modern(ist) History." *Modernism/Modernity* 7 (2000): 249–71.

Du Bois, W. E. B. *Darkwater: Voices from Within the Veil.* 1920. New York: Dover, 1999.

——. *The Philadelphia Negro: A Social Study.* 1899. New York: Schocken, 1967.

——. *The Souls of Black Folk.* 1903. Ed. Henry Louis Gates Jr. and Terri Hume Oliver. New York: Norton, 1999.

Dunbar, Alice M. "Wordsworth's Use of Milton's Description of the Building of Pandemonium." *Modern Language Notes* 24 (1909): 124–25.

——. *Masterpieces of Negro Eloquence.* 1914. New York: G. K. Hall, 1997.

Dunbar, Paul Laurence. *The Collected Poetry of Paul Laurence Dunbar.* Ed. Joanne M. Braxton. Charlottesville: UP of Virginia, 1993.

——. "Down De Lover's Lane (Plantation Croon)." 1900. Library of Congress American Memory, African-American Sheet Music, 1850–1920. http://memory.loc.gov/ammem/.

——. *The Life and Works of Paul Laurence Dunbar.* Ed. Lida Keck Wiggins. 1905. New York: Kraus, 1971.

——. *Lyrics of Lowly Life.* 1896. New York: Citadel Press, 1984.

——. *The Sport of the Gods.* 1901. New York: Dodd, Mead, 1981.

DuPlessis, Rachel Blau. "'Hoo, Hoo, Hoo': Some Episodes in the Construction of Modern Whiteness." *American Literature* 67 (1995): 667–700.

DuRose, Lisa. "Racial Domain and the Imagination of Wallace Stevens." *The Wallace Stevens Journal* 22.1 (1998): 3–22.

Eliot, T. S. *Complete Poems and Plays, 1909–1950.* New York: Harcourt, 1971.

——. "Marie Lloyd." 1922. *Selected Essays, 1917–1932.* New York: Harcourt, 1932. 369–72.

——. *The Sacred Wood.* 1920. London: Methuen, 1967.

Empson, William. *Seven Types of Ambiguity.* London: Chatto and Windus, 1930.

Epstein, Dena J. "The Folk Banjo: A Documentary History." *Ethnomusicology* 19.3 (1975): 347–71.

Erenberg, Lewis A. *Swingin' the Dream: Big Band Jazz and the Rebirth of American Culture.* Chicago: U of Chicago P, 1998.

Everdell, William R. *The First Moderns: Profiles in the Origins of Twentieth Century Thought.* Chicago: U of Chicago P, 1997.

Eversley, Shelly. "The Source of Hip." *Minnesota Review* 55–57 (2002): 257–70.

Fabre, Geneviève, and Michel Feith, eds. *Jean Toomer and the Harlem Renaissance.* New Brunswick: Rutgers UP, 2001.

Faulk, Barry. "Camp Expertise: Arthur Symons, Music-Hall, and the Defense of Theory." *Victorian Literature and Culture* (2000): 171–93.

Fauset, Jessie Redmon. "The Gift of Laughter." *The New Negro.* Ed. Alain Locke. 1925. New York: Atheneum, 1968. 161–67.

——. "The Symbolism of Bert Williams." *The Crisis Reader.* Ed. Sondra Kathryn Wilson. New York: Modern Library, 1999. 255–59.

Fekete, John. *The Critical Twilight: Explorations in the Ideology of Anglo-American Literary Theory from Eliot to McLuhan*. Boston: Routledge, 1977.

Fletcher, Tom. *100 Years of the Negro in Show Business*. 1954. New York: Da Capo, 1984.

Foley, Barbara. "'In the Land of Cotton': Economics and Violence in Jean Toomer's *Cane*." *African American Review* 32 (1998): 181–98.

———. "Jean Toomer's Sparta." *American Literature* 67 (1995): 747–75.

Foucault, Michel. "Nietzsche, Genealogy, History." *Language, Counter-Memory, Practice*. Ed. Donald F. Bouchard. Ithaca: Cornell UP, 1977.

———. *The Order of Things*. New York: Vintage, 1973.

Fowler, H. W. *A Dictionary of Modern English Usage*. 1926. Hertfordshire: Wordsworth, 1994.

Frascina, Francis, ed. *Pollock and After: The Critical Debate*. New York: Harper, 1985.

Freud, Sigmund. *Jokes and Their Relation to the Unconscious*. 1905. Trans. James Strachey. New York: Norton, 1960.

———. "The Uncanny." 1919. *On Creativity and the Unconscious*. New York: Harper, 1958.

Friedman, Allan Warren, ed. *Beckett in Black and Red: The Translations for Nancy Cunard's Negro (1934)*. Lexington: UP of Kentucky, 2000.

Friedrich, Otto. *City of Nets: A Portrait of Hollywood in the 1940s*. New York: Harper, 1986.

Friedwald, Will. *Stardust Melodies: A Biography of Twelve of America's Most Popular Songs*. New York: Pantheon, 2002.

Gates, Henry Louis, Jr. *Figures in Black: Words, Signs, and the "Racial" Self*. New York: Oxford UP, 1987.

———. "The Passing of Anatole Broyard." *Thirteen Ways of Looking at a Black Man*. New York: Random House, 1997. 180–214.

———. *The Signifying Monkey*. New York: Oxford UP, 1988.

Gordon, Avery F. *Ghostly Matters: Haunting and the Sociological Imagination*. Minneapolis: U of Minnesota P, 1997.

Gordon, Jan B. "The Danse Macabre of Arthur Symons' *London Nights*. *Victorian Poetry* 9.4 (1971): 429–43.

Gordon, Lois. *Reading Godot*. New Haven: Yale UP, 2002.

Green, Lisa. "Aspect and Predicate Phrases in African American Vernacular English." *African American English: Structure, History, and Use*. Ed. Salikoko S. Mufwene, John R. Rickford, Guy Bailey, and John Baugh. London: Routledge, 1998. 37–68.

Greenberg, Clement. "Avant-Garde and Kitsch." 1939. *Art and Culture: Critical Essays*. Boston: Beacon Press, 1961. 3–21.

———. "The Late Thirties in New York." *Art and Culture: Critical Essays*. Boston: Beacon Press, 1961. 230–35.

Greenblatt, Stephen. *Renaissance Self-Fashioning: From More to Shakespeare*. Chicago: U of Chicago P, 1980.

Guilbaut, Serge. *How New York Stole the Idea of Modern Art: Abstract Expressionism, Freedom, and the Cold War*. Trans. Arthur Goldhammer. Chicago: U of Chicago P, 1983.

Hamm, Charles. *Yesterdays: Popular Song in America*. New York: Norton, 1979.

Handy, W. C. [William Christopher]. *Father of the Blues*. 1941. New York: Da Capo, 1969.

———. "The St. Louis Blues." 1914. *American Poetry: The Twentieth Century, Vol. 1*. New York: Library of America, 2000. 89–90.

Harper, Frances E. W. *Iola Leroy*. 1892. Boston: Beacon Press, 1987.

Harrison, Daphne Duval. *Black Pearls: Blues Queens of the 1920s*. New Brunswick: Rutgers UP, 1993.

Harvey, David. *Spaces of Hope*. Berkeley: U of California P. 2000.

Heller, Adele, and Lois Rudnick, eds. *1915: The Cultural Moment*. New Brunswick: Rutgers UP, 1991.

Hicks, Granville, et al. *Proletarian Literature in the United States: An Anthology*. New York: International, 1935.

Hoffman, Frederick J. *Samuel Beckett: The Language of the Self.* New York: Dutton, 1964.

Hovey, Jamie. "Sapphic Primitivism in Gertrude Stein's *Q.E.D.*" *Modern Fiction Studies* 42.3 (1996): 547–68.

Huggins, Nathan. *Harlem Renaissance*. New York: Oxford UP, 1971.

Hughes, Langston. *The Collected Poems of Langston Hughes*. New York: Vintage, 1994.

———. *I Wonder as I Wander*. 1956. New York: Thunder's Mouth Press, 1986.

———. "The Negro Artist and the Racial Mountain." 1926. *The Portable Harlem Renaissance Reader*. Ed. David Levering Lewis. New York: Penguin, 1994. 91–95.

Hullfish, William R. "James R. Bland: Pioneer Black Songwriter." *Black Music Research Journal* 7 (1987): 1–33.

Hunter, Alberta. "Everybody Loves My Baby." *Complete Recorded Works in Chronological Order, Vol. 3 (1924–1927)*. Rec. 6 November 1924. Document, 1996. DOCD 5424.

Hurston, Zora Neale. "Characteristics of Negro Expression." *Negro: An Anthology*. Ed. Nancy Cunard. 1934. *The Sanctified Church: The Collected Folklore Writings of Zora Neale Hurston*. Berkeley: Turtle Island, 1981. 49–68.

Huyssen, Andreas. *After the Great Divide: Modernism, Mass Culture, Postmodernism*. Bloomington: Indiana UP, 1986.

Iser, Wolfgang. *The Fictive and the Imaginary: Charting Literary Anthropology*. Baltimore: Johns Hopkins UP, 1993.

Jacques, Geoffrey. "Listening to Jazz." *American Popular Music: New Approaches to the Twentieth Century*. Ed. Rachel Rubin and Jeffrey Melnick. Amherst: U of Massachusetts P, 2001. 65–92.

Jakobson, Roman. *Language in Literature*. Cambridge: Harvard UP, 1987.

Jasen, David A., ed. *Thirty-Five Songs by Great Black Songwriters: Bert Williams, Eubie Blake, Ernest Hogan and Others*. New York: Dover, 1998.

Jansen, David A., and Gene Jones. *Spreadin' Rhythm Around: Black Popular Songwriters, 1880–1930*. New York: Shirmer, 1998.

Jefferson, Thomas. *Notes on the State of Virginia*. 1785. New York: Harper, 1964.

Jespersen, Otto. *Essentials of English Grammar*. 1933. Tuscaloosa: U of Alabama Press, 1964.

Johnson, Charles. *The Negro Population of Hartford, Connecticut*. New York: National Urban League, 1921. Trinity College Hartford Studies Project. 23 March 2008: http://www.trincoll.edu/UG/UE/HSP/Collection_PD.htm.

Johnson, James Weldon. *Along This Way*. 1933. New York: Penguin, 1990.

———. *Black Manhattan*. 1930. New York: Atheneum, 1968.

———. *The Book of American Negro Poetry*. New York: Harcourt, 1922.

Johnson, James Weldon, and J. Rosamond Johnson. *The Books of American Negro Spirituals*. 2 vols. 1925, 1926. New York: Da Capo, 1981.

Jones, Gavin. *Strange Talk: The Politics of Dialect Literature in Gilded Age America*. Berkeley: U of California P, 1999.

Jones, LeRoi (Baraka, Imamu Amiri). *Blues People: The Negro Experience in White America and the Music That Developed from It*. New York: Morrow, 1963.

Kalaidjian, Walter. *American Culture between the Wars: Revisionary Modernism and Post-modern Critique.* New York: Columbia UP, 1993.

Kant, Immanuel. *Critique of Judgment.* 1790. Trans. J. H. Bernard. New York: Hafner, 1968.

Karl, Frederick R. *Modern and Modernism: The Sovereignty of the Artist, 1885–1925.* New York: Atheneum, 1988.

Keenaghan, Eric. "A Virile Poet in the Borderlands: Wallace Stevens's Reimagining of Race and Masculinity." *Modernism/Modernity* 9 (2002): 439–62.

Kenner, Hugh. *Samuel Beckett: A Critical Study.* New York: Grove, 1961.

Kermode, Frank. *Romantic Image.* 1957. London: Routledge, 2002.

Kern, Stephen. *The Culture of Time and Space, 1880–1918.* Cambridge: Harvard UP, 1983.

Keyser, Samuel Jay. "There Is Method in Their Adness: The Formal Structure of Advertisement." *New Literary History* 14 (1983): 305–34.

Knight, Arthur. *Disintegrating the Musical: Black Performance and American Film.* Durham, N.C.: Duke UP, 2002.

Knowlson, James. *Damned to Fame: The Life of Samuel Beckett.* New York: Touchstone, 1996.

Krasner, David. *A Beautiful Pageant: African American Theatre, Drama and Performance in the Harlem Renaissance, 1910–1927.* New York: Palgrave, 2002.

Krehbiel, Henry Edward. *Afro-American Folksongs: A Study in Racial and National Music.* 1913. New York: Frederick Ungar, 1962.

Kreymborg, Alfred. *An Anthology of American Poetry: Lyric America, 1630–1930.* New York: Tudor, 1930.

Kundera, Milan. *The Curtain: An Essay in Seven Parts.* New York: HarperCollins, 2005.

Lacan, Jacques. *The Seminar of Jacques Lacan, Book 1: Freud's Papers on Technique 1953–54.* Ed. Jacques-Alain Miller. Trans. John Forrester. New York: Norton, 1991.

Lauter, Paul. *Canons and Contexts.* New York: Oxford UP, 1991.

Leavis, F. R. [Frank Raymond]. *New Bearings in English Poetry.* 1932. Ann Arbor: U of Michigan P, 1960.

Lentricchia, Frank. *After the New Criticism.* Chicago: U of Chicago P, 1980.

Levenson, Michael H. *A Genealogy of Modernism: A Study of English Literary Doctrine 1908–1922.* Cambridge: Cambridge UP, 1984.

Levin, Harry. "What Was Modernism?" *Refractions: Essays in Comparative Literature.* New York: Oxford UP, 1966. 271–95.

Lewis, David Levering. *W. E. B. Du Bois: Biography of a Race, 1868–1919.* New York: Henry Holt, 1993.

Lieberson, Stanley. *A Piece of the Pie: Black and White Immigrants since 1880.* Berkeley: U of California P, 1980.

Lincoln, Abbey. *Straight Ahead.* Rec. 22 February 1961. Candid, 1961. CCD79015.

Litwack, Leon F. "Hellhounds." *Without Sanctuary: Lynching Photography in America.* Santa Fe, N.Mex.: Twin Palms, 2000. 8–37.

Logan, Rayford. *The Betrayal of the Negro: From Rutherford B. Hayes to Woodrow Wilson.* 1954. New York: Da Capo, 1997.

Lott, Eric. *Love and Theft: Blackface Minstrelsy and the American Working Class.* New York: Oxford UP, 1995.

Macey, David, ed. *The Penguin Dictionary of Critical Theory.* London: Penguin, 2000.

Mackey, Nathaniel. *Discrepant Engagement: Dissonance, Cross-Culturality, and Experimental Writing.* 1993. Tuscaloosa: U of Alabama P, 2000.

Magnis, Nicholas E. "Thomas Jefferson and Slavery: An Analysis of His Racist Thinking as Revealed by His Writings and Political Behavior." *Journal of Black Studies* 29 (1999): 491–509.

Mahar, William J. "Black English in Early Blackface Minstrelsy: A New Interpretation of the Sources of Blackface Dialect." *American Quarterly* 37 (1985): 260–85.

Major, Clarence. *Juba to Jive: A Dictionary of African American Slang.* New York: Penguin, 1994.

Mariani, Paul. *The Broken Tower: The Life of Hart Crane.* New York: Norton, 1999.

———. *William Carlos Williams: A New World Naked.* New York: McGraw-Hill, 1981.

Martin, Jay, ed. *A Singer in the Dawn: Reinterpretations of Paul Laurence Dunbar.* New York: Dodd, Mead, 1975.

Marx, Edward. "'The Idea of a Colony': Primitivism and Exoticism in Modern Poetry." Diss. City U of New York, 1995.

Marx, Karl. *Capital, Vol. 1: A Critical Analysis of Capitalist Production.* 1867. New York: International, 1967.

———. *The Eighteenth Brumaire of Louis Bonaparte.* 1852. New York: International, 1963.

Massey, Douglas S., and Nancy A. Denton. *American Apartheid: Segregation and the Making of the Underclass.* Cambridge: Harvard UP, 1993.

Matthiessen, F. O. *The Achievement of T. S. Eliot: An Essay on the Nature of Poetry.* 1935. New York: Oxford UP, 1958.

McGinty, Doris Evans, and Wayne Shirley. "Paul Robeson, Musician." Paul Robeson: *Artist and Citizen.* Ed. Jeffrey C. Stewart. New Brunswick: Rutgers UP, 1998. 105–20.

Mehaffy, Marilyn Maness. "Advertising Race/Raceing Advertising: The Feminine Consumer (Nation), 1876–1900." *Signs: Journal of Women in Culture and Society* 23 (1997): 131–74.

Melnick, Jeffrey. *A Right to Sing the Blues: African Americans, Jews, and American Popular Song.* Cambridge: Harvard UP, 1999.

Michlin, Monica. "Karintha: A Textual Analysis." *Jean Toomer and the Harlem Renaissance.* Ed. Geneviève Fabre and Michel Feith. New Brunswick: Rutgers UP, 2001. 96–108.

Miller, Cristanne. "Marianne Moore's Black Maternal Hero: A Study in Categorization." *American Literary History* 1 (1989): 786–815.

Miller, Nina. *Making Love Modern: The Intimate Public Worlds of New York's Literary Women.* New York: Oxford UP, 1998.

Moore, Marianne. *Complete Poems.* New York: Macmillan, 1981.

Morrison, Toni. *Playing in the Dark: Whiteness and the Literary Imagination.* Cambridge: Harvard UP, 1992.

Mufwene, Salikoko. "The Structure of the Noun Phrase in African American Vernacular English." *African American English: Structure, History, and Use.* Ed. Salikoko S. Mufwene, John R. Rickford, Guy Bailey, and John Baugh. New York: Routledge, 1998. 69–81.

"Negro." *Webster's Collegiate Dictionary.* 5th ed. 1942.

Nelson, Cary. *Repression and Recovery: Modern American Poetry and the Politics of Cultural Memory, 1910–1945.* Madison: U of Wisconsin P, 1989.

Nielsen, Aldon Lynn. *Black Chant: Languages of African American Postmodernism.* New York: Cambridge UP, 1997.

———. *Reading Race: White American Poets and the Racial Discourse in the Twentieth Century.* Athens: The U of Georgia P, 1988.

Nietzsche, Friedrich. *The Birth of Tragedy*. 1872. New York: Penguin, 1993.

North, Michael. *The Dialect of Modernism: Race, Language, and Twentieth-Century Literature*. New York: Oxford UP, 1994.

———. *Reading 1922: A Return to the Scene of the Modern*. New York: Oxford UP, 1999.

Odum, Howard W. "Folk-Song and Folk-Poetry as Found in the Secular Songs of the Southern Negroes." 1911. *Write Me a Few of Your Lines: A Blues Reader*. Ed. Steven C. Tracy. Amherst: U of Massachusetts P, 1999. 133–71.

Ogburn, Floyd, Jr. "Structure and Meaning in Thomas Jefferson's *Notes on the State of Virginia*." *Early American Literature* 25 (1980): 141–50.

Ohmann, Richard. *Selling Culture: Magazines, Markets, and Class at the Turn of the Century*. London: Verso, 1996.

O'Kane, Karen. "Before the New Criticism: Modernism and the Nashville Group." *Mississippi Quarterly: The Journal of Southern Cultures* 51.4 (1998): 683–97.

Olson, Charles. "Projective Verse." *Charles Olson: Selected Writings*. Ed. Robert Creeley. New York: New Directions, 1966. 13–26.

Ong, Walter J. *Orality and Literacy: The Technologizing of the Word*. New York: Methuen, 1982.

Ovington, Mary White. *Half a Man: The Status of the Negro in New York*. 1911. New York: Schocken, 1969.

Parry, Milman. *The Making of Homeric Verse: The Collected Papers of Milman Parry*. Ed. Adam Parry. Oxford: Clarendon Press, 1971.

Patterson, Orlando. *Rituals of Blood: Consequences of Slavery in Two American Centuries*. New York: Basic Books, 1998.

Perloff, Marjorie. *The Futurist Moment: Avant-Garde, Avant Guerre, and the Language of Rupture*. Chicago: U of Chicago P, 1986.

Peterson, Carla. "The Remaking of Americans: Gertrude Stein's 'Melanctha' and African American Musical Traditions." *Criticism and the Color Line: Desegregating American Literary Studies*. Ed. Henry B. Wonham. New Brunswick: Rutgers UP, 1996. 140–57.

Pickrel, Paul. "Identifying Clichés." *College English* 47 (1985): 252–61.

Poetry: A Magazine of Verse. Vols. 21–23 (1922–1924). New York: AMS, 1966.

Pound, Ezra. *Personae*. 1926. New York: New Directions, 1971.

Puckett, Newbell Niles. *The Magic and Folk Beliefs of the Southern Negro*. 1926. New York: Dover, 1969.

Rampersad, Arnold. *The Life of Langston Hughes, Vol. 1: 1902–1941*. New York: Oxford UP, 1986.

Reardon, John D. " 'Shakespearean Revival!!!' Satire of Elizabethans." *Mark Twain Journal* 21 (1983): 36–38.

Redding, J. Saunders. "Portrait Against Background." *A Singer in the Dawn: Reinterpretations of Paul Lawrence Dunbar*. Ed. Jay Martin. New York: Dodd Mead, 1975. 39–44.

———. *To Make a Poet Black*. 1939. Ithaca: Cornell UP, 1988.

Rexroth, Kenneth. *An Autobiographical Novel*. 1964. Rev. and exp. ed. Ed. Linda Hamalian. New York: New Directions, 1991.

Richards, I. A. [Ivor Armstrong]. *Practical Criticism*. 1929. New York: Harcourt Brace Jananovich, 1978.

Richardson, Joan. *Wallace Stevens, A Biography: The Early Years, 1879–1923*. New York: Beech Tree, 1986.

Riddel, Joseph. "Hart Crane's Poetics of Failure." *ELH* 33.4 (1966): 473–96.

Riis, Thomas L. *Just before Jazz: Black Musical Theater in New York, 1890 to 1915*. Washington, D.C.: Smithsonian, 1989.

———. *More than Just Minstrel Shows: The Rise of Black Musical Theatre at the Turn of the Century*. New York: Institute for Studies in American Music, Conservatory of Music, Brooklyn College of the City U of New York, 1992.

Rogin, Michael. *Blackface, White Noise: Jewish Immigrants in the Hollywood Melting Pot*. Berkeley: U of California P, 1996.

Ross, Andrew. *No Respect: Intellectuals and Popular Culture*. New York: Routledge, 1989.

Rowland, Mabel, ed. *Bert Williams: Son of Laughter*. 1923. New York: Negro Universities Press, 1969.

Rufus Jones for President. Dir. Roy Mack. Perf. Sammy Davis Jr. and Ethel Waters. Warner Brothers, 1933.

Sacks, Howard L. "Turning About Jim Crow." *American Quarterly* 51.1 (March 1999): 187–94.

Sánchez González, Lisa. *Boricua Literature: A History of the Puerto Rican Diaspora*. New York: New York UP, 2001.

Sanders, Mark A. *Afro-Modernist Aesthetics and the Poetry of Sterling A. Brown*. Athens: U of Georgia P, 1999.

Schuchard, Ronald. *Eliot's Dark Angel: Intersections of Life and Art*. Oxford: Oxford UP, 1999.

Schulman, Grace, ed. *The Poems of Marianne Moore*. New York: Viking, 2003.

Scott, Bonnie Kime, ed. *The Gender of Modernism: A Critical Anthology*. Bloomington: Indiana UP, 1990.

Seelye, John D. "The American Tramp: A Version of the Picaresque." *American Quarterly* 15 (1963): 535–53.

Seldes, Gilbert. *The Seven Lively Arts*. 1924. New York: Dover, 2001.

Sherman, Joan R. *Invisible Poets: Afro-Americans of the Nineteenth Century*. 2nd ed. Urbana: U of Illinois P, 1989.

Simonds, W. E. "The Three Rondeaux of Sir Thomas Wyatt." *Modern Language Notes* 6 (1891): 89–92.

Smedman, Lorna. "'Cousin to Cooning': Relation, Difference, and Racialized Language in Stein's Nonrepresentational Texts." *Modern Fiction Studies* 42 (1996): 569–88.

Smethurst, James Edward. *The New Red Negro: The Literary Left and African American Poetry, 1930–1946*. New York: Oxford UP, 1999.

Smith, Bessie. "The St. Louis Blues," by William Christopher Handy. Rec. January 14, 1925. *Bessie Smith: The Complete Recordings, Vol. 2*. Columbia, 1991.

Smith, Eric Ledell. *Bert Williams: A Biography of the Pioneer Black Comedian*. Jefferson, N.C.: McFarland, 1992.

Smolin, Lee. "The Other Einstein." *New York Review of Books*, 14 June 2007: 76–83.

Snyder, Robert W. *The Voice of the City: Vaudeville and Popular Culture in New York*. 1989. Chicago: Dee, 2000.

Soto, Michael. "Jean Toomer and Horace Liveright; or, The New Negro Gets 'into the Swing of It.'" *Jean Toomer and the Harlem Renaissance*. Ed. Geneviève Fabre and Michel Feith. New Brunswick: Rutgers UP, 2001. 162–87.

Southern, Eileen. *The Music of Black Americans: A History*. 2nd ed. New York: Norton, 1983.

Statistical History of the United States from Colonial Times to the Present. Stamford, Conn.: Fairfield, 1965.

Stein, Gertrude. *Fernhurst, Q.E.D., and Other Early Writings*. 1971. New York: Liveright, 1983.

———. "Tender Buttons." 1914. *Selected Writings*. Ed. Carl Van Vechten. New York: Random House, 1962. 459–509.

Stevens, Wallace. *Collected Poems*. New York: Vintage, 1982.

———. *Harmonium*. 1923. London: Faber and Faber, 2001.

———. *Opus Posthumous*. Ed. Samuel French Morse. New York: Vintage, 1980.

Stoljar, Margaret. "Mirror and Self in Symbolist and Post-Symbolist Poetry." *Modern Language Review* 85 (1990): 362–72.

Stormy Weather. Dir. Andrew Stone. Perf. Lena Horne, Bill Robinson, Cab Calloway, Fats Waller, Dooley Wilson, Ada Brown, and Flournoy Miller. Twentieth Century Fox, 1943.

Suisman, David. "Co-workers in the Kingdom of Culture: Black Swan Records and the Political Economy of African America." *Journal of American History* 90 (2004): 1295–324.

Sundquist, Eric J. *To Wake the Nations: Race in the Making of American Literature*. Cambridge: Harvard UP, 1993.

Symons, Arthur. *Selected Writings*. Ed. Roger Holdsworth. 1989. New York: Vintage, 1972. 459–509.

———. *The Symbolist Movement in Literature*. 1899. New York: Dutton, 1958.

Szefel, Lisa. "Encouraging Verse: William S. Braithwaite and the Poetics of Race." *New England Quarterly* 74 (2001): 32–61.

Taeuber, Karl E., and Alma F. Taeuber. *Negroes in Cities*. Chicago: Aldine, 1965.

Thomas, Lorenzo. *Extraordinary Measures: Afrocentric Modernism and Twentieth Century Poetry*. Tuscaloosa: U of Alabama P, 2000.

Tolnay, Stewart E., Kyle D. Crowder, and Robert M. Adelman. " 'Narrow and Filthy Alleys of the City'?: The Residential Settlement Patterns of Black Southern Migrants to the North." *Social Forces* 79 (2000): 989–1015.

Toomer, Jean. *Cane*. 1923. Ed. Darwin T. Turner. New York: Norton, 1988.

Top Hat. Dir. Mark Sandrich. Perf. Fred Astaire, Ginger Rogers, Edward Everett Horton, and Erik Rhodes. Choreographer Fred Astaire. Music Irving Berlin. RKO, 1935.

Tuckel, Peter, Kurt Schlichting, and Richard Maisel. "Social, Economic, and Residential Diversity within Hartford's African American Community at the Beginning of the Great Migration." *Journal of Black Studies* 37.5 (2007): 710–36.

Turco, Lewis. *The Book of Forms: A Handbook of Poetics*. Hanover, N.H.: UP of New England, 2000.

Twain, Mark. *Adventures of Huckleberry Finn*. 1885. Berkeley: U of California P, 1985.

Untermeyer, Louis, ed. *Modern American Poetry: A Critical Anthology*. 3rd rev. ed. New York: Harcourt, Brace, 1925.

Vendler, Helen Hennessy. *On Extended Wings: Wallace Stevens' Longer Poems*. Cambridge: Harvard UP, 1969.

———. "Stevens' 'Like Decorations in a Nigger Cemetery.' " *Massachusetts Review* 7 (1966): 136–46.

Waller, Thomas "Fats." "Oh! Dem Golden Slippers." Rec. 20 November 1939. *The Amazing Fats Waller: Then You'll Remember Me*. Solo Art, 2001.

Washington, Booker T. *Up from Slavery*. 1901. New York: Penguin, 1986.

Washington, Mary Helen. " 'Disturbing the Peace: What Happens to American Studies if You Put African American Studies at the Center?' Presidential Address to the American Studies Association, 29 October 1997. *American Quarterly* 50 (1998): 1–23.

Waters, Ethel. "There'll Be Some Changes Made." Lyrics by Billy Higgins, music by W. Benton Overstreet. Black Swan 2021. Rec. August 1921. *Ethel Waters, 1921–1923*. Classics, 1994. CD 796.

Watkins, Mel. *On the Real Side: Laughing, Lying and Signifying: The Underground Tradition of African-American Humor That Transformed American Culture, from Slavery to Richard Pryor*. New York: Simon and Schuster, 1994.

Webb, Barbara L. "The Black Dandyism of George Walker: A Case Study in Genealogical Method." *TDR* 45.4 (2001): 7–24.

Weber, Brom, ed. *The Letters of Hart Crane, 1916–1932*. 1952. Berkeley: U of California P, 1965.

Wentworth, Harold, and Stuart Berg Flexner. *Dictionary of American Slang*. New York: Crowell, 1960.

Whitman, Walt. *Leaves of Grass*. 1855 et al. Ed. Harold W. Blodgett and Scully Bradley. New York: Norton, 1965.

Whittier, John Greenleaf. "The Hunters of Men." 1835. *The Works of John Greenleaf Whittier, Vol. 3, Anti-Slavery Poems, Songs of Labor and Reform*. Boston: Houghton Mifflin, 1892. 33–35. 7 vols.

Wiggins, Linda Keck. *The Life and Works of Paul Laurence Dunbar*. 1907. New York: Kraus Reprint, 1971.

Wilder, Alec. *American Popular Song: The Great Innovators, 1900–1950*. New York: Oxford UP, 1972.

Williams, Bert. "The Moon Shines On the Moonshine." Rec. 1 Dec. 1919. Columbia A2849. *Bert Williams: His Final Releases, 1919–1922*. Archeophone ARCH 5002.

———. "Nobody." Rec. 1906 (twice). *Bert Williams: The Early Years, 1901–1909*. Archeophone ARCH 5004.

———. "Nobody." Rec. 7 January 1913. *"Nobody" and Other Songs*. Folkways, 1981. RBF 602.

Williams, Clarence. "Everybody Loves My Baby." Rec. 6 November 1924. "I'm a Little Blackbird Looking for a Bluebird." Rec. 17 December 1924. Perf. Clarence Williams, Sidney Bechet, Louis Armstrong, and Eva Taylor. Giants of Jazz, 1998.

Williams, William Carlos. *The Collected Poems of William Carlos Williams, Vol. 1, 1909–1939*. Ed. A. Walton Litz and Christopher MacGowan. New York: New Directions, 1991.

———. *Imaginations*. Ed. Webster Schott. New York: New Directions. 1970.

———. *I Wanted to Write a Poem: The Autobiography of the Works of a Poet*. New York: New Directions, 1978.

Wimsatt, William K., Jr., and Cleanth Brooks. *Literary Criticism: A Short History*. New Haven: Yale UP, 1957.

Wittke, Carl. *Tambo and Bones: A History of the American Minstrel Stage*. Durham, N.C.: Duke UP, 1930.

Wondrich, David. *Stomp and Swerve: American Music Gets Hot, 1843–1924*. Chicago: ACappella Books, 2003.

Wyatt, Thomas. *The Collected Poems*. Ed. Kenneth Muir. Cambridge: Harvard UP, 1950.

———. *The Poetical Works of Thomas Wyatt*. London: Aldine Edition of the British Poets, 1866.

Zijderveld, Anton C. *On Clichés: The Supersedure of Meaning by Function in Modernity*. London: Routledge, 1979.

INDEX

Adorno, Theodor, 71, 129n17
advertisements, 46–47, 79n11, 100
African American artists: attitudes of, 10–11;
role in modernism, 19, 108, 137–38; use
of nonsense, 19, 54. *See also* Dunbar;
Handy; Hughes; Toomer; Williams, B.
African American culture: as American
culture, 18, 56–57; American culture
impacted by, 1, 6–7, 17, 149–51; displacement of, 146–47; as modernist, 4, 56;
nadir of, 7, 16, 40; nonsense in, 54, 90, 91;
role in modernism, 6, 19, 108. *See also*
African American modernism; minstrelsy;
music
African American Imaginary: as an analytic
tool, 5, 16; concept of, 17, 18–19, 27–28,
56; displacement of, 121, 122–23, 125,
137–38; historical aspect of, 27. *See also*
language; music
African American literature, critics of, 146–47
African American middle class, 7–9, 11
African American modernism: approach to,
159, 160; authority of, 150; displacement
of, 121, 122–23, 125; marginalization of,
119–20. *See also* African American culture; *Cane*; modernism, literary
African American vernacular language, 14, 15,
17. *See also* "Negro" dialect
"All Coons Look Alike to Me" (song), 86
American culture: African American culture
as, 18, 56–57; contemporary, 3, 149;
ignorance of, 150–51. *See also* African
American culture; African American
Imaginary
"An Ante-bellum Sermon" (Dunbar), 74
Anthology of Magazine Verse (Braithwaite),
157–58
anxiety: in "The Comedian as the Letter C,"
31; in coon songs, 43; Crispin's, 34; in
"Portrait of a Lady," 37; role in the modernist subject, 33
Armstrong, Louis, 19, 42, 54
arts, visual, 129
aura in art, 65

"Avant-Garde and Kitsch" (Greenberg), 125–
28, 129

Baker, Houston A., Jr.: on African American
modernists, 5, 120; on Dunbar, 68–69,
81–83; on nonsense in minstrelsy, 91
Bakhtin, Mikhail, 84, 103
Baltimore, MD, musical significance of, 40
the banjo, 35–36, 77
barbers and barbershops: interracial contact
in, 1–2, 155; modernism in relation to, 1;
quartets in, 2, 3, 13
Beckett, Samuel: African American culture in
relation to, 102–3, 159; works: *Waiting for
Godot*, 1, 85, 101–2, 103–8
Behn, Aphra, 16
Bell, Clive, 112
Benjamin, Walter, 65, 84
Bergson, Henri, 143
Berlin, Edward A., 17, 59–60
Berthoff, Warner, 153
Bhabha, Homi K., 5, 33, 94, 103
"Black and Blue" (song), 42
blackface, 17, 41
blackness, 58, 146
Black Swan record label, 14, 15
Blake, Eubie, 21
Bland, James A., 60–61
Blesh, Rudi, 17
Bloom, Harold, 31
blues music: language of in *Cane*, 50, 139;
songs, 14; women singers of, 140. *See also*
"St. Louis Blues"
The Book of American Negro Poetry (Johnson),
15, 73
The Book of American Negro Spirituals
(Johnson), 2
Braithwaite, William Stanley, 121, 157–58
"The Bridge" (Crane), 100
Brooks, Cleanth, 122, 123
Brooks, Shelton, 9
Bruce, Dickson D., 72
Burleigh, Harry T., 34n1
Butler, Judith, 43–44